Emotional Milestones
From Birth to Adulthood:
a Psychodynamic Approach

Ruth Schmidt Neven

Jessica Kingsley Publishers
London and Bristol, Pennsylvania

First published in Australia in 1996 by
The Australian Council for Educational Research Ltd

First published in the United Kingdom in 1997 by
Jessica Kingsley Publishers Ltd
116 Pentonville Road
London N1 9JB, England

Library of Congress Cataloging in Publication Data
A CIP catalogue record for this book
is available from the Library of Congress

British Library Cataloguing in Publication Data
A CIP catalogue record for this book
is available from the British Library

ISBN 1-85302-456-2

Design by Noni Edmunds
Typeset by Mackenzies Typesetting
Printed and Bound in Great Britain by
Biddles, Guildford, Surrey

▓ CONTENTS

PART THREE: BRINGING UP CHILDREN IN A CHANGING WORLD

ACKNOWLEDGEMENTS

The idea for a book about the developmental stages and emotional milestones of development has had a long gestation period. It has evolved most particularly out of the training workshops that I have run on child development and parenting in Australia and the United Kingdom, and which first emerged out of the presentations on the emotional milestones in development which were run as part of the Exploring Parenthood model. It has also evolved out of my clinical work with children, adolescents and parents in Britain and Australia. I would like to thank all the parents, children and adolescents who have allowed me into their lives to work with them, hopefully to help them. They have always helped me to gain a clearer insight about the nature of development and the essential vital relationship between children and their parents.

I would particularly like to thank Joanna Goldsworthy, Parent Education Consultant at the Australian Council for Educational Research, for her support and encouragement for this project from its inception as a tentative idea. My thanks as well to Margaret Byron for her secretarial help with the manuscript; to my husband, Emil, for his generosity, support and editing skills; and my daughter, Hannah, who has interrupted me sufficiently to ensure I retain a firm grasp about development in the real world.

■ INTRODUCTION

Bringing up children is the most important job that we undertake in life. Yet it is often the one for which we have the least training and which we approach without very much preparation. This book on development from birth to adulthood is not intended as a manual to offer a fixed idea about how to bring up children; rather it tries to offer a perspective on the emotional milestones of development for children, parents and families. It introduces a psychodynamic perspective which focuses on the meaning of behaviour and on understanding how children grow in a relationship with their important carers, such as parents, extended family and significant others. In the book I repeatedly pose the questions: How do we grow emotionally? What do we need to thrive? What is the nature of our emotional and relational nourishment?

The book is based on my experience over many years of working as a child psychotherapist with children, parents and families both in Australia and the United Kingdom. I hope that the examples in the book, drawn from my clinical experience and from life experience, illuminate the particular areas of development that I describe.

The book has been written to be as accessible and user-friendly as possible. The issues which are raised in the examples I hope can be seen as universal. I have also included reference to particular areas of current concern, such as extended hours, child care, divorce, gender and sexual identification. These are the key issues for our time. The book is not written from a formal academic standpoint, though I refer to a number of theorists and clinicians who have influenced me greatly in my own work and theoretical development.

Useful references, which enable readers to go to the original sources, as well as to current psychodynamic understanding of the different stages of development, are listed at the end of the book.

For balance, the use of 'he' and 'she' is alternated when speaking about a child other than in specific examples drawn from clinical experience.

■ BIOGRAPHY

Ruth Schmidt Neven was born in London and trained as a child psychotherapist at the Tavistock Clinic in London, following an earlier training in psychology and then in psychiatric social work at the London School of Economics. She has over 25 years of experience as a clinician working with children, parents and young people.

In 1982, she founded and co-directed Exploring Parenthood, a national support service for parents in the U.K. Exploring Parenthood has pioneered taking specialist knowledge about child development out of the clinic into the community.

Ruth Schmidt Neven came to Australia in 1989 to take up the first position of Chief Child Psychotherapist at the Royal Childrens' Hospital in Melbourne, a position she held until 1994. At the Childrens' Hospital she established a Psychotherapy Clinic for children and parents, and in conjunction with the ACER a public talks series for parents.

In 1994 she set up the Centre for Child and Family Development in Melbourne, which offers a clinical service for children and parents, The Exploring Parenthood outreach program, and professional training. Ruth Schmidt Neven writes and lectures extensively on child development and parenting, and runs training programs in Australia and overseas.

PART ONE

A Psychodynamic Approach

CHAPTER 1

What is a Psychodynamic Approach?

SUMMARY

This chapter introduces the following key concepts associated with the psychodynamic approach.

- All behaviour has meaning and is always a communication between children and parents.
- The events surrounding our birth and early years of development inform the way we view the world. Thus, even as adults, we can talk of 'the child part of ourselves', which may influence the way we act as parents.
- Understanding a child's problem as a communication which has meaning helps us to reframe it and avoid blame and recrimination. It *opens up communication* between children and parents, rather than closing it down in an adversarial confrontation.
- The place of dreams, fantasy and play, which represent our 'inner world experience', and help us to build up important data about our lives and relationships is described.
- The provision of *containment* for children, parents and professionals is introduced as a key theme of the book.

The concluding section focuses on how a psychodynamic approach can help us to understand some of the conflicts which can arise in our professional work when we are trying to help people with difficulties.

A psychodynamic approach has been an active part of our everyday life for some considerable time. We may not be aware of the fact that psychodynamic ideas which have developed over the last century have now become so widely accepted that their integration into a wide area of human activity is almost imperceptible. For example, the focus in the Western world on childhood, on the importance of the first five years of life; the major changes in educational approaches to teaching young children; the closing of community homes, the reluctance to take children into care and separate them from their families; all these aspects of development would have been unthinkable without the influence of psychodynamic understanding, clinical experience and research.

In the world of the arts the same process has taken place. For example, we talk of the 'post-Freudian novel'. We are aware of playwrights and painters whose work is involved with a knowledge about 'life below the surface'; about the unconscious, about dreams and fantasy. This awareness has increasingly become part of the currency of life and the communication of ideas.

Traditionally, a psychodynamic approach is viewed as being synonymous with psychotherapy. Psychodynamic ideas are being used more frequently in brief interventions with families, for example in the case of sleeping problems in infants. However, in this book I will be describing the psychodynamic approach as a conceptual framework which helps us understand child and family development. Thus we go beyond seeing this approach as solely a treatment modality, part of the therapeutic process in the consulting room between patient and therapist.

What I hope to show is how a psychodynamic approach brings together theoretical understanding and practical observation in a way which leads to a new and exciting paradigm for the understanding of human behaviour. This understanding in turn can influence the way in which we organise services and facilities for children and parents. Thus it has a very practical application in our day-to-day lives. I hope that the examples in the book, drawn from my clinical experience and from life experience, illuminate the particular areas of development that I describe and help readers become more familiar with this approach, so they begin to find it a rewarding way of thinking about human relationships and behaviour.

Some of the terms used may be unfamiliar to readers; however they are useful terms with precise meanings which will become apparent in the text and can also be checked in the glossary.

I will start out by identifying some of the key components of the psychodynamic approach. These can be described as follows.

THE PSYCHODYNAMIC APPROACH TO CHILD DEVELOPMENT AND FAMILY LIFE

- All behaviour has meaning – behaviour is always a communication between children and parents.
- The child exists in the parent, and the parent exists in the child – the events surrounding our infancy and childhood shape our future.
- Behaviour is dynamic and changes all the time – it is not static.
- The tension and interplay between our inner world and our outer world.
- The Overt and the Covert in our behaviour.
- The place of dreams for children and parents.
- The place of play in psychodynamic thinking

I will now take each of these statements further by clarifying what is meant by each one, and use examples from clinical practice to illustrate each concept. When discussion about a child does not involve a specific example from clinical practice the use of 'he' and 'she' will be alternated.

All behaviour has meaning – behaviour is always a communication between children and parents

The psychodynamic approach puts forward the view that all behaviour has meaning, and that there is no such thing as communication and activity which has no specific communicable direction. In that sense, everything we do is part of a communication, and this of course is of vital importance in the communication between children and parents. For example, parents may be angry and irritated by what they perceive to be the destructive behaviour of their child. They may seek help and advice about specific ways of controlling this behaviour. A behavioural or cognitive approach to the problem would probably refer to ways of helping the parents to evolve 'strategies', or ways of managing the problem of destructiveness. However, in using a psychodynamic approach, one would view the problem in a different way. First of all, one would postulate that the destructive behaviour is in itself *an important communication*. It might, in the context of the family, be the only way in which the child is able to communicate something about what he or she feels. So we would ask the question 'What lies behind the destructive behaviour?' The other question we would ask is 'Why does this behaviour emerge *at this particular point in time*?' So the questions *'What does it mean?'* and *'Why now?'* are all-important.

Fundamental to the idea that all behaviour has meaning is the belief that the recognition of meaning behind behaviour is actually very important to our emotional well being. If we are not able to attribute meaning to our personal experience and to our relationships with the important people in our lives, it is difficult for us to exist in even the most fundamental state of relatedness to others and to the broader community.

As professional workers in our day-to-day work with children, parents and families it can be of enormous benefit to assist them to find meaning in what may initially appear to them to be a mass of confusion in the way their child behaves. For example, I have noticed in the clinic setting in which I work how, in taking a history from parents who present a child with a particular problem, parents inevitably describe their own childhoods as 'perfectly all right' or 'very happy'. However, on closer questioning, it will emerge that their lives and experiences have included very significant events such as loss, separation, even violent death. These events have been pushed into the background and become 'clouded by amnesia' until we are able together to make a connection between what has happened in the past, and how this affects the current problem they are presenting with their child. The following example may illustrate this point.

The Waa at the bottom of the toilet

A four-year-old boy was presented to the clinic with problems of failure to be adequately toilet trained. The difficulty for Mark was that he had a terror of using the toilet and sitting on it. When he looked into the bowl he was frightened of being attacked by a monster which he called 'The Waa'. As a result, Mark would only defecate into his nappies, although he would often go into the toilet and stand next to the toilet bowl to do his 'poos'. He managed to 'hold on' while he was at his play group, and his mother was concerned that he would never be able to go to kindergarten the following year if he was not properly toilet trained. Mark's parents presented as a very pleasant young couple who seemed well supported by extended family, and claimed that there were no difficulties in any aspect of their lives. However, when I asked Mark's mother if there had been any recent stresses or problems in the family, she said 'not really' and then, in a very matter-of-fact voice, added 'just that my husband had a serious accident with a chainsaw and nearly lost part of his hand' and 'a few weeks ago, the entire kitchen was set on fire'. The fact that Mark's mother's tone and manner did not change when she recounted these horrifying events, suggested that, for her, they had no meaning and that she could make no connection between the accident that Mark's father had experienced, the near-death escape from the fire and Mark's worry about the monster 'Waa' at the bottom of the toilet. As our work progressed it became clear that Mark's mother was worried about letting out problems of any kind which might mar the superficial coping exterior of the family's life. For example, Mark's mother prided herself on managing Mark when he had a toileting accident by being able to change him, even when he was playing with friends, so speedily and with such little fuss that not only would his friends not need to know that he had made a 'poo', but neither would he. In working with this family, it was possible to help Mark's mother, particularly, to be able to make connections and feel less worried about maintaining a facade of control about difficult events. This enabled Mark in turn to be able to give up some of the control that he was exercising in not becoming fully toilet trained. He was, after a short period of time, able to quite spontaneously overcome his terror of the toilet and go on as planned to kindergarten.

This example illustrates that instead of interpreting Mark's difficulty to become toilet trained as troublesome or defiant, we can see the problem of the toilet training as a very important communication in this family. There may have been many things that Mark was struggling to say. In fact he did have some difficulties with his speech so that being able to in a sense to 'talk with his bottom' was the only available communication open to him.

The following example illustrates how through physical illness the body struggles to communicate what cannot be put into words.

A matter of life and death

I attended a regular ward round in a busy children's hospital run by the Consultant Paediatrician and Registrar and Resident. The ward round is a fascinating learning experience as it offers an opportunity to be in touch with the nitty-gritty of hospital life. It puts one in touch with the struggles of the nursing and medical staff who work often in demanding circumstances, and with the parents who in their turn struggle to adapt to the complexity of the organisational dynamics of the ward to ensure the best for their children.

On this occasion, we arrived at the bed of a 12-year-old girl said to be suffering from asthma. For some reason the girl was away from her bed, and the discussion about her condition took place in a disembodied way between the medical staff that is often so typical of these ward rounds. It appeared that her physical condition was not very serious. Most significant however, was the girl's fear that she would die, although there was nothing in her history or in her current condition to suggest that she was in any danger. The medical staff were discussing some recommendations. They suggested that more medical tests should be run to reassure her, and that she might see a psychiatrist to talk about her anxiety. Towards the end of the discussion, the junior doctor mentioned in an incidental way that the girl's father had in fact died of asthma. Here we can see an example of how vitally important information that goes to the heart of the problem should really have been discussed at the very beginning of this exchange. The medical staff believed that since the girl's father had died when she was very young, she had not been aware of the nature or cause of his death. Here we can see how the meaning that this event had for the particular patient was negated and misunderstood, rather than used positively to influence the effective treatment of the patient.

The problem of denial

The importance of understanding that all behaviour has meaning is one that is slow to be recognised. Very often, in working with parents and families, one becomes aware of the cultivation of an attitude in which there is a denial of the links between life events, between the childhood experiences of parents and their own children and between making connections at all. The reasons for this are complex and may largely lie with the fear that we all have, at times, of becoming emotionally overwhelmed if we allow ourselves to recognise and make links between the different experiences in our lives. I will illustrate this with another example.

It's all the same to me

I was talking to an experienced and sensitive maternal and child health nurse whose work I knew to be of the highest quality and who was totally committed to providing a good service to the mothers and babies she saw every day. However, on one occasion, when she referred to the nature of her day-to-day work, she said that in her opinion the work of the maternal and child health nurse tends to be repetitive and monotonous as it involves repeating a set of inquiries and giving out information and instructions about the care of the baby. Her description of the work and the way I had seen her operate indicated a complete discrepancy. It seemed to me extraordinary that she could describe as repetitive the emotional and highly charged relationship that mothers often have with maternal and child health nurses, and which of course has its parallel in the highly charged emotional relationship between infant, mother and father. It seemed to me of course that indeed the opposite was true. Every baby is different, every mother and father is different, and every situation is different. However, in trying to reflect on this later, I came to the conclusion that perhaps the work is so emotionally involving and highly charged that this maternal and child health nurse, as well as many other professionals, feel they have to defend themselves against being overwhelmed by their own internal baby feelings. In our work with mothers, fathers and babies, very early worries, anxieties and emotions associated both with being a baby, and with being a mother are aroused. We may feel we have to defend ourselves against observing the meaning of what we see so that we do not become overwhelmed. The problem with this is that it then may lead us to cut off the possibility of exploration, both for ourselves as professionals, and for the parents and children we are trying to help.

The erosion of meaning and the effects on childhood

We may consider another factor which is that, in an increasingly technological and consumer-oriented society, the capacity to attribute meaning to children's behaviour, particularly, and therefore to be able to understand children, has become increasingly eroded.

The capacity to attribute meaning to behaviour in itself requires that we develop a 'process' which enables us to allow ourselves time to step back and think a little about what is going on. This can be difficult to do when we may feel under pressure to control, manage or eradicate what is seen as troublesome, defiant or difficult behaviour in children. The psychodynamic approach to child and family development, which I formulate in this book, requires not only a different process of thinking, but also an appropriate time frame. *Children and parents need time to develop together.* They need a time frame which can allow for trial and error rather than one which has to do with fitting into an instrumental and mechanistic world view. There is a danger if we do not fully attribute meaning to a child's behaviour, or try to step back to more fully comprehend the context of the problem, that we as professionals may fall back on a wish or need to feel in control. One way of doing this is to separate out one single aspect of the problem and focus on this rather than to attempt to encompass the complexity of what the child or parents' behaviour may mean in a particular context. It is sobering in this regard to consider the current language and discourse of the parent advice literature which is resonant with terms such as 'managing', 'fixing', 'taming', and with placing children's developmental experiences within the limited currency of behavioural problems, disobedience and discipline.

In putting forward the basic tenets of the psychodynamic approach, namely that all behaviour has meaning, we are faced with the dilemma of having to accept the limitations of our understanding. We are faced with the problem of not knowing and having to deal with our own uncertainty. If we cannot stand uncertainty then there is an understandable tendency to want to reduce human growth, development and behaviour to a more instrumental and limited understanding which can be encompassed without challenging us too much internally, or posing too much of a threat to the existing order of things, and the way in which we see the world.

As this book unfolds, I return to a fundamental point about how hard it is for us to be able to tolerate uncertainty, and how, paradoxically, the 'containment of uncertainty' lies at the cornerstone of child, adolescent and family development.

The pitfalls of focusing on managing a problem without trying to understand what it means to the child is that it creates a situation in which the child is seen as the adversary of the parent, or of the adult world, and needs to be shown his or her place.

A recurring justification for favouring a more instrumental approach with clients or patients, which does not seek to understand the meaning behind behaviour, is that many families, it is said, have little capacity for understanding complex psychological and emotional issues. These families are often described as inarticulate or ill-educated people who cannot benefit from a psychodynamic approach which tends to be seen as the reserve of middle-class and educated people. Again, I believe we are dealing with a rationalisation whereby professionals, perhaps understandably, try to protect themselves from what they feel will be a deluge of painful information and revelation from people who may have experienced a long-term cycle of deprivation and unhappiness. Unfortunately, this rationalisation can relegate a whole class of people into a perpetual state of not being properly informed and of not being listened to, which in turn doubly deprives the children. Ultimately, the capacity to attribute meaning to behaviour has very little to do with education or intellect. Rather, it is connected with the availability of time and our willingness to listen to people and to facilitate them to give a powerful account of their lives. Almost invariably they are able to truly find their own voice which will serve to provide them with the potent source of change for their children and themselves.

I will conclude this section on all behaviour has meaning with the following example.

Keeping Daddy alive

A three-year-old boy was referred to the Clinic for wilful, defiant and difficult behaviour. Harry's father had died suddenly a year before, when he was two years old, from a brain tumour. Harry's mother, who was pregnant at the time, gave birth to a child with multiple handicaps who had spent most of his sixteen months at the hospital. With the death of her husband, Harry's mother had lost her home and her financial security, and had to move in with her own parents. When Harry and his mother arrived at our clinic we were struck by two things. One was that Harry appeared a delightful little boy who played contentedly with the toys and was listening carefully to everything his mother said. Harry's mother, by contrast, hardly seemed to want to touch on the events of the last two years, as though they were of little consequence. She was concerned to know whether we could 'fix Harry's behaviour' and 'manage his discipline problems'. She said he would hit out and become very angry. His mother was exasperated and had to resort to asking her father to hit Harry on the hand in desperation. However, nothing that they had tried to do had succeeded in having any effect on Harry, and she wanted to know what 'strategies' we would recommend. While Harry, his mother and brother were living with the grand-parents he was not allowed to go into any other room of the house apart from the family room in case he spoiled the cream carpets, and he was not allowed to go into the landscaped garden in case he spoiled the plants.

The first thing we tried to explain to Harry's mother was that we saw Harry as a very healthy boy, who was trying hard to let her know that he could not forget what had happened to him and to his early baby relationship with his mother, and indeed his father. His behaviour was viewed as split off from the context of what had happened to him and to the family, and was seen as having no meaning. Rather, it was seen simply as behaviour which was aggressive and which had to be stopped at all costs. We could see that the vehemence of Harry's mother's insistence that something be done about his behaviour suggested her great anxiety about beginning the process of mourning all the losses for herself. The process of mourning is quintessentially a process of attributing meaning to our lost significant relationships and contains within it the seeds of developing emotional well being. Harry's mother had as well never explored her feelings towards her handicapped child. For example, when we asked how old he was, she said, 'Oh, he is 1.4' and then said, 'He is sixteen months old'. Later we wondered whether the 1.4 suggested the figure that she had seen on the chart on his bed on the ward. In this way, her second child, Jeremy, had become not so much a real person for her, but perhaps still remained a safe statistic. The complexity of how relationships between people contribute to our understanding of the meaning of behaviour was further highlighted by the fact that Harry's mother had returned to her parents' home, and in the process she had returned to being a child again. She appeared to have lost the authority to manage any limit setting and discipline with her own son, and resorted to her father to literally be the heavy hand.

The child exists in the parent and the parent exists in the child: the events surrounding our infancy and childhood shape our future

The recognition of the importance of early infantile and child development and its impact on later life is fundamental to an understanding of a psychodynamic approach. Here we can observe the child self, remaining in the parent and in the adult, and the experience of the parents beginning to mould and shape the experience of the child.

In subsequent chapters, I describe in detail the emotional milestones of development and the particular attributes of each age and stage.

What is important to keep in mind is that the process and the experience of childhood does not end with childhood itself. It remains within all of us as a live and informative experience that influences our current and future relationships and activities. In this sense, we can speak of the child in ourselves or the child part of the adult. We are all aware on an everyday level of some of the fears and worries of childhood which may still remain with us in adult life, and may have been difficult to overcome. The idea that we must renounce childhood experiences or worries in adult life denies the validity of this experience and suggests that we must strive towards overcoming our childhood to become rational adult beings. In fact the opposite is the case. In order to become fully integrated as adults, and in order to be successful parents, we need to be able to encompass and use in a constructive way our significant childhood experiences.

Thus, far from trying to eliminate or control childhood events, it is important for us to be able to integrate them as data which can be illuminating in informing current problems and concerns.

Send for the police!

A thirteen-year-old boy was referred with his parents because of his difficult and uncontrolled outbursts of aggression. Both parents, who had received marital and couple counselling in the past, were now said to be at a loss to know how to manage their defiant and unhappy son. Nicholas was the middle child of three, with one older sister of 14 and one younger sister of 10. In making the referral, the therapist who had previously worked with the parents made the comment that she felt that much of the problem was due to the fact that both parents had come from different cultures, the father from an Australian Anglo-Saxon background and the mother from an Asian background. They had fought for many years about different ways of bringing up the children, and this was said to be the conflictual problem in the family.

I was particularly struck by the event which had precipitated the referral. One week before, Nicholas and his father had had a fight which had led to Nicholas becoming out of control and trying to attack his father. In the course of these events, both parents had felt at such a loss to know what to do that they had in fact called the police. I was concerned to know what had driven these parents to such an extreme position where they felt like children themselves, unable to exert any authority either over themselves or over Nicholas, but had needed to take the drastic measure of calling for an outside source of control and authority.

At my first meeting with Nicholas and his parents I had the impression that both parents were caring, and had done a great deal for their children. Nicholas's father opened the interview by expressing his despair at the difficulties he had in communicating with his son. He described the problem as being one almost beyond his comprehension, and spoke of his feelings of loss for his relationship with his son. At times, he said, he felt so desperate that the feelings he had were worse than having cancer. 'At least if you have cancer, you know what you have.' In his troubled relationship with Nicholas he could not identify why things had gone so badly wrong. Nicholas himself was so desperate that he had asked his parents if they could find a foster home for him, or if he could move in with his grandfather. His parents were beginning to consider this as a real possibility, and it struck me that this was not dissimilar to the way in which they had invited the police in to manage the family row.

As the interview progressed, I tried to explore with Nicholas and his parents not only how they saw the problem, but also what had happened to all of them in developmental terms. So, for example, I was interested to know what sort of baby Nicholas had been, and was interested to hear from his father that he had been referred to as 'the cuddle king' because he so loved to be cuddled and had such an intense attachment to both his parents, and they to him. He had been a happy and contented baby and little boy, right up until the birth of his younger sister when he was about three and a half years of age. It was pointed out to me that Nicholas' mother had breastfed him until the third child was born, which is the custom in her culture, and he had spent a considerable amount of time in the marital bed and had been very close, particularly to his mother, and also to his father. However, with the birth of the new baby all this changed very abruptly. Nicholas was weaned, almost overnight, and his place in his parents' bed was taken by his sister. When we talked about these events, Nicholas pointed out to his mother that he remembered very vividly shaking his sister's cradle in the hope that she would fall out. It appeared that Nicholas' idyllic extended babyhood had ended abruptly at this point, and he was forced to go to school shortly afterwards when he was only four and a half. Although he had fitted in well and succeeded academically, it was as though he had not been able to complete a critical part of his early childhood. He had moved from infancy straight into school with nothing in between, and little to prepare him. Nicholas' resentment towards his younger sister has remained a major feature of the family's life.

In the process of trying to understand what had happened to Nicholas, I also asked both parents to explain something of their own experiences as children. Nicholas' father recalled that he was the seventh child of eight children, and that he too, like his son, had enjoyed being the baby in the family until the eighth child, a girl had arrived. He had also been about the same age as Nicholas when his sibling was born. The most significant aspect of his sister's birth was the fact that his mother had, in the course of this last pregnancy, become ill with polio and had a paralysed arm. At this point, Nicholas' father recalled a vivid memory of his mother sitting in a rocking chair with her arm in a sling, and he supposed that there was a housekeeper who had come in to look after the eight children, but clearly, at that point, life had changed for him very abruptly. When I made the point that Nicholas' father's experience parallelled the experience that Nicholas had just described, his father broke down and wept. It seemed significant that Nicholas had not known about this experience of his father's, and that it was very important for him to hear it. It clarified for me, in my puzzlement, how the battle between Nicholas and his father could not be handled in any reasonable way, but had so flown out of control.

In making the link here, between the child in the parent and the parent in the child, we can see that the powerful emotional events of our childhood can force us into repeating precisely the same experiences. If these experiences have been difficult and destructive, then our repetition of these events will be made in a way which can be unhelpful to our present experience and present parenting. By enabling Nicholas' father to make the connection between Nicholas' experience and his own experience as a baby and young child, Nicholas' father could hopefully use this information as important data to be brought into everyday awareness rather than to act it out in the mindless way it had been, when the police were called during their row.

In considering the child in the parent, and the parent in the child, as a dynamic process in the relationships between different members of the family, the psychodynamic approach invites us to be able to make hypotheses about this process which can be useful both for ourselves as professionals and also for the clients and patients with whom we work. For example, we could make a hypothesis that for Nicholas' father, his own experience as a child had been every bit as traumatic as Nicholas' had been, but in different ways. They had both had to move abruptly from babyhood into a later stage of development without much preparation. Nicholas had felt the abrupt loss of his mother, who had then become devoted to his younger sister, while he was forced to become the grown-up boy. Nicholas' father experienced the loss of his mother, not only through the birth of a sibling, but also through her terrible illness which incapacitated her in the long term. We can hypothesise further that Nicholas' father was unable to express his confusion and his mixed feelings of love, hatred and rage towards his mother for withdrawing from him. Since her incapacity due to the polio would have continued, it would have made it more difficult for him to have felt able to express any of these concerns.

We can therefore postulate that, in seeing Nicholas relive some of these almost identical experiences, Nicholas' experiences had become merged with his own and he had no way of separating out who was the child and who was the parent, or to ask the important question 'What belongs where'? Hence the poignancy of his language when he first arrived, talking about his terrible sense of loss and despair concerning his son.

Behaviour is dynamic and changes all the time - it is not static

A psychodynamic approach suggests that behaviour is dynamic and constantly changing and evolving. A psychodynamic approach takes as its starting point a focus on the developmental thrust of child, adolescent and human growth and development. It is the opposite of a traditional medical model with its emphasis on symptom, pathology and cure.

A psychodynamic approach is the opposite of what one might call a 'reductionist' approach, or a 'mechanistic world view' approach.

There is an essential interdependence between children and parents. The relationship between them is the fuel of their entire existence, but it remains invisible until it breaks down. The psychodynamic approach rests on the assumption that one cannot begin to describe the behaviour of an individual without taking into account how the individual relates to others. We will see in subsequent chapters how the internal and psychological life of the baby, for example, and what we might call 'the baby's personality' only exists in so far as it is acknowledged by, and drawn out and interacted with, by both his parents.

We also recognise in a psychodynamic approach how malleable behaviour can be, depending on the surrounding events. We observe the extraordinary adaptability of children who may have to struggle to make sense of their world, and hang on to a childhood often in very deprived or violent circumstances. It follows that if we view behaviour as dynamic and changing, then this will necessarily alter the way we as professionals are able to facilitate change in our patients and our clients.

The tension and interplay between our inner world and our outer world

The psychodynamic approach offers a link or bridge between our inner individual and inner world perceptions and our experiences within the family, and in the broader community and culture. For example, within a family there can be six children, all of whom have a completely different vision and perception about their experiences of life in that family. Thus it is our *inner construction of outer reality* that often creates the different experience.

The overt and the covert in our behaviour

In describing the psychodynamic approach thus far, I have indicated that this approach encompasses an understanding of human development which places great emphasis on the earliest experiences of infancy and early and later childhood. It follows, therefore, that a psychodynamic approach gives credence to the importance of what we can call 'the unconscious world', the world of fantasy and of dreams. Another way of putting this is to say that a focus on the unconscious is quite different from an approach which focuses purely on behaviour as it is presented. A behaviourist might say 'what you see is what you get'. Thus the problem that is presented is seen as the total field within which the worker would operate. However, a worker using a psychodynamic approach would say what you see is not what you get. Thus, in a psychodynamic approach we would be working towards carefully observing the situation and discussing the problem with the child and parents in such a way to be able to move beyond the manifest behaviour to what is latent. The recognition of overt and covert processes, and of manifest and of latent behaviour, leads us to a greater awareness of the place of the unconscious. At its most simple level, the unconscious refers to wishes, hopes and fears which in a sense are not quite known to the individual. Paradoxically this does not mean that these unconscious processes, thoughts, hopes and wishes do not influence action. In fact all too often they do, sometimes with unfortunate results. My description of Nicholas' father, whose experience in early childhood was so similar to that of his son, is one such example. His own deprivation and sense of loss had weighed heavily upon him all of his life. One could say that it lay like a heavily undigested unhappy part of his personality of which he was only fleetingly aware. Nevertheless, he acted on this unconscious information by repeating something unhelpful with his own son. The fact that he was not able to digest the experience, and had not come to terms with it, meant that he acted it out unhelpfully with Nicholas rather than learning from it and helping Nicholas with his own sense of loss when his younger sibling was born.

An important condition for making the unconscious conscious is the availability of the right environment for this experience to be thought about and worked through.

We know from clinical experience that a vital part of helping parents who harm their children or fear they will harm them is to help them to put these fears and impulses into words. Thus making the unconscious conscious in a supportive environment can help to avoid destructive behaviour.

The place of dreams for children and parents

In the next chapter I refer specifically to the work of a number of theorists whose work underpins a psychodynamic approach to child development. I also refer to how the beginning of psychodynamic thinking, or, more specifically, psychoanalysis and its application to treatment and other aspects of human development, was first developed by Sigmund Freud. Freud described dreams as 'the royal road to the unconscious'. What he meant by this was that during sleep we are able to slough off the more inhibited, rationalised versions of our life experience, and are able to succumb to the world of our dreams which represents another important reality for us. At its most simple level, one can describe the work of dreaming as follows.

Suppose you are feeling concerned about a current crisis at work or at home. Inevitably you will struggle to find ways of dealing with it, or rationalise it away perhaps to make it more bearable. At night you may have a dream which 'tells a story' about this current tension or difficulty, albeit in an indirect way, with different people perhaps appearing in the dream. Nevertheless, your primary worry may be very much to the fore. In listening to the dream, one may be able to find not just a solution to the problem, but a way of gaining some greater understanding of why the particular problem causes so much distress. This in itself might lead to asking a different question about the problem, and to a possible solution.

I have used the term 'work' for the process of dreaming, because it is indeed working through the problems and experiences of the day or the week that dreams address. The importance of dreaming has been confirmed as well by current neurological studies which show that, where dreaming is not able to take place for various reasons, sometimes due to the taking of sleeping pills, people's functioning and capacity for cognitive thought is severely hampered.

The place of play in psychodynamic thinking

Play features as another cornerstone of psychodynamic thinking. Play can be said to be both an experience, a product, work, fun and a vital part of communication. A key feature of play, particularly in children, is that it operates on the boundary between the inner and the outer world. It is a safe place, and an important place for discovery and for experimentation in which experiences from the here and now of the present, and tasks that are still required to be mastered, are combined with wishes, hopes, fantasies and dreams. Current research and literature on early childhood and education confirms that play is recognised as a crucial part of early childhood development and leads to the development of personality. It contributes significantly to the way in which children learn, solve problems and maintain social relationships in the subsequent school years. If we postulate as Freud did, that in adults, dreams are the 'royal road to the unconscious', then in children, play represents the 'royal road to the child's unconscious', unverbalised wishes, fantasies, hopes, fears and expectations. For young children, and even older children, it is mostly through play rather than in verbal discussion that they are able to give us an account of the most significant aspects of their lives.

In the next chapter, I refer to the work of Donald Winnicott and some of his specific writings on the nature of play and its importance for cognitive and creative development. We may pause for a moment to consider how redolent our language is with images and metaphors that explain how play is utilised in terms of everyday experience. For example, we talk about 'playing with ideas', which suggests that far from being an irrelevance or a distraction, play provides a central foundation to the beginning of being able to engage in a higher level of reasoning and abstraction. One could say that playing with ideas is an important prelude to conducting research. The capacity for play and imaginative thought is a precondition for mental health in children as well as in adults. Because it is such a vital process which mediates between the inner world and the outer world, play and imaginative thought and fantasy enable 'the worst scenario' to be played out, thought about and fantasised about in a way that can make it more manageable and less threatening. It can also enable us to take some internal distance from frightening and overwhelming experiences. A typical example of this is the way in which children play out frightening and desperate events almost immediately after they have taken place. We witnessed this after some of the shootings that took place in Northern Ireland and in other war-torn parts of the world. The fact that children are driven to repeat what they have witnessed or heard about through play does not mean that they are bloodthirsty or unkind. Rather it indicates that they need to find a safe and helpful way to be able to process these events to enable them to be made more manageable, internally and externally. Thus the commonly used phrase 'It's just child's play' misrepresents the complexity of what is actually taking place. Indeed we need to have a far greater respect for both adults' and children's need to play, to help extend their imaginative life.

As I have emphasised before, far from being irrational or a diversion or irrelevant, play is an important developmental process which requires to be nurtured and supported because it contains within it the prerequisites for the capacity for health and integration, and also creativity in human development.

HOW CAN A PSYCHODYNAMIC APPROACH HELP US IN OUR PROFESSIONAL WORK

The tension and interplay between our inner world and our outer world is very much to the fore in our everyday working life.

In providing services for people who are ill, whether physically or mentally, and in trying to offer support for children and parents in a wide range of settings, great demands are placed on professional workers within these settings and on the institutions that try to carry out these particular services. At times, the demands of the work may produce some odd paradoxes. For example, doctors working round the clock in a hospital can become so immersed in the task and the demanding nature of their work that their own health begins to suffer. In some organisations the outside workings or structure of the system can take precedence over any capacity to think about what is going on within the system. The need to fit in with deadlines and administrative procedures can override the purpose for which these procedures have been set up in the first place.

It is often striking, when we observe organisations, how we can hypothesise that the problems which the organisations or services have been set up to solve become manifest within the organisation itself. For example, one can postulate that warders in a prison are themselves in prison in view of the amount of time they spend within the walls of the prison. The problems that many professionals face in dealing with some of the complex and demanding social and emotional problems of their clients can be very similar at times to the problems they may be facing within themselves or in their own families. As professionals who try to help people in difficulty we are all also in the process of conducting a form of 'personal research' into our own needs and difficulties. This can result in a positive healthy experience if it is properly acknowledged and supported.

We can thus speak of a 'mirroring' which takes place where there is a parallel line or connectedness between our personal and our professional experience. There is also a parallel between the way in which an individual operates between the inner world and outer world, negotiating between fantasy, dreams and demands of the outside world. An organisation can be said to operate on what we would call the boundary between the inner world and the outer world, and in relationship with other organisations.

If we are to work successfully with children, parents and families, then it is essential that we are open to and aware of the particular dilemmas that we face in providing appropriate services. This means that the organisations and services themselves need to be thought about and reflected upon in the same way that we would reflect and work out the best ways of trying to help our clients. Where this process does not take place problems start to gather, and very often there are difficulties either associated with the service becoming idealised, or people feeling that they can only carry out the work if they make unrealistic demands on themselves. This may lead to an experience of feeling burned out after a time, or to a cynical view of the service and one's capacity to help people. The extremes between either a cynical or an over-idealised response leads to professionals fleeing from their work and/or to a concern that clients have been abandoned and professional workers have been exploited.

The psychodynamic approach allows us to consider the link between our internal individual experience as well as the group and organisational experience in a way which can attribute meaning to both. In describing the individual experience of attributing importance to the meaning of behaviour, I have used the term 'gathering important data' that can be thought about and used to enhance people's relatedness to themselves and within the family. The gathering of data about the meaning of work within settings and services specifically devoted to helping people is of equal vital importance to the maintenance of that service. For example, services concerned with any aspect of mental health are subject to enormous projections by everybody in the community, most particularly by the patients and by referring agencies. It is not surprising therefore that these services may find that their internal workings become quite fraught when there are differences of opinion about how things should be handled. At times it may seem as though the pressures from the outside come into the organisation in a way which cannot be thought about or properly digested or made sense of.

The overt and the covert in groups and organisations

The acknowledgement of what lies beneath our actions and activities is as much a part of group and organisational life as it is of individual and interpersonal experience. For example, we have all been in meetings ostensibly set up to discuss a particular problem or meet a particular task only to find that neither has been achieved. Sometimes we discover that a different task emerges, in the committee meeting or the group meeting, from the one that we had anticipated. This process is often referred to as the 'hidden agenda.' It may be an agenda that is known only to a few members of the group. At other times the 'hidden agenda' emerges and can take everyone by surprise. For example, a group may come together with the ostensible task of developing a new service, or setting up a new project. Despite everyone's best intention, it seems to be impossible to get this new project or task off the ground, and group meetings are taken up with members meandering off in all sorts of different or opposing directions. Here it may be important to acknowledge that different members of the group may have different conceptions of what the task represents for them. Groups or committees often find it difficult to pursue their task where it is impossible to acknowledge rivalry or differences between members or aggression within the group. Similarly, many groups depend for their existence on the belief that they have to oppose a group or service outside of themselves. Often the outside aggressor is the enemy force which unifies the group, albeit in a tenuous way.

In the following example I try to illustrate how there can be a close link between the needs of a professional group concerned with the care and support of children and parents in difficulty, and the needs of the clients.

Left holding the baby

I was asked to give a talk to a group of child-care staff on the subject of 'depression in mothers'. At the first meeting with the group, I was struck by their youth and idealism and their wish to do as much as they possibly could for many of the children who suffered from emotional deprivation, and the parents who were primarily single and had also suffered from the cycle of emotional abuse. Following this initial discussion where we focused on how depression manifests itself in young mothers, the group became enthusiastic about the possibility of continuing consultation sessions, and it was arranged that I would visit them once a week to talk about issues of concern in the group. However, once these sessions started, it did not take the group long to begin to present to me and to each other the depression and anger that existed in themselves and between themselves. While, on the one hand, they were concerned to help the children and parents in their care, on the other they felt that they too were in many ways abused. For example, they felt, in many cases, that they were left literally 'holding the baby' by fickle parents. The professional staff also felt unsupported by the administration heads who they believed did not fully understand their work and did not offer them sufficient resources.

In the course of the consultation, a parallel consultation was offered to the senior administrators. They described the childcare staff as greedy children who made constant demands on them, and who refused to share the resources available with other nurseries in the area.

In this consultation, we can see how the job that the service had set out to do, namely the care of deprived children and their parents, had become intertwined with the way in which the service was carried out, and the style of management of senior staff. At times it became difficult to know 'what belonged where'. For example, phrases such as 'the greedy children' were applied as much to the children and parents as to the staff. The idea of the 'withholding uncontaining management' also has its parallel in the everyday experiences we have of parenting.

Thus, in this example, we can see how a psychodynamic approach is particularly useful in enabling us to recognise the powerful intrapsychic, interpersonal and organisational forces which come into play in all the work in which we are involved, whether in health and community services, early childhood services or education. In the nursery I have described, the staff were thrown into turmoil in the process of working with deprived infants, young children and their parents, because they were also reminded of some of their own early infantile experiences which may not have been entirely resolved and understood. The senior management for their part were not sufficiently in touch with this process themselves and thus could not offer sufficient 'containment' for the young staff.

A psychodynamic approach suggests that we can reflect on these processes within organisations in a way which can inform appropriate action rather than acting out in a way that may be unhelpful to the professional staff and to the service as a whole. Thus we can see that the emotional support of staff working with children, parents and families needs to be seen as a key to the provision of safe and sustainable services.

CHAPTER 2

The Psychodynamic Heritage

SUMMARY

The discussion in this chapter:
- Offers an overview and introduction to some of the key theorists and clinicians who have contributed to our psychodynamic understanding of child development in the twentieth century and whose work informs the way we manage many problems today.
- Refers to the impact of the Second World War, with the development of psychodynamic ideas in Britain and the United States occurring in its aftermath, as well as an enormous wealth of ideas, clinical work and research in child development.
- Creates a bridge to link our understanding of the individual child within the context of the family, which includes family dynamics and the development of gender and sexual identification.
- Refers to the work of clinicians who applied these ideas of individual and interpersonal experience to help us better understand the workings of groups and organisations.

I n this introductory chapter on the psychodynamic tradition I do not intend to give an exposition of all psychodynamic thinking to date. Rather, I would like to introduce a perspective on some psychodynamic thinkers who have radically influenced the way in which we view child and family development.

My own conviction is that the most interesting and useful psychodynamic theories and ideas have derived from child development rather than from a focus on adult psychopathology. This contradicts earlier perceptions which suggested that if we focused on understanding in detail illnesses such as schizophrenia, we would know more about the workings of the mind. Within traditional clinical frameworks psychotherapy with adults has generally been accorded more status than psychotherapy and work with children. Anna Freud, Sigmund Freud's daughter, and one of the founders of child psychotherapy, had spoken of the tendency for adult psychotherapists to be more interested in what she described as 'the reconstructed child' (1971) who exists in the consulting room in the form of the adult patient, rather than in the real child who poses a challenge for the therapist because he is *in* the full thrust of development.

In the last 50 years, however, the body of psychodynamic clinical work and research into child development and family life has expanded beyond all expectations. It has been pointed out that our past attention to a focus on understanding psychotic processes in adult patients, in the hope that this would inform our understanding about the workings of the mind, has actually drawn some work in the adult psychotherapy field into a cul-de-sac (Meltzer, 1989). These findings have contributed to our understanding of how the mind can go utterly wrong with its functioning but they have contributed little or nothing to how it can go right. The burgeoning growth of interest in child development and family life has forced a shift away from pathology towards an interest in development. The exciting initiatives that have taken place in this field are testament to the need for clinicians and researchers to address the needs of the real child. Practical solutions have had to be found, as well as ways of supporting a variety of workers in the community concerned with children's needs. This in turn has influenced the way in which psychodynamic theory has evolved. Thus we can say that the very urgent thrust of development, which is the core of childhood experience, has forced clinicians and researchers to reshape their theory in the light of changing external circumstances and demands.

We can see how psychodynamic work has addressed some of the key issues of our time, such as the effects of separation from their parents on children, the effects of deprivation, loss and grief, the effects of child abuse, the essential connection between emotional difficulties and problems in learning, and many other areas of difficulty. The application of the psychodynamic approach therefore has enabled us to understand not only what goes on within the consulting room between patient and therapist, but has also taken us further into thinking about and understanding the nature of parenting and family life, as well as group and organisational life.

 # THE ORIGINS OF THE PSYCHODYNAMIC APPROACH

The very beginnings of psychodynamic thinking started with the work of Sigmund Freud. From Freud's earliest writings we can see that he started out as a biological theorist, a step away from his original commitment to neurology. Freud's subsequent theories, observations and clinical work which so revolutionised our ideas about the existence and the development of our inner worlds of perception and sexuality were created in a climate of hostility and vilification. The British psychoanalyst Harry Guntrip (1967, pp. 384-385) states:

> Freud's supreme achievement was to rise superior to his scientific origins and to challenge science to go beyond treating human beings as laboratory specimens to be investigated and manipulated and to see them as persons whose lives mean something to themselves and others. Persons who can only really be known and helped by someone who does not just objectively diagnose their illness and prescribe treatment but who knows and in a way shares the experience of suffering and goes along with them in seeking to understand and offers them a relationship in which they can rediscover their lost capacity to trust and love.

Guntrip discriminates between what he calls the 'object' of study and the 'subject' of experience in identifying the main difference between a conventional scientific approach and a psychodynamic approach. Thus, in biology, neurology and behaviouristic psychology, for example, live subjects i.e. human beings are studied as objects, whereas in psychodynamic understanding the objects we are concerned with, namely human beings, are subjects of experience.

Freud and his followers developed the earliest theories of psychoanalysis before the onset of the Second World War. Vienna was a primary focus for the psychoanalytic movement but there were strong links as well with other thinkers who were working along similar lines in Germany and in Eastern Europe.

The Influence of the Second World War

We should not overlook the fact that the Second World War provided an enormous catalyst for change for the psychodynamic movement. The dispersement of Freud and many of his followers from Austria, Germany and Eastern Europe to Britain and the United States, despite its potential personal upheaval, created a crucible from which so many of the most influential and potent ideas about child development and family life have emerged during the twentieth century.

There are a number of key interweaving threads which have influenced the way in which clinical work, theory and research in child development has progressed. The impact of the Second World War involved these clinicians in direct contact with major social, interpersonal and intrapsychic upheaval. They found themselves, for example, working with refugee children and evacuated children. Many of the clinicians entered the Services and were involved in establishing rehabilitation programs for servicemen. It is striking to note that much of the work and research that was carried out at this time on behalf of dislocated children and families, both during and after the war, involved clinicians who were themselves refugees and who had to make a new start in a new culture with a totally new language.

Another factor to keep in mind is that, as a result of this dispersement to both sides of the Atlantic, mainly Britain and the United States, similar ideas and preoccupations within child development could take place in parallel, so to speak, in different countries. This is a factor which is often overlooked as there is a tendency for people to assume that there is only one thinker or one group to arrive at a particular form of understanding. Instead, what we see in retrospect is that particular forms of thinking emerge out of a critical climate of receptivity or readiness within the culture and society. Thus new ideas are rarely totally unique. They often occur simultaneously in different places because they have found their time.

The psychodynamic clinical work and research which was produced immediately after the War and in the following approximately 25 years represents an era of startling richness and discovery. This period is also characterised by major differences of opinion which were expressed by these practitioners on both sides of the Atlantic and also within their own different groupings. The divergence of opinion and the passionately held convictions of different psychodynamic theorists suggests that understanding about the emotional world of children and families can only be produced out of sometimes painful dissension; that there are no absolute truths. Thus, as in any scientific endeavour, the tolerance of uncertainty is part of the vital process of creativity.

We must keep in mind that the great postwar clinicians and researchers that I refer to below came to their conclusions via the arduous path of continual clinical work and experience. Thus their research was not confined to having ideas about a subject and writing about it: rather their theoretical ideas were formulated out of extensive clinical experience and application.

The work of Anna Freud

I have referred before to Anna Freud's view that adult psychotherapists preferred to work with the reconstructed child in a consulting room rather than with the actual child. Anna Freud herself became a highly influential contributor to the body of knowledge about child development. In 1938 she and her father, Sigmund Freud, emigrated to Britain following the Nazi occupation of Austria. Anna Freud's earlier training had been in the field of education. Her work contributed to laying the foundations for an understanding of psychotherapeutic work directly with the child through the medium of play. Freud had described dreams as providing the royal road to the unconscious. By paying attention to play, Anna Freud showed that it was possible to elucidate ideas about the child's inner world, preoccupations, fears and fantasies.

Anna Freud's theoretical contributions to child development and understanding are very extensive. She is particularly well known for her work on identifying a theoretical framework for the understanding of defence mechanisms. These ideas have been taken up particularly by American psychotherapists who have expanded her ideas into the sphere of ego psychology and self psychology. Anna Freud's work *Normality and Pathology in Childhood* remains a classic in the field and outlines the ages and stages of development in terms of 'developmental lines' and behaviour which is relevant and appropriate for each stage.

Through her forced migration, Anna Freud's clinical and theoretical work had an immediate practical application. During the war she and an American colleague, Dorothy Burlingham, established the Hampstead Wartime Nurseries in London which were attended by a large number of refugee children, many of whom were orphaned. The Hampstead Wartime Nurseries subsequently became established as a psychotherapy and training centre known as the Anna Freud Centre. Today the Anna Freud Centre carries out extensive training in child psychotherapy for students from Britain as well as from all over the world. The theme of applying psychodynamic ideas within the broader community was fostered at an early stage at the Anna Freud Centre: first in the form of a well baby clinic and then a nursery attached to the Psychotherapy Centre. This provided both a service to the community as well as an opportunity for students on the intensive child psychotherapy training to observe and study children in the course of their normal development.

The work of Melanie Klein

Another major figure in the field of child development is Melanie Klein. Melanie Klein was born in Austria. She was much influenced by the work of Freud and saw herself as continuing his work and ideas in her therapeutic work with children. Klein moved to London in 1926 and remained there for the rest of her life. Melanie Klein's pioneering work with children has enabled us to gain insight into some of the earliest configurations of personality, particularly the pre-verbal period of infancy. Klein's most significant contribution was to identify the way in which the interaction between the infant and mother, in all its aspect, produces those states of mind which are the precursors for the way in which the child and adult perceives the world. Klein was particularly concerned with understanding the nature of anxiety and the way in which negative and angry feelings occur between the therapist and patient. Klein's views were, and still are, regarded as highly controversial.

She was specifically concerned as well with the earliest origins of the nature of persecution and envy, the idea of reparation and the wish to repair relationships. She emphasised the importance of depression which, instead of being viewed solely as a syndrome to be eliminated, she perceived as a dynamic process by means of which thoughtful integration can occur in the individual. Klein's particular contribution to our understanding of the psychological life of the infant and young child lay in her identification of the specific mental experiences which the baby has in relation to her dependence on the mother. These revolve around her capacity for dealing with her mother's coming and going, with feeding, with separation and with the intrinsic good or bad relationship she has with her mother. Klein puts forward the idea that the baby, up to six months of age, cannot encompass the whole mother but splits off parts of her mother in her mind as a way of managing her immediate environment. These split-off part objects themselves become imbued with intense feelings of good and bad, love and hate, which require to be contained by the mother. Klein postulates what she calls the 'paranoid-schizoid position' for this period, which can only be resolved by the subsequent emergence of 'the depressive position' after six months, where the baby can begin to see her mother as a whole. In this state of mind she can integrate the previously split off parts of her experience of her mother. Klein introduces the concept of reparation as the dominant emotion during this period. These processes of splitting and integration are seen by Klein as the continuing work of psychic life for everyone and manifest themselves in many different ways.

Klein's ideas have been particularly illuminating in furthering our understanding of the development of psychotic processes. They have also been of enormous importance in helping us to understand the effects of separation and loss for infants and young children, particularly in the first year of life. This understanding, for example, is very relevant when we consider the effects of separation on young children who may be removed from their parents at a critical stage for fostering or adoption, or even spend a great deal of time in long-term day care.

Klein has been influential in developing what has become known as the 'Object Relations School' of psychodynamic thinking. This particular approach has been taken further by thinkers such as Donald Winnicott and Wilfrid Bion among others. This idea of object relation refers to the way in which our personalities are made up of intrapsychic interpersonal relationships based primarily on the first relationship between the infant and his parents. These are of course made up of negative as well as positive attributes.

The work of Donald Winnicott

The early work of Anna Freud and Melanie Klein was taken further by Donald Winnicott, who worked simultaneously as a paediatrician, child psychiatrist and psychoanalyst. Winnicott's prolific writings span a period of over 30 years from approximately 1930. In this book on child development I draw extensively on Winnicott's ideas, which, more than any other psychodynamic thinker, I find extraordinarily contemporary and apt. Eric Rayner (1991), writing about Winnicott, says:

> If one were asked wherein lay Winnicott's particular greatness it would be hard to be specific. It was perhaps in the way he showed how special ordinary real human relationships were... Freud and then Klein had illuminated the individual unconscious inner world. Winnicott showed how these determine and are determined by a myriad interpersonal relationships.

Winnicott first trained as a paediatrician and was for many years paediatrician at the Paddington Green Children's Hospital in London. His formulation of understanding about aspects of child development and parent development was thus informed by what I have described as the urgency that is needed to address children's problems. Winnicott saw literally hundreds of children and parents during the course of his work as a paediatrician. His descriptions of clinical consultations indicate how psychodynamic insight and understanding can be used remarkably effectively in such brief consultations. It lays to rest the erroneous notion that psychodynamic understanding is only synonymous with long-term psychotherapy or with articulate educated people.

Winnicott's work in paediatrics enabled him to start from the position of development and growth, rather than from the position of pathology. Winnicott was in many ways one of the first preventative mental health practitioners. His talks to parents on the radio during the 1950s were unique at the time in totally instating parents and their own instinctive understanding of their children. These talks were collected in 1964 under the title of *The Child, the Family and the Outside World*, a book that remains as fresh today as when it was first published.

Winnicott was particularly helpful in avoiding idealisation of both the parent and the child by introducing the helpful concept of 'the good enough mother' as opposed to the perfect or wonderful parent.

I stated in the opening chapter of this book that the psychodynamic approach helps us to understand our essentially paradoxical position as human beings of existing simultaneously in our inner world of hopes, dreams and fantasies and in our outer world of demands and realities. Winnicott describes the very nature of development as a paradox in which, for example, separation and individuation for the child are experienced simultaneously. Among the many ideas that he has introduced, one is of particular importance in assisting us to understand this in-between phase of managing ourselves at one and the same time in our internal world and our external world. This is the nature of what he calls 'transitional experience'. Winnicott puts forward the idea of a space between the infant and his intimate and appropriately dependent relationship with his mother and father and the demands of the outside world. The infant and young child cannot go immediately from one to the other. Winnicott postulates the idea of an intermediate space between the two which he calls 'the transitional space'. This transitional space is often represented by a physical object, such as a blanket or a toy, which the child carries around with him – the transitional object. This transitional space acts as a safety zone so to speak between the inner and outer worlds. In later life, it is also used as a vehicle through which actual thought, imagination and play can take place. We are always negotiating our inner and outer reality as part of the daily process of living. In adults, a transitional space, Winnicott argues, can also be seen operating in imaginative life such as the arts, in religion and in creative and scientific work.

The work of Margaret Mahler

In the United States, paediatrician and psychiatrist Margaret Mahler developed ideas along not dissimilar lines to Winnicott's. Margaret Mahler was a refugee from the Nazi Holocaust and had trained as a paediatrician while still in Vienna. Much of her work was concerned with writing about what she called the psychological birth of the infant and young child. Mahler's work focuses particularly on understanding more thoroughly the meaning of separateness and the establishment of selfhood. In her clinical and research work she posed questions such as, how do normal children separate their self images from the images of the mother? how do they go through the gradual process of psychological birth? Mahler's work describes particular phases of separation and individuation of the young child. As with Melanie Klein and Winnicott, Mahler believed in the vital significance of the pre-verbal mother-child interaction and also in the value of direct child observation.

The influence of Infant Observation

The area of infant observation and young child observation is now becoming one of the key features and cornerstones of the psychodynamic approach. Infant observation has emerged specifically out of child psychotherapy training. It is now utilised in a wide range of training concerned with child and family development. For the observer, the act of actually being with the baby and parents immediately after birth is a profound and moving experience. It is also a most appropriate form of research and offers an opportunity to test hypotheses about the nature of infant development and the way in which earliest relationships with parenting figures emerge. The observer records the observation in detail for later discussion. At the same time, the process of observation in itself transforms the observer. Much of the uncertainty that is experienced during the infant and young child observation and the deeply emotional feelings that are aroused is seen as one of the best foundations for subsequent clinical work, both with children and adults.

It is interesting to note, of course, that one of the first baby observations was carried out by Freud himself. In his paper, 'Beyond the Pleasure Principle' (1920), he describes an observation of an 18-month-oldboy. The child had a wooden reel with a piece of string tied around it. Instead of pulling it along the floor behind him he held the reel by the string and very skilfully threw it over the edge of his cot, so that it disappeared into it. When this happened the little boy uttered an expressive 'Oooh'. He then pulled the reel out of the cot again and hailed its reappearance with a joyful 'There'. This, as Freud commented, was the complete game – disappearance and return. The interpretation of the game for Freud was related to the way in which the child could manage his mother's coming and going from him. As Freud says, he compensated himself with this, as it were, by staging the disappearance and return of the objects within his reach. The mother's departure had to be re-enacted as a necessary preliminary to her joyful return and it was in the latter that lay the true purpose of the game.

Understanding the effects of separation and loss on children

One of the particular concerns of psychodynamic theorists working in the field of child development has been that of understanding the child's response to separation and loss, as well as, of course, to try to understand how much of the personality of the child is potentially damaged by experiences of loss in early childhood.

The work of René Spitz

In the United States the work of René Spitz was pioneering in the field. René Spitz was an American psychoanalyst of French descent. His work centred mainly at the University of Colorado in Denver. René Spitz contributed to laying the foundations for developing observational research methods in the field of psychodynamic studies. He is renowned for his research work on the impact of separation on infants and young children, particularly children in long-term institutional care. Spitz's research elucidated the nature of the young child's reaction to arbitrary separation from his caregiver which takes the form of denial, protest and then withdrawal. Spitz's work was illuminating in describing the severe states of what he called 'anaclitic depression' in young children in long-term residential care, who had little or no opportunity to create a relationship with one caregiver (Spitz & Wolf, 1946). Spitz's work highlighted the trauma for the young child who is handed from one caregiver to the other and has no consistent person whom he can call his own.

The work of John Bowlby

At about the same time John Bowlby, in England, was developing his ideas about attachment, separation and loss. Similarly to Spitz, Bowlby conducted research on the long-term effects of maternal deprivation on the developing infant and young child. His book, *Child Care and the Growth of Love*, first published in 1951, conveyed the message that the essential relationship of the infant and young child to its mother was vital to subsequent mental health and that deprivation of that continuing closeness would bring severe risks of emotional disturbance and delinquency repeated over generations. Bowlby's work at this time was based on a postwar study of homeless children for the World Health Organisation. Bowlby had described the emotional damage resulting from deprivation as a kind of social infection which was as real and serious as that of diphtheria and typhoid. Bowlby's dictum that a bad home is better for a child than a good institution has informed many of the ideals of contemporary public child care.

Bowlby is best known for introducing a new and different perspective to accepted thinking about the nature of the relationship between mother and child through the then-revolutionary comparison of human young with other animal species. These researches led him to conclude that attachment is as necessary to emotional survival and mental health as food and shelter is for physical survival. Bowlby saw attachment as deriving not so much from the feeding relationship itself, but from physical closeness which allows intimacy between the mother and baby to develop. In his work on attachment, separation and loss, he has shown that there are at least five innately based instinctive patterns of response which the baby initiates by sucking, clinging, following, crying and smiling. These serve the function of linking the child to the mother and of obtaining her care and protection in return. The result of this interaction is that the child remains in proximity to the mother. Bowlby sees the process of developing attachment as fundamental to shaping subsequent human relationships.

Bowlby's original work on childhood experience of attachment, separation and loss has led to the continuing development of his ideas through research carried out in Britain and in the United States. His original co-worker, Mary Ainsworth, and subsequently Mary Main, for example, have carried out research on the attachment patterns of children. Mary Main, in her research, has distinguished four main forms of attachment in young children: anxious avoidance, secure, ambivalent-anxious, and disorganised.

These four categories of attachment were identified in babies from 12-18 months using the 'Strange Situation' test. In this test, the baby and mother are observed together, during a brief separation with the observer, and on reunion. At the mother's return, the different categories of attachment described above are used to describe the quality of the infant/mother interaction on reunion. For example, secure attachment is characterised by the infant who can respond positively to her mother's comfort on reunion. The 'ambivalent baby' may allow the mother to comfort him intermittently, while the 'anxious/avoidant' baby may actively withdraw from the mother and seek to comfort himself. The 'disorganised' baby, most typified by early experience of abuse or neglect, may not know to whom to turn. Main and Ainsworth's research suggests that these early patterns of attachment provide diagnostic indicators for subsequent adjustment and parent/child interaction.

The work of James and Joyce Robertson

The dual focus of psychodynamic clinicians at this time on working directly with children and on observed and actual experience brought home to parents and policy makers alike the reality that parents mattered to children. The films of children separated from their parents made by James and Joyce Robertson further reinforced this position. James Robertson had worked with John Bowlby at the Tavistock Clinic as a social worker. He subsequently trained as a psychoanalyst at the Anna Freud Clinic. His wife, Joyce, worked for several years at the Anna Freud Centre observing mothers and babies in the Well Baby Clinic and later in the residential nursery.

The work of James and Joyce Robertson focused particularly on the effects on young children of separation of various kinds. They addressed the need at the time for urgent reform of arrangements at hospitals whereby children were separated from their parents and a regime was favoured which fitted in with the needs of the bureaucracy but not with the needs of a small child. In order to convince professional staff and administrators about the importance of parental visiting in hospital, the Robertsons made a film about a child's admission to hospital which recorded in detail the experience of the child from the point of admission to the point of discharge. This enormously vivid and moving film helped to educate hospital staff about the emotional needs of children and influenced arrangements regarding the access of young children to their parents – a different way altogether of looking at the link between paediatrics and child mental health.

James and Joyce Robertson went on to make films about the effects of brief separation on young children, particularly in residential care and also in short-term foster care placements. The Robertsons were frequent visitors to Australia and helped in the establishment of the Association for the Welfare of Children in Hospital. Their films, made in the late 1950s and 1960s, are still available for training purposes and are as relevant and poignant today as when they were first made.

The work of Selma Fraiberg

We can see how many of these clinicians focused their attention on the earliest stages of infant and young child development. In the United States the work of Selma Fraiberg is particularly noteworthy in this regard. Rather like Winnicott, her writings about early childhood and development were written for a wider public and distributed through magazine articles and radio. Her book written mainly for parents, called *The Magic Years*, helps them to understand the nature of their child's experience through focusing on the child's world of play and how different kinds of behaviour can be understood to have very special emotional meanings. Fraiberg's later work was concerned with the support of deprived mothers and babies. Like Bowlby and other clinicians and researchers in the field, she was concerned with the repetition of deprived and brutalising experience. In one of her papers, called 'Ghosts in the Nursery' (1980), she describes the important and careful work that is required by a professional team who are able to work closely together to support deprived mothers and help them work through the traumatic and difficult experiences that they had themselves as babies. The work of Fraiberg and her associates demonstrates clearly how broadly and flexibly the psychodynamic approach can be applied, since much of the work carried out by Fraiberg and her associates with these mothers took place in the mother's own home.

Work with severely disturbed and psychotic children

The work of Bruno Bettelheim

In the United States the work of Bruno Bettelheim has been a particular inspiration. I have mentioned before that the Second World War and the trauma of dispersement paradoxically provided an opportunity for a generation of significant ideas in this field of human development. Bruno Bettelheim had been imprisoned for 12 months in the concentration camps of Dachau and Buchenwald. He moved to the United States where he established the pioneering Orthogenic School at the University of Chicago which focused particularly on clinical psychodynamic work with severely disturbed children and adolescents. In 1987, towards the end of his life, Bruno Bettelheim published a book, *A Good Enough Parent*, which he acknowledged had been derived from Winnicott's concept of the idea of the good enough mother. Bettelheim's book finds an echo in Winnicott's original work, *The Child, the Family and the Outside World*. Bettelheim, like Winnicott, invokes the centrality of the relationship between the child and his parents as the core point from which all advice about parenting must follow.

The work of Erik Erikson

Also in the United States, Erik Erikson, working as a clinician with children and adolescents, made a unique contribution to the field through his analysis of the psychosocial factors in the formative years of childhood. He studied also the process of growing up in a variety of cultural and social settings. His work *Childhood and Society*, with its core chapter on 'the Eight Ages of Man', remains a classic in the field.

The work of Wilfrid Bion

Another thinker of the British Object Relations School, Wilfrid Bion, has contributed widely to psychodynamic thinking and understanding on a number of different levels. His ideas have been useful in helping us to understand the intrapsychic processes at work in the infant-parent relationship. Bion's work during the Second World War as an army psychiatrist enabled him also to become concerned with the nature of group and organisational processes.

In the course of this book I refer to Bion's ideas about the 'container and the contained', that is to say how the infant-parent relationship from the outset can be viewed as a containing experience. The parents need to be able to contain the baby and growing child and, in the process, to be able to contain whatever the baby produces – tears, hunger, fear, anxiety. Bion has pointed out how a specific part of the containment process involves the parent in being able to transform the negative or anxious communication of the child so that it is in a sense reintegrated within the child as a tolerable experience. Where the parental caregiver is not able to provide this containment, then the child is left with the undigested anger or despair or feelings of persecution which cannot be transformed or transmuted into more tolerable states of mind.

Bion's model of containment can be applied to individual and family developments as well as to groups and organisations. As I indicated in Chapter 1, we can extrapolate from the containment required within the infant-parent relationship to the appropriate containment required in a child centre or kindergarten. Similarly, the therapeutic relationship has as its core the need for the therapist to be able to contain the patient in order to facilitate the joint therapeutic endeavour.

The importance of the organisational setting

With the establishment of the National Health Service in Britain after the Second World War came a belief that the clinical work and experience of psychodynamic thinkers could be brought together in a way which could be applied to a much wider community. This thinking led to the expansion and formal establishment in London of the Tavistock Clinic and Tavistock Institute of Human Relations shortly after the war. The Tavistock Clinic still exists today and is funded by the National Health Service and offers psychological facilities for a wide range of patients. It offers a child and adolescent service, as well as an adult service, and has a distinguished record of initiating and developing training for psychotherapists in the child, adult and adolescent fields. Perhaps the effects of the horrors of the Second World War and the vicissitudes of migration had contributed to a need to invest in the future of successive generations, and certainly in a more preventative approach.

If we look at the extraordinary contribution of so many of these clinicians and thinkers in Britain and the United States, we can see that the work was part of an international movement at a particularly given time and place. However, the best of the work emerged not just from clinicians working in isolation but from clinical work taking place in organisations and institutions which fostered ideals about the furtherance of understanding about human development generally. We can see the flowering of this work through institutions such as the Tavistock Clinic and the Anna Freud Centre in London, and the Menninger Clinic in the United States.

In the previous chapter I referred to the wide application of psychodynamic theory and observation to group and organisational life. The immediate postwar period saw a significant expansion in this area, both in Britain and the United States. Bion's work as an army psychiatrist had led to his developing theories about the way in which people relate in groups. He put forward the idea of 'the basic assumption', a strong belief shared by members of a group. Generally, this belief or assumption is not grounded in reality but nevertheless dominates the functioning of the group to make it difficult for the group members to pursue their task.

Later developments of these ideas led to formulations about the 'culture' of an organisation or company. For example, Isabel Menzies Lyth, a psychoanalyst in Britain, also undertook large-scale organisational studies. Her work for the nursing department of a London teaching hospital led her to identify a theory about 'social defences'. She found that nurses used procedures and routines in a defensive way to avoid contact with the patient. This was the nurses' way of managing their own fear and anxiety.

In subsequent chapters I refer to the way in which similar defensive manoeuvres can be used in how we think about many of the challenging issues raised by the young child and adolescent.

The impact of family therapy

In describing the clinical psychodynamic tradition thus far, I have focused on those clinicians and theorists who have identified the complexities of human development from the perspective of intrapsychic and interpersonal phenomena, focusing mainly on the child-parent relationship, most frequently the dyad of mother and infant or child. An understanding of the tradition of psychodynamic thinking must include as well those theorists who have developed primarily a family therapy or family-oriented approach.

Many of the founders of family therapy have been steeped themselves in the work of individual psychotherapy. The movement of family therapy, particularly over the last 30 years, has seen a particular flowering in the United States. Family therapy introduces the idea of systems thinking into our understanding of relationships. The work of Gregory Bateson, originally an anthropologist, is of particular significance in this context (Luepnitz, 1988). Bateson's description of systems as organisations of interdependent parts led to an interest in understanding how family systems, for example, can exchange information with the environment around them and exhibit particular ways of organising themselves. One of the basic tenets of systems theory is that it is not possible to create change in one aspect of the system without affecting change in another aspect of the system. The dynamic interdependent nature of systems thinking is not dissimilar to the way in which I would view the interaction between the infant and his parents. I describe this in Chapter 3 as a mutually transforming experience in which the infant is not the passive recipient of activity; rather the infant creates his own input into the system which in turn will affect the way in which his mother responds to him. We can of course postulate that the very birth of the child sets in motion major changes in the family and extended family systems.

Purists from either the individual psychotherapeutic world or the family therapy systems world may probably take issue with this approach and argue that the two views are incompatible with each other. However, I would tend to disagree because I would see the psychodynamic perspective as encompassing more than intrapsychic experience. Put most simply, one can say that there can be no 'inside the self' without an idea of 'outside the self'. External experience in turn has to be processed by the meaning that we give to events. Thus, in all my clinical work, I would not consider seeing a child for psychotherapy on their own without contact with the parents or arranging for a close colleague working in the same centre to offer parallel therapy to the parents.

In the same way, I believe that family therapy and systems ideas, linked to an understanding of developmental and intrapsychic functioning, has tremendous potential for helping children and families. The presentation of a family, for example, at a first interview enables us to view simultaneously the parental-marital interrelationships, the child-parent interrelationships going both ways, and the relationships between the children. The room can also be filled in a sense with the absent members who may be very significant in the family's life, for example extended members of the family and dead relatives. The idea of how a problem becomes manifest in one particular family member is also able to be identified at such family meetings, where we can see what the child's problem means not only in terms of his intrapsychic development, or in terms of the two-person or three-person relationship, but in terms of the broader family system. The diagram below shows how I perceive the interconnectedness of these different levels of experience, going from the internal intrapsychic experience outwards to influence external events, and coming back from external events through to influence intrapsychic configurations.

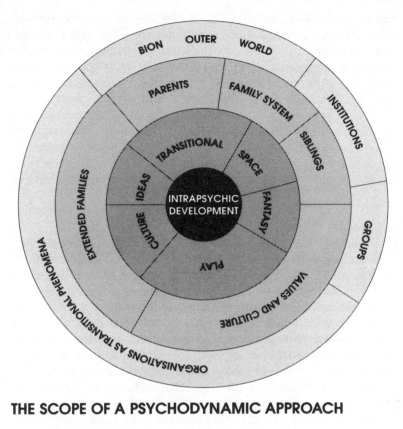

THE SCOPE OF A PSYCHODYNAMIC APPROACH

Broadening the scope of psychodynamic understanding

I have mentioned before that much of the thrust towards the development of family therapy models has come from the United States. However, a considerable amount of work has also been undertaken in Britain and in Europe, most particularly in Italy. This suggests again that ideas, particularly as they relate to assisting children in need and their parents, do not develop in isolation but emerge from broader felt needs both in the community and in professional groups. Many of the founders of the different family therapy movements, as I have mentioned before, had themselves been steeped in individual psychotherapy with children and adults. Perhaps, as a way of struggling to identify a new discipline and profession, there has tended to be a tension within family therapy either espousing a purely systems approach or trying to combine a psychodynamic, intrapsychic interpersonal approach with an understanding of systems theory. I see the counter-pulls towards either the pure systems direction or pure individual direction as rather missing the point, because the needs of children and parents demand that we are able to perceive a more complex and many-layered view of development and life experience.

The focus of the earliest family therapists such as Nathan Ackerman, Virginia Satir, Salvadore Minuchin and Carl Whittaker in the United States and Robin Skynner in Britain, served to broaden the entire discourse about child development and family life. In this book I write about the different levels of human development which involve an irrevocable crossing of a boundary, such as the birth of a baby or the move to adolescence. In theoretical and conceptual terms we can view the introduction of family therapy as producing such a similar irrevocable boundary, following which theory and conceptualising about family life could never be the same again. For example, in my own experience of working in child guidance clinics in London, the arrival of family therapy ideas in the 1970s in the form of training seminars run by family therapists from the United States heralded a change of enormous proportions. This change took place not only in terms of everyday clinical work, but affected the policy and structure of the kind of services we offered. It now seems inconceivable that a child psychotherapist, although trained in intensive individual work with children and adolescents, could refuse to see the value of conducting an initial assessment or subsequent meetings with the family of the child they are treating.

Another significant feature in the development of family therapy is the recognition of the place of the father. Family therapy actively encourages, and indeed in some cases insists upon, the presence of all the members of the family, and the role of supporting and instating the father has been a particular feature of this work. We could say that, from a professional perspective, the mother-infant dyad mirrored by the professional mother dyad, for example, in Winnicott's consultations has been superseded by the family-professional constellation.

The focus in family therapy on family of origin is also another way of comprehending the idea of the child within the parent and the parent within the child. This intergenerational impact is another area that family therapy has made ripe for exploration.

I have stated earlier that family therapy has been particularly helpful as an approach in enabling fathers to become more involved. An exploration of the dynamic of the family and the relationship between the family and intrapsychic processes enables us as well to consider some of the crucial aspects of the formation of gender and sexual identity. A recent contributor to this field, Deborah Anna Luepnitz, in her book *The Family Interpreted* (1988), has made a dazzling contribution. Her book explores the relationship of family therapy to both psychoanalysis and to feminism. She sees the continuity between psychodynamic theory and family therapy as providing the most promising foundation from which to develop a conceptual framework that can address these key issues as we move towards the twenty-first century. It is interesting to note her reference to the many passages in Freud's writings which have what she calls 'a family systems ring'. For example, she refers to the following from *An Outline of Psychoanalysis*:

> Freud states that no one who has any experience of the rifts which so often divide a family will, if he is an analyst, be surprised to find that the patient's relatives sometimes betray less interest in his recovery than in his remaining as he is (Luepnitz, 1988, p. 171).

Here we come full circle with the first origins of indepth psychology seemingly in tune with feminist family therapy of the late twentieth century. Luepnitz further points out how she finds the work of the British Object Relations School, particularly that of Melanie Klein, Bion and Winnicott, most useful and compatible with feminism because of their particular emphasis on the earliest mother-child interactions. Luepnitz refers as well to Winnicott's ideas of the 'holding environment' or the 'facilitating environment', which refers to the atmosphere of safety and trust which the parent provides for the child, and similarly the environment which the professional offers their client. The holding environment and the place of containment, which informs so much of the developmental thinking of this book, can thus be seen to provide a bridge between the earliest developments of psychodynamic practice and current experience. We thus come full circle at the end of the twentieth century to what Winnicott has so appropriately called 'the child, the family and the outside world'.

For details of references used and a comprehensive suggested further reading list see the endmatter pages at the back of this book.

PART TWO

Development

CHAPTER 3

The Beginning of Life and Before: Birth and Early Infancy

SUMMARY

This chapter on birth and early infancy presents the following core ideas about birth.

- It is a time of transition and involves crossing a boundary from being someone's child to becoming someone's parent.
- For this transition to succeed an opportunity for reverie is needed, particularly for the mother.
- The role of the father is crucial.
- How parents and professionals cope with mixed feelings at the birth of a baby must also be addressed.
- Parents are not made at birth but become parents over time.
- The theme of container and contained enables us to see that the mother cannot 'hold' or contain her baby if she does not feel contained herself.
- From birth the baby is a partner in shaping her earliest relationships and is already 'primed' for interaction with her parents.
- The need to help the baby 'give voice' and the method of infant observation are also discussed.

'There is no such thing as a baby,' said Donald Winnicott, the famous paediatrician and psychoanalyst. What he meant by this was that the infant and the personality of the baby develops within a context. The infant's development can only take place within total social embeddedness. The infant's development exists in a relationship with his mother, father, family and significant others. This suggests that the beginning of life for the infant actually takes place in the mind of the parents before the baby is born, since the baby is held in mind for nine months and the ideas, thoughts, fantasies and worries about this developing baby in the mother's body have a significant effect on the way the baby comes into the world, and the type of welcoming committee he will have. We know from the emotional experience of women who have suffered miscarriages or have had terminations of pregnancy how the developing infant is perceived as much more than a collection of biological cells. From the start of pregnancy the mother and father will create a meaning for the existence of this particular child, which paves the way for subsequent development of identity and personhood.

A TIME OF TRANSITION: CROSSING A BOUNDARY

The state of pregnancy itself represents a transition and the irreversible crossing of the boundary from being someone's child to becoming someone's mother. It represents, in a sense, one of the last major significant steps towards full adulthood. In recognising the transitional nature of this experience, particularly for first-time parents, it is important to acknowledge that pregnant women can have mixed feelings about having the baby, and that they should not be put under pressure or made to feel that everything is wonderful all the time.

Throughout this book I will return to the core theme that parents are not made at birth but become parents over time. This process of 'becoming' involves a lot of mixed feelings, and at times a quite ambivalent attitude towards the developing baby. Women may feel anxious about not having what they feel are instinctive maternal feelings. Some women enjoy the change in their bodies, while others dislike it. Their pregnancy may be an apprehensive time. The birth of a first child for both men and women also offers an opportunity for the cycle of development to come full circle, in that both men and women reflect on how their own mothers and fathers coped with pregnancy, motherhood and fatherhood. Do they wish to be the same as their mothers and fathers, or would they like to be different, and in what way?

Donald Winnicott has found a poetic and apt way of describing this phase of transition and crossing of the boundary, which he refers to as the need in the mother for 'maternal reverie' and maternal preoccupation. By this he refers to the spontaneous need of the woman, particularly in the later stages of pregnancy, to withdraw somewhat into herself and become preoccupied with the growing baby, who increases in size and activity every day and makes his or her presence known. There is both a biological as well as an emotional imperative involved in this kind of reverie and preoccupation because it evokes a final stage of allowing the baby to become a real person. One can speculate at this time that in the mother's mind, and the father's, there are all sorts of ideas about what this child will look like, how the child will appear, as well as anxieties about possible damage to the child.

The opportunity for reverie which Winnicott has described also incorporates within it the opportunity for play, and for both parents to have playful ideas about their forthcoming child. This may involve giving the baby a nickname or speculating about the sex of the baby.

With the advent of the use of the ultrasound technique a powerful visual image is introduced which enables us to see the miracle of life as it literally unfolds. In some maternity centres in Australia parents are actually given a photograph of the ultrasound, which represents a permanent capturing of this period of fascination and preoccupation with the developing baby.

In the first chapter on laying the foundations for a psychodynamic approach, I referred to one of the tenets which is the cornerstone of the psychodynamic approach, namely that this approach is concerned both with the inner world of our dreams, fantasies, hopes and wishes, as well as with the outer world of reality demands and needs. The period of pregnancy and preparation for parenthood represents par excellence the inner world/outer world preoccupations in process. I have mentioned that pregnancy can be seen as a state of transition and also represents the crossing of a boundary from being someone's child to becoming someone's mother. There is also the transition in terms of the inner space in which the baby is developing and the outer world. Here the physical, the psychological and emotional all come together. Indeed one can say that in order for the mother and father to be optimally prepared for the birth of their child, these are the processes that ideally need to take place. The mother needs to move into a different time frame and perhaps distance herself from immediate external preoccupations as the birth of the baby becomes imminent. The dreaminess that is often commented on in mothers is actually a very important working through process. What is vital is that society allows for this time process to take place.

As we go through the different stages of development I will refer to how each stage of development requires an appropriate time frame. Often this is not available for a variety of reasons. An appropriate time frame which allows the processing of maternal reverie, paternal reverie and maternal and paternal preoccupation to take place is absolutely essential in order for the proper groundwork to be done to prepare for the birth of the baby.

The point at which the inner and the outer intersect in pregnancy has its parallel in biological reality in what is known as 'the common hormonal pool' shared between the mother and the developing baby. Whatever the mother takes into her body in the form of foods and whatever is happening to the mother physically and biologically will inevitably affect the baby. We can postulate that the mother's emotional state, and the emotional and psychological experiences which surround this period of the pregnancy will also affect the common hormonal pool.

What happens when maternal reverie and maternal preoccupation are interrupted?

It is not always possible for mothers and fathers to be in this state of optimum preparedness or maternal and paternal reverie and preoccupation, particularly when a variety of external stresses may get in the way. For example, when a woman has experienced repeated miscarriages she may find herself almost determinedly not thinking about the life of the baby or the personality characteristics of the baby-to-be in case she creates too much of an identity of the baby for herself which could lead to disappointment and hopes being dashed again if the pregnancy is miscarried. Similar difficulties may occur with couples who have experienced long-term infertility problems and who may have been on fertility programs for many years. The high level of anxiety associated with such difficulties in conception, together with the fear of losing the baby again during pregnancy, may contribute to a difficulty in establishing this process of reverie and preoccupation with the idea of a real baby. Other factors, such as stress associated with financial difficulties or a poor relationship with a partner, will make it difficult for a mother to be exclusively concerned with the coming baby. These difficult circumstances would steer her away from her reverie to deal with these pressing external issues.

An area that is often overlooked is the impact of bereavement during the course of pregnancy, particularly of a close relative such as the potential grandparents. Here the task of preparing for a new life is complicated by the need, at the same time, to mourn for a death. The birth of a new baby requires all the mother's energy and concentration, and the process of mourning may often have to be delayed until after the baby's birth, which may complicate the first few months of the mother's experience of motherhood in relation to her baby.

The effect of external transitions on the internal transitional process

In order for the process of preoccupation and maternal reverie to take place in a satisfactory way it is important for the mother and father to be living in reasonably stable circumstances, that is not to have to be on the move. It is important for a mother, particularly for the birth of a first child, to be in familiar circumstances, with a known and supported network of family and friends.

We may pause for a moment to consider that Australia is a country made up of many migrants who have come from a variety of different countries, some of them from very difficult circumstances. One could say that the issue of migration for families across cultures and continents is one of the key issues of our time and is currently taking place on an unprecedented scale. Families from Eastern Europe, Central Europe, Asia and Africa find themselves putting down roots in Australia, in a country which is totally different from their original country of origin and culture. What effect will this cultural change and transition have on the young mother and father who are about to start a family, or where the mother may be already pregnant while in transit. We can see how the effects of an external transition, which can be very traumatic in some cases, can make the work of preparation for the pregnancy very difficult. It is interesting to note, for example, that we talk about 'a mother tongue' as though the beginnings of language and identity are very much caught up with and related to our earliest experiences of the mother's body and identity. How difficult it must be then for the mother herself who has, in a sense, lost her own mother tongue to come to a new culture where she may give birth surrounded by people and customs that are totally alien to her.

Most recently, I have been involved in an international project called Parents in Transition which attempts to explore the effects of this kind of migratory dislocation on the developing infant-parent relationship. We are able to make some hypotheses about how migration, particularly when it has been preceded by traumatic circumstances such as persecution and experiences of war, seriously hampers the capacity of both the mother and the father to engage with the normal process of preoccupation with the infant which is part of this essential preparation for life. The importance of having a base and being on familiar territory is described in the following example.

Being away from home

A young professional couple migrated to the United States when the mother was in her final trimester of pregnancy, awaiting the birth of her first child. Her husband was keen to take up the offer of a course of further study at an American university. Although there was a possibility of postponing this until at least after the birth of the child, he was reluctant to do so and put great pressure on his wife to arrange for their departure as soon as possible. In this situation one might speculate that, as this young man's wife was about to give birth to the baby, he perhaps needed to feel a separate sense of importance in being able to give birth to his own new baby, that is the special course for which he had been accepted. This might be one way to enable us to understand the extreme urgency and pressure he created in his insistence that he and his wife migrate before the birth of the child. In the event, the couple found themselves in difficult circumstances on their arrival in the United States only two months or so before the birth of the baby, and had no opportunity to put down any roots or make contact with friends or a social network. Later this young woman described the birth of the baby and the subsequent months as one of the most traumatic in her life. She described her total sense of isolation and how her own depression, and one can imagine anger with her husband, was echoed by her child's almost inconsolable crying. She described how she struggled to find a way to stop the baby crying and found that the only way she could do so was to settle into a position lying on the floor of the hallway of their tiny flat and place the baby against her diaphragm. In this way the baby, hearing his mother's heartbeat, was able to settle and be comforted for a while. Here one can see how this woman had been wrenched away from her normal maternal preoccupation and reverie into a situation of extreme stress settling into a new country where, for a time, she became overwhelmed by her own infantile needs and was left, in a sense, huddling together with her baby.

Bringing the baby into the world

When one enters a birthing unit or post-natal ward there is a sense of the very air reverberating with intense emotion. The birth of a new baby is a poignant, powerful and miraculous event, and it is these very facts that in turn engender such powerful, and at times confusing, experiences both in the parents themselves, in the professionals who assist them, and in the families and friends who are also part of the birth experience.

For many women preparing for a baby, it sometimes becomes difficult to see beyond the actual labour. An enormous amount of energy and time seems to go into the preparation for birth classes which, while laudable, may sometimes convey the impression of working towards a huge crescendo or climax, but may offer little preparation beyond the point of birth. The primary task of all professionals involved in childbirth is to facilitate the key relationship between the mother, the father and the baby. It is important that the childbirth setting and any surgical or other interventions that need to take place should, at all times, work towards facilitating this relationship and its potential in the most optimum way. Unfortunately, this does not always take place and, in fact, on many occasions women particularly are drawn into relationships with the staff who are attending them when their concentration really needs to be focused much more on the baby and their relationship with their partner in beginning to understand this new being who is coming into the world.

It is now widely recognised that the presence of fathers at the time of the birth of their children is critical in facilitating their connectedness with the child and their investment right from the beginning This needs to parallel that of the mother which is created more directly through her biological connection.

Understanding ambivalence at the beginning of life

I have referred to the fact that the beginning of life represents a powerful emotional experience which reverberates not only for the parents themselves but also for those people around them. Sigmund Freud has made the classic remark that 'Death arouses ambivalence', by which he means that it arouses in us a wide range of mixed feelings: sorrow, grief, rage, anger with the person who has left us, perhaps a sense that they were not as wonderful as we had thought them to be. In the same way one can postulate that birth, an equally powerful event – the start of new life – also arouses mixed feelings in everybody concerned. First-time parents, in particular, may feel extremely vulnerable. They may find themselves open to a wide range of suggestions made apparently in good will by professionals and other helpers, family and friends, although this advice may be contradictory or even unhelpful. For example, it is not unusual, particularly for first-time parents, to be warned before the birth of the child, or even at the birth, of the difficulties lying ahead with an expression such as 'You won't know what hits you once the baby is born'. Here the suggestion is that the gilt will be taken off their miraculous gingerbread and the parents will fall from their state of grace and joy into a pretty miserable state.

In the first chapter I stated that one of the cornerstones of the psychodynamic approach refers to the connection of the child in the parents and the parents in the child. At the time of the birth of the baby, the experience of the infant in the parent and in the adult is very much to the fore. Their memory of infancy, which may have been very distant, through this powerful experience comes flooding back to both parents. The sight of a newborn baby nuzzling against its mother's breast and body, a combination of fragility and toughness, arouses an extraordinary range of emotions in all of the people who may be attending to the mother and baby at this time. Feelings may be aroused about the infantile self, the baby in oneself as an adult, that may yearn for a similar experience. There may be feelings of envy of the parents and their achievement in giving birth to a healthy baby. The professionals who attend to the baby, the mother and father are not immune from these powerful emotional experiences. It may be for this reason that childbirth, more than any other human experience, appears to be subject to so many vagaries and changes, and such powerful ideas of what is right and proper. This suggests that there is a need to control the experience of childbirth, thereby also controlling the powerful emotions which this experience engenders in all of us. It is sobering to recall, for example, that as recently as 40 years ago many mothers in the Western world were subject to the ideas of paediatrician Truby King with his emphasis on rigid feeding practices and the separation of the mother and baby after birth. This intrusion into the infant/parent relationship is also reflected in the commonly used expressions such as 'making a rod for your own back', which admonishes the mother for daring to be too intimate and close with her baby.

An exclusive focus either on the type of childbirth or the way in which feeding schedules should be organised, or whether the baby should be rooming in with their mothers or not, or what type of feeding is best, tends to fragment and partialise the total experience of the relationship of the baby to its mother and father, and they to him. The tendency towards fragmenting the childbirth experience denies the total configuration of the infant mother and father relationship, which needs the full attention of the professionals involved. Specific decisions about what type of feeding or what sort of childbirth must be seen as dependent on the needs and personalities of the individual mother and father and their circumstances, rather than a dogma which is issued by the professionals or the birthing centre.

Many mothers, years after their children have been born, recall extremely vividly some of the trials and difficulties associated with their baby's birth. It is not uncommon for mothers to recall how they found themselves engaging in a battle, for example with nursing staff, about 'whose baby is this?' when their baby was whisked off to the nursery and the mother may have wanted it to be with her either in bed or next to the bed. Current thinking about feeding babies tends to support the idea that breastfeeding is best for babies as well as demand feeding. However, at times, the insistence with which this can be promoted for mothers can smack of the same rigidity with which the Truby King four-hourly feeds were instigated.

THE FIRST 18 MONTHS

Parents are not made at birth but become parents over time

Infancy and the beginning of life shows us that there is no such thing as a baby, as Winnicott has said, because the baby is totally dependent and interdependent with his mother and father and other social relationships. We can also postulate that there is no such thing as a ready-made parent. The idea that parents, particularly of a first-born child, should be all-knowing and coping is frankly ludicrous. Parents can only become parents over time in a relationship with their baby and young child. This is a process of learning through experience rather than of having an assumption of knowledge. One of the greatest difficulties for parents in a consumer-oriented, technological society is that we have become used to the idea of gaining knowledge and expertise, as though everything can ultimately be known and mastered. It is difficult for us to acknowledge that human processes of development are rather more complex and require a different kind of learning. I recall seeing a family with a little boy, aged three, said to be hyperactive and out of control. His mother was a very anxious, over-controlling young woman who had difficulty making sense of his ordinary development. She had herself grown up in a very rigid family. Her husband took a much more relaxed attitude to the problem and remarked 'She believes that she will find the manual that will help her to work the child'. Regrettably, this way of thinking about child development and the parenting experience is becoming more widespread. When I refer to the fact that parents become parents over time, the issue of time is literally of great importance here. I have mentioned the importance of preparing for the baby. The parents need time for reverie and preoccupation. They also require an appropriate time frame and structure in order to carry out the important task of getting to know their baby once it is born.

One of the most common misconceptions about the developing infant is that he comes into the world as a blank slate, as a tiny creature who only eats and sleeps. In a sense he only needs to be 'fed and watered', but has no real capacity for responding or knowing what is going on until very much later. Happily, in the last 20 years, there has been a tremendous resurgence of interest in the emotional life of the infant. This interest has spawned a considerable level of research around the world into different aspects of the infant's experience and also into exploring optimal conditions for the development of the infant and parent relationship. It is interesting to note that many of the findings of these infant researchers confirm the clinical findings and reports of clinicians such as Donald Winnicott. For example, Daniel Stern, an eminent research scientist in the field of infant mental health, makes the point that, far from being a blank slate, the infant comes into the world bringing formidable capacities for human relatedness. Daniel Stern says that the infant is immediately a partner in shaping his first and foremost relationship.

The word 'partner' is here the operative one. Far from being passive and inert, the infant is active, alert and continually in interaction with his environment and the key people within it. Thus the first task for parents in learning from the experience is actually to feel, to believe and trust that they can learn from the baby. We can then see the partnership between the parents and the child as having a 'mediating function', that the parents mediate on behalf of the child in relation to the outside world, certainly in relation to his immediate physical needs and in translating the outside world, in assisting the baby in not feeling too over-whelmed, and in protecting the baby. In turn, the infant is able to communicate his needs through a wide and complex range of interactions to assist the parents to understand his inner world. What is critical in this process of mediation and partnership is that parents need to be able to learn from the infant, but they also need to be in a position of being able to observe the infant. By this I don't mean to observe the infant as a scientific curiosity or dis-tancing themselves from the experience; rather that they need to trust in the infant's formidable capacities and try to understand what the infant is actually trying to communicate. This requires that the parents are able to contain a considerable degree of uncertainty and are able, to some extent, to experiment with ideas about what may be going on for the baby.

The container and the contained

I have referred before to Wilfrid Bion's helpful concept which he uses to refer to this early experience of the parents and the baby getting to know each other. He describes this as 'the process of the container and the contained'. That is to say that the task of the mother and father is to be able to contain the anxiety of the baby and also their own anxiety. The baby requires to be contained by parents. However, it is extremely difficult for the parents to be able to contain what the baby produces, whether it is tearfulness or sleeplessness or an illness, without themselves becoming at times quite anxious. So they in turn need to feel that there are helpful grandparents available or extended family or friends, or a helpful professional person. In this way we can see that containment takes place on a number of different levels. Here we can imagine the image of Russian dolls, one within the other, so that the infant is contained by the parents, the parents are in turn contained by family friends, or professionals, and that there is containment available in the surrounding network.

The feeding relationship

Feeding for the baby is more than just taking in her mother's milk or nutrients from a bottle; rather we need to understand that feeding, right from the beginning of life represents part of a relationship which involves the child and her partnership with her mother, father and caretakers. It is striking how often parents will describe their child's particular interest or lack of interest in food right from the word go. Sometimes the difficulties in establishing feeding in infancy may be associated with later difficulties. To some extent this depends on the interaction which has been set up within the partnership between the child and her parents. The area of food and feeding is one which can easily turn into a battleground because of the intensely powerful emotions associated with the process. Feeding, of course, is necessary for life and survival, but it also indicates for the mother, particularly, her capacity to be satisfactory, to be able to offer food either through her own body and breasts or with some satisfactory alternative.

I recall a colleague telling me that, when her first child was born, she was tremendously relieved to witness his regurgitating the milk he had swallowed after a feed which landed on an exquisite little coverlet that had been handed down through the family. She recalled the overwhelming sense of reassurance that the baby was actually feeding on her milk and that she had enough to give him. One can understand how the opposite can hold true: that where mothers may not have sufficient milk or where the circumstances inhibit the possibility of satisfactory breast feeding to be established, the mother particularly may feel that she has not been able to offer enough to her child. In some cases parents will talk about a fretful 'colicky' baby where perhaps the tension that gets set up between the mother and the child contributes to an inhibition and anxiety for both of them, so that the process of feeding becomes imbued not with calm and pleasure and fulfilment, but with an anticipation of anxiety or rejection. Perhaps for the baby there may be a sense of not being able to get enough food or having too much food forced into his mouth. A woman who had satisfactorily breastfed her first child was having some difficulties with her second newborn baby girl and felt that this child was not quite as accepting of the breast as the previous one had been. When I visited her in hospital I noticed that she tended to force her nipple into the baby's mouth. She said, 'Come on, kid, this is what you need to do.' We talked for a while about how there had been a difference for her in the feeding experience with the first child because, in a sense, both she and the baby had been novices at this joint enterprise. This allowed her to, in turn, allow the baby to explore the breast and in this way for them to both to set up a pattern that was reward- ing and satisfactory to both. For her second baby it seemed as though she felt that she knew it all and somehow she had to teach the baby and perhaps force her before the baby was ready to experience her own exploration on the breast, and in a sense to get to know her mother.

Feeding as a social and interactive experience

In attempting to fit into a routinised idea of 'managing' a baby, parents may emphasise the baby's need for food and for sleep in a concrete way which denies the other real need of the baby, which is for intimate engagement and social exchange.

A young mother with a three-month-old baby contacted a Parent Advice Line. She was convinced that she had a severe sleeping problem on her hands. The problem, as she put it, was that she had been told by her mother that once the baby has fin- ished its feed, it needs to be wrapped up in its blanket and put down into its cradle. She had tried to do this several times but found that her baby had refused to go to sleep and indeed protested. It seemed, as we talked a bit more, that the baby, far from having a problem, was really trying very hard and actively to communicate with her mother. I tried to suggest to this young mother that the baby so enjoyed her company that, at the end of the meal, she wasn't always ready for sleep but that she wanted to be sociable. She was letting her mother know that she wanted to have a conversation with her. This mother was quite surprised to hear that her baby had a distinct social need.

What is striking about this example is how parents manage to deprive themselves of the opportunity for play and of getting to know their babies when they try to fit into rigid managing patterns.

Helping the baby to give voice

If the beginnings of the capacity for attachment and relatedness are rooted in the earliest infant-parent interactions, then certainly the act of giving voice for the baby is a crucial part of this process. The baby's cries, cooing and singing seek to find a response in his mother. The quality and tone of her voice – her own crooning, talking and singing – forms part of creating the language of the mother-infant interaction. The amazing aptness of the mother's contribution which 'appears to come from nowhere' suggests that she too is primed, like Daniel Stern's infant, for an intense relatedness which, in ideal circumstances, has the quality of an intoxicating love affair. The baby, as he grows, can also delight in the use of his voice to communicate a wide range of emotions and experiences which act as indicators of his parental relationship and pathfinders for his exploration of the outside world. The talking, chirruping, whooping, laughing baby lets us into his world. Thus we can see how 'baby talk' has a vital developmental function. Baby talk may be disparaged by some parents who may be uncertain about their own infantile needs and who sadly wish to push their child into what they perceive to be a more 'adult' form of communicating. There are also other ways of eliminating baby talk altogether.

When we observe babies and their parents, we may wonder how the capacity of the baby to find its own voice or give voice is affected by the continued use of a dummy. I have been struck by how, in Australia, the dummy appears to be part of the essential kit that is bought together with all the other basic things that are needed for the baby's birth. What, it seems to me, happens when the dummy is used is that the baby cannot readily give voice to his experience. In not being allowed to give voice, there is yet another missed opportunity for a potentially important communication between the parents and the baby. It is as though there is a confusion about the meaning of the baby's cry. The baby's cry may be construed as negative, or there may be a sense in which the parents feel themselves unable to cope or bear the crying. There may also be anxiety about the disapproval of others if they are in a public place, which leads them to feel unable to consider that there may be another way in which to respond to the cry rather than simply to offer the dummy.

We can speculate that a continual use of the dummy may diminish the range of the infant's communication and limit the possibility for a wider repertoire of interchange and dialogue between infants and parents. The continual use of a dummy may also reflect the parents' anxiety about containing the negative experience which the baby's cry might elicit in them, for example, making them feel useless at not immediately understanding what the baby needs.

A continual use of the dummy also illustrates the lack of appreciation of the complexity of the infant's capacity for emotional relatedness. For example, the baby's cry represents giving voice as well as being different, of being in a state of having mixed feelings, of showing the beginnings of differentiation. What is concerning about the continual use of the dummy to stem a baby's cry is that it is as though every cry is construed as having the *same* meaning, and therefore requiring the *same response*, namely the giving of the dummy. This parental response has its parallel in the description given earlier by the maternal and child health nurse in the first chapter of the book when she described her work with mothers and babies as highly routine and repetitive.

The paradox of development

I have referred to Daniel Stern's comment that the infant brings formidable capacities into the world for establishing relationships. Winnicott talks about understanding the paradox of development, which is that at the point at which the infant comes into the world she is already developing, so that in a sense we can see that dependence and interdependence, the beginnings of separation and individuation, go hand in hand. The very fact and reality of physical growth in the infant can be enormously reassuring to parents. We should not underestimate the extraordinary resilience of babies and the fact that they will grow no matter what. I recall, at the birth of my daughter, being enormously reassured by the fact that her physical growth was in a sense outside of my control and there is an overwhelming reality of the infant's surge towards growth and health.

Dependence versus separation

The paradox which is involved in this early stage of the infant's life, namely that the infant requires the total commitment, involvement and attention of the parents, but is at the same time beginning his life as a separate and individuated person, makes considerable demands on both parents. It requires an extraordinary degree of flexibility and, at times, imaginative leaps for both parents. As we begin to explore further the psychodynamic perspective of human growth and development we begin to understand how vital the processes of interchange are for the development of the child, and how these processes are related to the particular needs of the stage that the infant and the parents are going through. Difficulties may arise when the particular process that is characteristic of a specific phase of development for the child and its parents continues into subsequent stages of development where it is either not required or no longer appropriate. An interesting example of this process is what I will refer to as the 'psychosomatic interrelationship' between the mother and the baby. Donald Winnicott describes what he calls the mother's 'natural hypochondriacal state' in relation to her child. That is to say that, instead of thinking of the term 'hypochondriacal' in the pejorative sense or negative sense, he says that a mother must naturally be hypochondriacal if she is able to notice certain symptoms in her child or changes that may affect the course of the child's development. Another way of putting this is to suggest that the relationship in the early stages of the baby's life is a psychosomatic one in relation to the mother. The child has only recently emerged out of the mother's body and is getting to know another life environment. We need to understand that the boundary between the internal and external worlds that I have described in the preparation for pregnancy continues through the early months and at least until the first year of the child's life. Here the physical and the psychological, appropriately and healthily, are to some extent fused. Maternal preoccupation develops on a psychosomatic level with the mother being able to respond to the cues which the baby presents. Within this psychosomatic mind/body state the mother is able to intuit the baby's needs and possible difficulties. The fact that this almost symbiotic state takes place alongside the baby developing as a separate individual simultaneously can make the situation quite complex. Under the best of circumstances it will lead to a spontaneous resolution with the continuing independence and development of the child. However, where this process is not worked through, in later life we may see examples of children who develop specific physical or hypochondriacal symptoms where the relationship between the mother and the child can almost only take place through a preoccupation with an illness in the child.

The role of the father

I have talked of the almost symbiotic nature of the relationship in the early weeks and months between the infant and his mother, but what of the role of father? One of the ideas which I return to at various times in this book concerns the nature of the partnership between parents and child since parents are not made at birth but become parents over time, through trial and error and learning from experience. In understanding the nature of partnership in this process, we must of course identify the core partnership which exists between the father and mother, husband and wife, man and woman. The strength of this partnership right from the outset will be a determining factor in promoting positive development for the child. For this reason it is regrettable that much theoretical and research work on infancy tends to focus on a rather exclusive mother-infant relationship, rather than seeing the infant as an active partner within a dynamic interchange and one that includes the father. We can postulate that the child's capacity for mental health and growth in later life is as much dependent on the existence of fathers and the quality of relationship with fathers as it is with mothers. The inclusion of men at the time of birth is often added as an afterthought. In preparing for the baby, women may be advised that they may need to take account of their partner's jealousy or rivalry with the baby, or may be surprised when this occurs after the baby's birth. Here the father's role is diminished by characterising him as 'another child'. We may wonder why this has come about. Pregnancy and maternity have for centuries had their own myths, and in traditional societies pregnancy and birth are kept separate as a woman's area apart from the world of men.

There are traditional differences about how men and women develop and think about their bodies, about partnerships and having children. For women the mental and physical preparation for becoming a mother does not have a necessary parallel in the life of men. The majority of men find themselves taking a kind of crash course in understanding a woman's reproductive system at the point that their partner has a baby, when the whole idea may have been very detached beforehand. Men may feel that they are pulled into intimacy with the female physical world which may generate a fear that they may lose a masculine part of themselves. At the same time we need to acknowledge that there is reality in men's envy of women's capacity to bear children. This can result in childbirth being both idealised and also denigrated. There is a further factor in that birthing centres or hospitals may tend to reinforce this attitude and pull the mother into a relationship with the professionals when the primary task at the birth of the child and immediately after is for her to establish a strong connection with her partner.

In order to find their way out of this dilemma men may try very hard to become as good as their partners, as good as women, perhaps even competing with their partners to see who can be a better mother. However, the primary task for men at this time is not that they should compete with their partners to become a better sort of mother, but rather that they need to find ways of combining their different qualities of masculinity with that of nurturing. The family therapist Robin Skynner has made some interesting comments on this topic. He has referred to the state of symbiosis between mother and baby, similar to the psychosomatic relationship I have described above, as one in which the father may see the mother as 'drowning in maternity'. Robin Skynner asserts that the task of the father is to draw the mother back into a relationship with him. As the baby grows and develops this may be a task which the mother is unable to do on her own and she is dependent on her partner to be able to assist. The father's role then involves the critical re-establishment of the parenting and sexual relationship, which in turn will enable the child to be able to develop positive mental health, grow and thrive.

The role of mediation between mother, father and the baby

The concept of mediation is useful in understanding the early critical process of the development of relationships and the development of the fundamental core of personality. The parents need to mediate on behalf of the child in relation to the external world, but they also need to be aware of the child's capacity to act as a mediator and indicator about his own internal world. This suggests a more three-dimensional model where the child is not just a passive recipient of interactions from the mother and father. That is to say that we do not refer to the child being 'done to', but of a dynamic interactive process. In this way the mediating process can be seen as a teaching process in which the infant teaches the parents how to become parents. Donald Winnicott has a wonderfully descriptive way of describing this process when he says the infant 'looks at the mother and sees himself'. By this he means that the infant makes up a picture of himself and of how he appears to the mother by scrutinising the mother's face and expressions, so that the mother's joy and delight in him will reverberate within the child himself and he will see himself as a valued, loved and delightful person. The opposite, of course, can hold true where the mother's depressed or averted gaze, or her anger, or her incapacity to stand what the baby produces, whether it is his physical poos or his tantrums or crying, will develop within the child an internal construct of his own personality as unacceptable and unlovable. However, here I would say that the infant not only looks at the mother and sees himself, but looks at the mother and father and sees himself.

If we are to fully understand how mental health and development takes place, we must move out of the focus of the dyadic relationship into the three-person relationship, and indeed the broader relationship of the outside world. Another way of putting it is to say that the presence of the third person is all-important in facilitating this process of development. For example, if we go back to the idea of the mother who needs initially to have a hypochondriacal or psychosomatic relationship with her child, as the relationship develops and the baby grows there is a requirement for more than this type of fused relationship, for the promotion of mental health. What is required is the presence of a third person who can take a step back, observe what is happening, make a comment about it, and interpret the interchange both for the mother and the baby. Most commonly, this would be the father of the child, but, where mothers are parenting on their own, it may be a sympathetic and supportive grandparent or a professional. The inclusion of the third person has a transforming effect on this dyadic interchange. For example, we can all imagine a mother, perhaps with a first-born baby, who, after the initial euphoria, is left mostly on her own in her home to cope with the child. She may begin to feel some depression creeping in, a feeling of the sameness of the routine of every day, and feel very anxious about the reality of the total dependence of the baby upon her. So, after a while, the mother's own capacity for observation of her baby can become rather blurred or a bit numb. What is required at this stage is the intervention of the third person, ideally the father, who, through making a comment about what might be happening, can actually facilitate the process. At this time the intervention of the third person through language or by trying to make sense of what might be happening for the baby, is all-important. This may be the intervention of a friend, another parent of a baby, maternal or child health nurse, particularly where no partner is available. What is important here is that a comment needs to be made about the interaction between the mother and the baby which can take the form of describing the baby's action, for example 'Look at the way the baby is looking at you, she really likes what you are doing', or perhaps suggesting some alternative way of going about managing the care of the baby, where this may involve some difficulty or where the mother and the baby may seem to be stuck.

Being a good enough parent

Donald Winnicott makes the point that what is required of the mother is not that she should be a superwoman or to be fantastically available to her baby and intuitive all the time; rather she only needs to be what he calls 'good enough'. However, in order for the mother to feel that she is good enough, she and her partner need to be in a position to be able to deal with the at times overwhelming uncertainty of coping with a new baby and of knowing what to do. In the three-person relationship of the mother, father and the baby, the father can take on the role of this third person and of offering what Bion has referred to as the 'necessary containment'. The father, by holding the mother and the baby in mind enables the uncertainty and anxiety to be contained long enough for both of them to be able to think together about what might need to be done. Thus both the mother and father are 'good enough'. Where no partner is available, we should not underestimate the potential importance of the role and sensitivity of professionals who may be required to work in this capacity.

Understanding the baby – the place of the significant other

I have stated that the main tenet of the psychodynamic approach is that all behaviour has meaning. One of the most difficult things to deal with, particularly for parents of first babies, is to understand the meaning of their baby's behaviour. How is it possible to attribute meaning to what at times seems very chaotic and confused behaviour when parents feel overwhelmed by their own worries and anxieties. Indeed, often parents are thrust back into memories of what it was like for them as babies. For this reason, the three-person interaction is absolutely vital, where the father or a significant other can act as a mediator in order to transform and attribute meaning to the interaction between the mother and the child, and the behaviour of the child. Many men may either be excluded at this early stage of the infant's development or tend to exclude themselves, thinking that their role as fathers only comes into its own when the child has reached the stage of walking or talking. Even Winnicott refers to a sequential involvement for the father. He says: 'Fathers must allow me to use the term maternal to describe the total attitude to babies and their care. The term paternal must necessarily come a little later. Gradually, the father as male becomes a significant factor.' (1965b) As our understanding of the mental development and mental health needs of children increases, we become aware that fathers have more than just a scene-setting function. Fathers must necessarily be involved in interaction of equal intensity with the mother right from the start of the baby's life, and feel that they have a critical role to play in the child's development. The critical role that both parents play as partners in understanding their baby is illustrated by the following example.

In this example one can see how parents, particularly of a first baby, can become flooded with anxiety and uncertainty about everyday tasks such as helping a young child to sleep. We can see how the mother's own experience in her first year of life affected her capacity to think clearly about how she might help Michael.

Our baby won't sleep

A couple in their thirties came to seek help with the problem of sleeping behaviour in their one-year-old boy. When they arrived at the clinic it was striking that they were obviously devoted parents and the child Michael was the apple of their eye. He was a highly responsive, interactive little baby who communicated extremely positively with both parents. He was carried in very tenderly by his father while he was asleep and, on waking, had a very animated exchange with both parents and myself in the room – making noises, chattering and singing. His parents explained that he had never in fact slept in his own bed or cot for any length of time since the birth. They had wanted their relationship with Michael to be as spontaneous and natural as possible, and had been advised that they should take the baby into their bed with them after his birth. However, he had never really left their bed. At one time he spent a few weeks in his own cot, but developed a cold and came back into the parents' bed. The difficulty now was that Michael, no longer a tiny baby, had developed sleeping patterns and rhythms which tended to dominate the household. When he went to sleep his parents would have to go to sleep at the same time, as Michael would not tolerate falling asleep in the parental bed without his mother's presence. The situation was further complicated by the fact that Michael's mother continued to breast feed him, so that Michael's presence in the bed would involve a virtual sleepless night for his mother. The impression I gained from Michael's parents was that they seemed to view the establishment of any limit setting or boundary, or any notion of a separate space, as imposing an intolerable cruelty on Michael. At the same time, when they spoke of trying to help Michael to sleep on his own, they suggested moving him into a completely separate room. Thus, on the one hand, they felt unable to create a reasonable separation between themselves and Michael, but the consequences of this drove them into a sufficiently exasperated state to consider that they would banish him to another room.

As part of the consultation process, I obtained a brief history about both parents' experiences and of what had happened to them as young children and babies. Michael's father tended to be rather reserved and said very little about his early experiences, which suggested perhaps that there may have been aspects of this which he did not care to remember. Perhaps one could speculate that they were too painful to remember. Michael's mother, on the other hand, was very forthcoming about her early experience. She had grown up in another country. When she was only a few weeks old her family had migrated from the Far East, where she lived, to the United States. Her own first year of life had been punctuated by transition and change, and she knew from her mother's description in later years that it had been an extremely traumatic time for her mother. Thus, in her own early infantile experience, Michael's mother was exposed to a sense of uncertainty and loss. So one might postulate, for example, that her own mother might have reacted by keeping all the children close and having them all in the bed with her.

The parents also mentioned that, quite aside from sleeping difficulties, Michael was a child who could not be left with anybody else, not even his devoted grandmother. They mentioned an example of how, on one occasion on one of their very infrequent evenings out, they had gone to a restaurant to celebrate an anniversary, and how this evening had been cut short by grandmother phoning the restaurant to say that Michael had cried so much that they would need to come home. It seemed, therefore, as though there could be no opportunity for containment of anxiety within this family or the tolerance of uncertainty. Both the parents were extremely anxious about the establishment of separation or boundaries and could not find a way of clarifying things for each other. The maternal grandmother, in turn, also became overwhelmed with anxiety at the crying baby as though, despite her own experience of bringing up children, there was something about the nature of this crying baby that had to be stopped at all costs.

During this initial consultation I made various practical suggestions about how the parents might organise the transfer of Michael to a separate sleeping place, and suggested that it would not be helpful for Michael to be moved into a separate room straightaway as the transition from the parental bed to a totally separate room on his own would be traumatic for him. I suggested instead that, since the parents had mentioned there was a cot in their room, Michael should be placed in the cot and that they should also be quite specific about the bedtimes that they set, so that Michael did not have to pull the whole family to bed at the same times. We also talked about how important it was to establish a bit of a routine before Michael went to bed, and that the parents, either separately or together, might need to sit with him for a little while to accustom him to being in his cot. I also suggested the use of some little cuddlies or a favourite blanket that he might be able to relate to as a way of holding on to a part of Mummy and Daddy.

I knew that the parents were going to embark on a process of change that would be quite hard for them to carry out because it involved not only an external change, but also having to change aspects of their own internal expectations and anxieties. I therefore suggested that they should telephone me to let me know how things progressed, and I also arranged a follow-up meeting.

About a week later, I received an anxious telephone call from Michael's mother explaining that it had been extremely difficult to implement my suggestions, and that really nothing seemed to work. However, when we explored in detail what had actually happened and why it was so difficult for this plan to succeed, it emerged that in fact Michael's parents still had some reluctance in implementing the plan. She would postpone the time of bedtime or make it very erratic, or allow Michael to engage in extended play once he was actually in the room. I suggested to Michael's mother that my recommendations seemed like a cruel action, and that she and her husband could not bring themselves to go through with it. I tried to explain as well that nevertheless some positive limit setting and the possibility of some separation between Michael and themselves would almost certainly enable Michael to feel more confident about his own capacity to put himself to sleep and to have some sense of mastery for himself which would also facilitate his move into the next stage of his development. When Michael's parents arrived for their next session a week later, they were absolutely delighted with the fact that, shortly after the telephone call, they had been able to be firm about putting Michael into his cot and setting a proper bedtime. In enabling themselves to be both convinced and convincing about what needed to happen, both parents had acknowledged the sense of pleasure and mastery that Michael was experiencing. It seemed for both of them that a load had somehow slipped from their shoulders.

In this example we can see how parents, particularly of a first baby, can become flooded with anxiety and uncertainty about everyday tasks such as helping a young child to sleep. We can see how the mother's own experience in her first year of life affected her capacity to think clearly about how she might help Michael. Interestingly, her own mother was similarly paralysed and was unable to offer the advice or support or observation of the third person, and the parents had become rather fused in their concern and anxiety about being cruel in suggesting any type of separation or individuation for Michael, or indeed themselves. My role in this regard was to act as 'the third person' as a container for the parents' anxiety, to support them, to give them permission to assert their authority as parents and make a decision that seemed to be appropriate for the development of all concerned.

Infant observation: what it can teach us

I have referred to how parents can learn from their child and how a capacity to take a step back and observe what is happening is an important part of this process. The establishment of infant observation as a learning tool in understanding the intricacies of the pattern of early development has considerable potential.

As a part of their training for child psychotherapy, students are required to undertake a detailed infant observation of a baby from the first weeks of life, generally to two years of age. This particular technique of infant observation was developed in the United Kingdom at the training institutions for child psychotherapists such as the Tavistock Clinic and the Anna Freud Clinic. It requires that the student visits an infant for an hour once a week, generally at an appointed time, and attempts to observe in detail the developing experience of the infant and its relationship with parents and other members of the family. While the observer is encouraged to take a positive attitude and interest in the developing baby, it is important for the observer not to feel under any particular pressure to take action or initiatives in relation to the direct care of the baby which is often seen as distracting to the process of observation. The observer is placed in a position of privilege and explains to the parents that they are engaged in a course concerned with child development, and that it will be of great importance and relevance to be able to observe an infant from the first few days or weeks of life. This process of detailed observation enables the student to be involved as an observer of the normal vicissitudes of development, the day-to-day life of bringing up a baby and young child in the family. Inevitably, the observer will experience very strong emotions aroused by being in such close proximity to the infant at the beginning of life, and some of the struggles and vicissitudes associated with development. For example, at times observers feel concerned about the baby or concerned about the mother. At various times they feel inclined to attribute blame. The task of the observation is, however, not to apportion blame but rather to enable the observer to gain some insight into the complexity of development as it unfolds and changes; and secondly, to develop skills in maintaining an observational stance which can be applied to other learning situations and experiences.

Infant observation as a learning tool has been gaining increasing recognition around the world and has now become firmly established as part of the training for psychotherapists in Australia, as well as for other professionals who are engaged in understanding the nature of childhood and family development.

An essential part of the observation process and learning is the weekly seminar to which participants in an infant observation course bring their detailed written observations. It is important for the observer not to take notes in the course of their session which will interfere with the whole process of their observation. An infant observation seminar represents a rich opportunity for inquiry into the variety and complexity of development. We can see how an infant's development progresses at different stages and levels; how the meaning of an infant's behaviour may be construed very differently, depending on the different life circumstances and indeed the view of the observer. The task of each infant observation seminar, which should be led by an experienced practitioner, is to reflect on these different levels of development and on the meaning of behaviour as it occurs. The task of the seminar is also to offer containment and support for the observers who may be experiencing strong or disturbing emotions associated with their proximity to the new baby and his family.

I will give brief vignettes of this type of infant observation. The examples all come from an infant observation seminar which I ran for paediatricians who had embarked on a year's course in child development. The notion of being in an experience, rather than 'having to do something', at times was quite difficult for the doctors since their professional training had trained them rather differently, to act upon situations and to take decisions and initiative. The idea of thinking about the interrelationship between mother and baby from the psychological, as opposed to a physiological, point of view also posed a particular challenge. Nevertheless the three different observations all indicate how quickly the observers were able to enter into the psychological world of the infant and mother and father. In some of these observations we will see how parents are coping with the birth of a first child, and also the birth of a second child.

Baby Martin

This visit took place when baby Martin was seven-weeks-old and . his parents, Marian and Bill, had been married for 10 years. They were both in their mid-thirties. Marian worked to the end of her pregnancy, which was described as wonderful, with no morning sickness or complications. She now recalls her 15-hour working days as nothing compared to the work involved with caring for a newborn baby.

Aged seven weeks

Marian greets me warmly at the door. She is welcoming and not at all anxious about my visit or the reason for it. She is wearing track pants and a sloppy-joe. We walk through the immaculate lounge room with baby grand piano, and numerous paintings adorning the walls, into the cosy kitchen where baby Martin is lying on his back in the pram, looking at a brightly coloured rattle mobile strung across the front of his pram. His arms and legs are moving in a playful way, and their movement is increased when Marian's face is brought close to him over the pram, and she talks to him. I note a Baby Development book on the kitchen bench, and later a copy of Christopher Green's book on babies and young infants on the coffee table in the lounge.

Marian starts to make us a cup of tea, and during this baby Martin starts to grizzle. Time for a feed, and we go into the lounge and sit on the leather couch and baby Martin is offered his mother's breast. He fusses at first and doesn't want to attach. Eventually the attempt is abandoned, and he is nursed over Marian's shoulder. This sequence is repeated on a few occasions. I started to feel uncomfortable and eager for Martin to feed. Marian didn't seem bothered. Eventually he attached and fed well for 8 minutes, looking constantly at Marian, his free hand moving gently and his legs outstretched and still. This peaceful and relaxing scene was interrupted by one episode of 'conversation' between Marian and baby Martin, where Marian would talk to him and he would coo softly in response. A similar conversation ensured after the feed finished. Overall the feed time was a very pleasant experience.

Back into the kitchen and time for a nappy change. Baby Martin looked around the room during this event, frowning as his eyes fell to rest on me, and with a more peaceful and happy expression as his interest returned to Marian. Marian then asked if I would like to nurse him while she set about preparing the dinner. Initially he was grizzly and tense but snuggled quickly into my shoulder and relaxed, looking around the room contentedly. After about 10 minutes he started to grizzle again, looking at Marian move around the kitchen. 'Maybe he is still hungry'. Back to the lounge-room for another attempt at feeding.

He fussed and wouldn't attach on three attempts. Marian concluded that he mustn't be hungry after all and carried him around the room showing him the pictures and mirrors which covered the walls. He seemed alert and interested, although fussed occasionally, yawning and rubbing his face on Marian's shoulder. 'It's as if he's fighting sleep,' Marian commented. He was again offered her breast, and attached readily on this occasion. This feed was again followed by a cooing conversation.

Marian commented that this was how most of her day passed, and that it took hours to prepare the usual evening meal. She said that her husband Bill was very happy to help with the cooking and that she found it hard to imagine how mothers with less obliging husbands managed. Today baby Martin had slept for only 15 minutes. He was often grizzly for a few hours in the evening (colic, I thought), and seemed better if he was nursed at these times. There seemed to be no obvious cause for his disquiet compared with similar episodes during the day when his grizzling seemed to be related to wanting either a feed or nappy change. She said that she wouldn't have believed before having baby Martin that you could differentiate between cries, but she really felt that she could.

Relatives had commented that she would spoil him by carrying him around so much, but she didn't think this was so. She was determined to enjoy her baby. He usually slept well at night despite the unsettled periods in the evening. At present he was sleeping with his parents, which made night feeds less disruptive. Sometimes he would feed without waking up properly, and settle back to sleep for five hours. He seemed more unsettled if left alone in his cot.

Marian was happy to take baby Martin to visit relatives, but did not take him shopping yet because of the crowds. She was still attending a postpartum physio group at the hospital, and took baby Martin to a baby massage group which he really enjoyed. She doesn't miss the frequent dining out.

Time is well and truly up. We have chatted past the hour visit. On my way out Marian showed me two brightly coloured jumpsuits which Bill had bought his son. They were different sizes, both quite large. Bill had been unsure of which size to buy. Baby Martin will soon grow into them.

Comments

At the beginning of this observation it is interesting to note that, while baby Martin does not feed at first, his mother is able to contain her anxiety about this and to nurse him and cuddle him until he is actually ready to feed. She does not believe that she knows best and must, in a sense, force her nipple into the baby's mouth. Rather she waits for Martin to decide that he does want to eat, and it is striking that the anxiety is in fact carried by the observer in this case, who comments on how uncomfortable she felt and how eager she was for Martin to feed. One might postulate that perhaps if the observer was able to carry the anxiety, it was possible for the mother to feel a little bit more contained, thus indicating the importance of what I have described earlier as the three-person interaction. The observer has noted the very real nature of the conversation between Marian and baby Martin, which can be seen as an example of Winnicott's statement that the baby looks at the mother and sees himself. The conversation continues after the feed is finished, which suggests that Marian was correct in assessing that Martin wanted social interaction with her as much as he wanted a feed; that the two in a sense went hand in hand.

Martin is not happy to be handed to the observer and tries to communicate this to his mother in order to be back in close proximity to her.

This observation is a lovely example of the feeling of timelessness and slight loss of boundaries that accompanies the birth of a baby, particularly a first baby, when Marian comments, for example, that most of the day seems to pass without her noticing and how it takes hours to prepare the usual evening meal. When she describes the fact that Martin is a bit grizzly for a few hours in the evening the observer comments that this must be colic. This suggests that as observers, when we are confronted by a situation that seems difficult, we will tend to try and understand it in terms of our most immediate past experience, in this case a medical one.

The comment that a relative had made to Marian that she would spoil her baby by carrying him around too much can also be seen as an example of what I have described earlier as the ambivalence that surrounds the beginning of life and birth; of how difficult it is at times for people to see a tiny baby relishing the intimacy of his mother's body. It is, of course, the child's ability to be dependent and supported and contained by his mother that will truly, at a later stage, enable him to be more independent, rather than the other way around.

Baby Lisa

Aged two months at the first visit

I rang Ann to arrange for an appointment. She had been expecting my call and said that she was pleased to help. I arrived at the appointed time of 4 pm and was greeted at the door by Ann, who had Lisa in her arms and Andrew. Ann introduced herself and the children, then we proceeded to enter the lounge-room. Ann placed Lisa in the bassinette and went to the kitchen to make a cup of tea. Lisa lay in the bassinette and looked at a mobile placed in front of her. Andrew, aged two, continued to play with his toys and paid little attention to either myself or to Lisa. Lisa soon fell asleep with her right arm flexed and with her head tilted to one side. Andrew looked up from his playing and then ran over to the bassinette. He gently rocked it. Ann returned and Andrew then went back to his toys. Ann started to tell me about Andrew's delivery. He developed foetal distress and needed resuscitation. He was a difficult baby and had trouble establishing breastfeeding. She persisted for four months before ceasing. She said that he sucked much better from a bottle than from her breast. After much reluctance, she eventually decided to use a dummy and said that he seemed to settle much better. She then talked about not liking the first eight weeks of a baby's life because one just 'gives, gives, gives' and gets nothing in return. She described a low point with both babies at six weeks of age, when she wanted 'to give them back' but remembers waking the next morning and feeling happy again. She said she loved it when Lisa smiled at her and felt it made it all worthwhile.

Lisa then woke up, stretched, and Ann picked her up and cuddled her. Lisa again stretched and yawned and started to cry. Ann took off her nappy, saying that that always seemed to settle her. She lay her down on the floor where she settled. She kicked for a while and then smiled at her mother, who responded by smiling and cooing at her. Andrew, who had been running in and out of the room, came over and joined in. He bent over Lisa, then kissed her. He then climbed onto his mother's back and tried to distract her attention. Lisa continued to kick vigorously and Andrew began to play hide and seek with her. Lisa smiled and kicked. She then looked at her mother and cooed. Ann put her nappy back on and placed her on her lap. She didn't cuddle her, but placed her over the inside part of the arm of the chair. Lisa maintained good head control in this position. She started to roll over and to slip down the arm. Ann caught her and again placed her in her lap. Lisa stretched and yawned, and I decided to leave. We made arrangements for the following week.

Comments

In this observation we can see the vicissitudes associated with bringing up young children. Here the mother shares with the observer the difficulties of her first child's delivery, the problem of his foetal distress and how he was a difficult baby, and her trouble establishing breastfeeding. The fact that she remembers this experience so vividly and relates it to the observer indicates perhaps something of the lack of resolution of this problem. One might wonder whether she had received any help and support for this very difficult first experience, and one might speculate about how much this initial difficulty might influence her relationship with her second child. Certainly, she perceives the first weeks of living with a baby as very demanding, as though the baby is draining everything from her and, as she says, gives nothing in return. Perhaps we can see something of the mother's ambivalence in the way she subsequently handles Lisa. For example, after she changes her nappy she doesn't cuddle the baby but plays with her over the arm of the chair, where Lisa subsequently rolls over and starts to slip down the arm. Her mother captures her just in time. One might speculate whether this process might repeat itself as a way for the mother to enact some of her mixed feelings towards this baby and the birth of the older child. Again, in this observation, it is worth noting that the mother, on this first occasion, has not actually mentioned her husband and it is uncertain, at this stage, what sort of support he is able to offer.

Baby Rebecca and brother Kevin

Rebecca, aged 9 weeks and Kevin, aged 2 years at the third visit

As I drive up the street, I can see Karen outside talking to a woman across the road with a youngster. They wave goodbye as I pull up, but she then begins to chat to another lady and toddler strolling up the street. Karen explains that they live in a very sociable position with the shops just down the street. I have arranged a visit during a less tranquil time of the day with Kevin's sleep over and Jim (father) not yet home.

Kevin is sitting on the front doorstep eating some crackers and sultanas. Karen is busy threading the ivy in and out of the fence while carrying Rebecca in a front pouch. Rebecca is awake and making little grizzly noises which Karen interprets as working up to a feed. It starts to rain but Karen does not seem to notice until I ask her if she has any washing on the line. This is followed by a mad rush to the back of the house to retrieve the nappies.

Having assisted with this task, I see a very different picture to the immaculate 'home beautiful' I had visited just a few weeks ago. The laundry is piled high with linen clothes and nappies, both dirty and clean, some to be folded and put away. The breakfast dishes are still on the kitchen table, the beds unmade, the shopping by the front door, and Kevin's toys strewn from one end of the house to the other. I knew something must have changed but decided not to be tactless and wait until Karen felt ready to tell me in her own good time.

Kevin grabs his mother by the hand and drags her to his bedroom. He is cross that I follow. Rebecca, by this stage, is hollering, so we all sit on Kevin's bed while Karen feeds her. Kevin jumps up and down vigorously on the bed, making it difficult for Rebecca to attach herself to the breast, but Karen does not stop him, instead praising him on his improving balance. Kevin empties his toy box with a thunderous crash. Karen continues to talk to him, attempting to persuade him to actually play with some of his toys. There is no interaction between Rebecca and Karen throughout this time. Kevin then climbs into his wardrobe, the old-fashioned sort that is free-standing and easily tipped. Karen asks him to remove himself but her request is ignored. She stands Rebecca, still attached to her breast, and pulls him out of the wardrobe, locking it as she does so. A dreadful noise and lots of tears follow. Karen gives Kevin a hug, then I go with Kevin to help him retrieve his bottle from the kitchen bench.

We move into the living room, Rebecca still in the previous position. Kevin is encouraged to play with his Fisher Price zoo, newly acquired from the toy library. He does so momentarily, then hides behind the couch, daring his mother to find him. Karen enters into this game, pretending to have lost him until his little fingers begin to creep over the edge of the sofa. She tires from this game before he does and asks him to find the photos to show me. We look through these for a short while but Kevin becomes bored and starts to demolish the lounge.

Karen begins to tell me how Rebecca's behaviour changed three weeks ago, and that she now demands to be carried around continuously. Even if placed carefully down while asleep, within two minutes she will be distressed and needing a great deal of comforting. Karen now finds it difficult to accomplish any work through the day. She makes us a cup of coffee, Rebecca still attached, then, as she sits down, explosive noises herald time for a nappy change and Rebecca emerges from her secure place with a beautiful smile.

Rebecca now enjoys this time of freedom around her bottom. She sees me and puts on the most wonderful display of smiles and coos. Her whole body moves in the pleasure of being able to interact with me. Karen continues to talk to me while she changes the nappy, making comments on what a gorgeous baby she has. She does not talk to Rebecca. From another room Kevin yells to his mother amidst the ominous noise of heavy objects dropping to the ground. He enters the room, requesting to look at the photos again despite his previous boredom with them. Karen fits a disposable nappy on Rebecca because she has run out of clean, dry, cloth ones. At this point, I feel very guilty and ill at ease. I wish to fold some linen, wash the dishes, or at least take the baby off Karen's hands for a few moments. I feel compelled to tell her that I really need to be a fly on the wall, and she reassures me that she understands.

It is time for 'Playschool'! With great enthusiasm, Karen and Kevin rush to the television but disaster strikes. The picture works but there is no noise. After several minutes of fiddling with knobs and a huge sigh of relief, the familiar song comes forth from the set.

Karen and I finally sit down to have our coffees and a chat. Karen explains that this is the time that she normally rushes around the house tidying up the day's mess. Today she would like just to sit and the mess can wait until her husband comes home. She again tells me of Rebecca's changed behaviour. Rebecca is very happy while being carried around in anyone's arms, and for this she is grateful. Rebecca rarely cries inconsolably if being cuddled but is resistant to being put down. She is slightly more tolerant if propped up in a beanbag so she can view the goings on. Kevin, now safely absorbed in 'Playschool', Karen feels free to indulge in cuddling and caressing her baby. She props her on her knee, and they exchange smiles and baby noises.

My hour up, I feel free to have a cuddle with Rebecca, who is perfectly happy with her new cuddler. While Rebecca and I enjoy this short time together, Karen slumps in her chair and looks forward to her husband arriving home and taking the two children for a walk.

Comments

In this visit to Rebecca, aged 9 weeks, we can see at first hand the tension that is evoked in the mother struggling to deal with the sibling rivalry and envy of her little boy towards the new baby, and how hard it is for her to be able to think clearly enough to give each of them the attention that they need. The observer suggests that, prior to this visit, the mother had tried to maintain an image of perfect order and calm but, by this session, perhaps she feels safe enough with the observer to allow her to see some of the mess and confusion that reigns, not just in the external sense of the house being messy but of struggling to meet the needs of two young children. Karen comments that Rebecca's behaviour had changed in the last few weeks as she insists on being carried by her mother and does not wish to be put down. This may coincide with Kevin's increasing anger about his sister's presence and the suggestion that he might become a threat to her. However, Karen finds it difficult to acknowledge the intensity of her son's feelings. Her solution, to pick Rebecca up all the time to keep her out of Kevin's way, probably serves to further fuel Kevin's envy. At one point the observer became caught up in the sense of chaos which these powerful feelings engender and wished that she could create some order by folding the linen, washing the dishes or taking the baby 'off Karen's hands'. How is it possible to understand what is happening to Karen, Kevin and Rebecca, and contain some of the anxiety, without wanting to rush into activity and clear the problem away?

SUMMARY

This chapter covers the following areas in discussion of this transition.
- The importance of play.
- The need to recognise that early childhood is a time when the child is struggling to negotiate a number of tasks simultaneously.
- The use of 'the transitional object' (a blanket or soft toy).
- Feeding, sleeping and toilet training, which are areas of development often construed as problems by parents.
- The emergence of sexual identity and the beginnings of sexual differentiation.
- Problems which are not resolved at this stage of early childhood frequently continue into later childhood and particularly adolescence.
- The idea of helping children to deal with depression and anxiety, which is also part of normal healthy development, is introduced.
- The importance of providing appropriate limits and boundaries, which represent another version of 'containment' for the young child, is emphasised.

S elma Fraiberg, an American child psychotherapist, has described this period of development as 'the magic years'. The young child at this stage does not fully comprehend her relationship with the outside world and construes her own actions and those of others as having particularly magical properties. Thus it is quite characteristic for toddlers and slightly older children at this stage to believe that they are the centre of the world; that they in a sense control the world in a magical way. Magical control can, of course, backfire. Hence this is often the beginning of a period when children feel anxious about going to sleep on their own, or begin to have nightmares.

THE PLACE OF PLAY AND FANTASY IN DEVELOPING PERSONALITY

The hallmark of the magic years is the capacity of the young child to develop fantasy and an imaginative life. This also depends on the parents' abilities to allow for imagination and fantasy in their child without feeling too worried or annoyed by it. For example, I was travelling on a bus and overheard a young child describe what she saw on the street. She described the scene in terms of a fantasy world of suns and trees and people moving around in all sorts of extraordinary ways. The person whom she was with, whether her mother or an older sister, cut her short by saying in an irritated voice: 'No, that's not what's out there. It's just trees and buildings.'

This extreme example of a wish to do away with any imaginative or fantastical idea about the outside world denies the reality of a child's experience. It also misunderstands how learning actually takes place. It is possible that the mother or older sister seemed to think that the fantasy of the child needed to be brushed away in order to make way for rational, logical thinking. However, the opposite is in fact the case. Logical, cognitive development takes place through the capacity for play and fantasy and imagination. We can thus say that for the young child 'play is literally work'. It is the work of discovering a sense of their own body, of the world outside, of what is inside their body and outside their bodies. Donald Winnicott says that one of the main tasks for the young child at this stage is to establish the idea of 'what is me and what is not me'. That is to say, the child needs to understand where the boundaries of his body end and the world begins. Sometimes this can be very confusing, for the child has not yet developed a sense of real time or space. The idea that monsters, for instance, can live in the bedroom or hide under the bed forms a part of this whole process. It is also related to the child's concern with what is real and what is not real.

Throughout this book I refer to the core tenet of the psychodynamic approach, which is that our emotional world and life is seen as operating on a boundary between the internal world – the world of our fantasies, dreams and ideas – and the external world. It is at this stage of toddlerhood and early childhood that this link between the inner world and the outer world is at its most visible and almost tangible. It is rare for this process of integrating the inner world/outer world to be perceived with so much clarity, except possibly later in adolescence.

I have referred to the paradox of how the child is both simultaneously dependent and also moving towards separation and individuation. In the stage after babyhood, the young child is beginning to walk and to seek some control and mastery of his world. The young child has an omnipotent idea of feeling at times that he may be the centre of the world. However, at the same time, he is still close to babyhood and needs the reassurance of mother, father or caretaking figures close by. The contradictions of this phase of development are beautifully captured by the A.A. Milne poem 'Disobedience':

James James
Morrison Morrison
Weatherby George Dupree
Took great
Care of his Mother,
Though he was only three.

James James
Said to his Mother,
"Mother," he said, said he;
"You must never go down to the end of the
town, if you don't go down with me."

THE TRANSITIONAL OBJECT

In order to be able to manage this complex transition, that is the state of struggling for mastery and at the same time being dependent and becoming anxious about separation, the child needs to find some concrete way of symbolising and managing this process. Thus many parents report that it is at this time that an object like a little blanket or a cuddly toy, or a teddy bear, or even a rag, is taken up by the young child and carried from room to room, or taken out of the house. A special term that Donald Winnicott has coined for this – attachment to the little rag or toy or blanket – is 'the transitional object'. By this he meant that the toy, or teddy bear or piece of material, stands as a physical object that can be touched and smelt and felt. It is a link with the parents and reminds the child of the smell of the mother's body or the caregiver's body. At the same time, because this object can be moved around from room to room or taken out of the house, it has a very special function, that is one of transition. It is an object that can really go places and be adaptable, and stay with the child as a direct link with parents and so cover the space between the child and his parents when they may not be in the same room or even in the same house.

One of the hallmarks of a transitional object is that it is totally in the control of the child. It can at one moment be wrapped around her head or used as a cuddly shawl or a blanket. At another moment it can be thrown on the floor as though it has been forgotten, only to be gathered up again when the time is right for the child and she requires it again. Sometimes parents make the mistake of thinking that the transitional object represents a lack or a gap in their own caretaking of the child, as I describe in the example below.

A blanket to help me breathe

Abigail, a child with severe asthma was referred for psychotherapeutic help, together with her adoptive mother who was, in fact, her aunt by marriage. The adoptive mother had taken the child into her home when her own children were in their late teens. Abigail's early life – she was now five years old – had been extremely traumatic. Her mother had a history of severe psychiatric illness and, although she had struggled to look after Abigail, had been unable to do so. Abigail had been left for long stretches of time on her own and had been quite seriously neglected, both physically and emotionally. Her adoptive mother described how, in the early days when she was taken into her care, just after she was a year old, Abigail could not bear to be held and could not stand to look at anybody. Her adoptive mother had worked very hard to encourage and promote Abigail's capacity for relationships and she was by now, by and large, a fairly happy and settled little girl. The severe asthma attacks, however, caused great distress and suffering for Abigail and her adoptive mother, and there was a suggestion that they were provoked by stress. What was striking in my discussions with Abigail's adoptive mother was that, despite the fact that she was in many ways understanding and devoted to Abigail, she had difficulty in accepting one aspect of Abigail's behaviour. This was with regard to a little blanket which Abigail had had from when she was a baby, which she tended to carry around with her and particularly wanted to take when she left the house. Abigail's adoptive mother tried to resist this as much as possible and explained to me that she saw it as Abigail showing the world that there was something not quite right about the way in which she cared for her. We may speculate that this may have had something to do with the fact that Abigail's adoptive mother felt guilty about taking on the mothering of this little girl. She was very angry with Abigail's mother and perhaps, in a sense, felt that she had somehow stolen this child. Perhaps for her Abigail's use of her blanket was an indication that she still longed for a 'real' mother or a mother whose smell or feel she may still have associated with the blanket, and this was very distressing for her. Because of these difficulties it was hard for Abigail's adoptive mother to understand that the use of the blanket represented an important aspect of Abigail's capacity for development. The blanket showed Abigail's need and capacity for a relationship and her valuing of the link with her adoptive mother. For a child who experienced such frightening asthma attacks in which it seemed at times as if she had lost control of her body, the ability to be able to control the blanket and to take it with her, particularly to the Hospital, contributed to the healing process concerning separation and loss, both physically and also emotionally.

MILESTONES AND MASTERY

One of the main features of this early developmental phase is that, for the young child, intense activity of a very complex nature happens simultaneously. The young child is beginning to learn to speak, to be able to feed himself and, more than that, to begin to develop a choice about food. Toilet training will be introduced around this time as well as, in many families, the suggestion that the child may want to sleep in their own room, or certainly move from a cot to a little bed. Thus we can see that, for the young child, there are many expectations, both that he has for himself and that parents and other family members also have on his behalf. Another way of putting it is to say that the young child at this stage has a number of different tasks which have to be negotiated, be they eating, speaking, sleeping, or toilet training. For many parents these tasks are often construed as particular problem areas. Thus we may pause for a moment to discuss these different areas.

Feeding

One of the most common anxieties for parents, particularly with a first child, is the worry about whether their child is eating enough or getting enough food. On occasions, there may also be anxiety about whether their child is eating too much. Food, like the dummy that I have mentioned before, can be used as a pacifier by parents as though if the child has something in his mouth continually, or feels full, or is given treats, then parents can deal with his distress. I will elaborate on different ways in which parents may be able to understand difficulties or sadness in their child later on in this chapter.

The fear that parents have about their child either not getting too much or not being able to control the amount of food that they eat suggests that their view of the child is one in which the child represents a passive receptacle into which food is either poured or not. It echoes the theme that I have tried to develop from the outset, which is that the nature of a healthy relationship between parents and child is one which encourages and facilitates a partnership between them. The parent needs to be able to trust that the child has his own ability to choose food that, largely, will be right for him and that he will be unlikely to starve. I have talked about how, in infancy, the emphasis on 'getting the baby into a routine' to the exclusion of all else does not make for a good partnership between the parents and child. It suggests that there is a formula from outside of this relationship which must be applied. We know, as Daniel Stern has said, that the infant comes into the world bringing formidable capacities to relate and interact. We might also consider that the child is physiologically and neurologically equipped, even at this young stage of development, to maintain himself for survival and growth.

The circumstances in which feeding takes place for the young child will, of course, be important and relevant. For example, just as it is important for the baby's feeding at the mother's breast or the bottle to take place in a quiet, peaceful environment, so it is important for the toddler's mealtimes to have a reasonable regularity and for the child also to feel that eating is part of a social experience. Contemporary family life is often so compartmentalised, with different members of the family having to be involved in different activities, that this may necessitate them eating in a staggered way at various sittings throughout the evening. The lack of any social content and interaction to the feeding experience can make it very lonely, particularly for a child on her own. Tensions and difficulties within the family will certainly exacerbate any feeding difficulties.

I have mentioned before that the young child at this stage is preoccupied with omnipotent fantasies about his power and mastery, and a sense that he is at the centre of the world. The battles regarding feeding and mealtimes are often a time when these omnipotent fantasies become acted out and the authority of the parents may be challenged. In an extreme example I knew of, parents found themselves racing through the house holding a spoonful of food which they hoped to pour into the mouth of their small child who was leading them a merry chase through all the rooms. In this situation the child perceived the implications of his eating or not. He had enormous power and a hold over his parents. The parents, for their part at this point, were driven by a belief that one spoonful would make all the difference to the child's physical survival and were hell-bent on getting it into his mouth.

Sleep and the young child

Another vexed area for many parents is the one of sleeping. As with feeding, the inbuilt rhythms and capacities of the infant and the young child need to be acknowledged and respected. Of course, the particular innate rhythms with which the child comes into the world may not fit into the particular family needs or routines which have to be established, and it is here that the problem often emerges. It is also surprising to note how parents have very different ideas of when sleep should occur.

We have to keep in mind that for the young child the process of going to sleep becomes a much more self-conscious act than it had been in infancy. The young child is moving into a new world of curiosity, exploration and understanding of the world around him. We must recognise that, in going to sleep, we are asking the young child to make the transition from a waking state to a sleeping state, which poses a considerable challenge. The young child may at times be aware that some of his more omnipotent ideas or fantasies about being the centre of the world come home to roost when he goes to bed, in the form of worries about monsters under the bed or behind the curtains or in the flicker of shadows. The young child also has to deal with what is real and what is not. At this stage of his development he is not able to internalise his fears and worries. Thus, if he feels he has been naughty during the day or has met with disapproval from his parents, or has felt himself to be very much in charge, he may feel that there will be retaliation in the dark and quiet of his room in the form of the monsters under the bed.

Another important feature of sleeping and sleep problems in young children which is often overlooked is that, for the young child, going to sleep constitutes a separation from the parents.

Even in the best of circumstances the child has to manage to negotiate leaving his parents, going to another room and settling into a state of sleep different from wakefulness, and being in control. If the family is experiencing difficulties such as emotional divisiveness between the parents or the parents are contemplating divorce or separation, then the child may express his distress by not sleeping.

The way in which sleep is handled for the young child depends as well on the parents' own experience and their own history. Again, the question of 'What did my parents do in this situation?' is very much to the fore. Sometimes parents who have difficulty understanding what lies beneath the problem that their child presents in not being able to sleep or not fitting into a sleep routine take the view that the child must be forced or coerced into a routine. They may find themselves following particular schedules or even becoming quite brutal in locking the child in his room. These solutions almost invariably fulfil the worst fantasies and fears of the young child. They may have a short-term effect because the child will be coerced into going to sleep, but the reason for the sleep problem may emerge in another part of the child's development.

In my clinical work I have been struck by the number of occasions when parents have complained about their child's sleep problems, when in fact it has been a problem of their own inability to sleep at times. For example, parents may invite the child into the parental bed if one parent is away. Children can be taken into the parents' bed as a cure for loneliness and a need for comfort. When the child becomes annoying they are then pushed out of the bed and naturally begin to resist. In this situation we can see that a confused message is being given to the child who may be invited into the maternal bed one day and thrown out the next. For example, a mother whose husband went on long work trips would regularly invite her son into her bed. It was a clear message that he was there to keep her company and help her with her lonely feelings. However, when his father returned, the boy was promptly given his marching orders, which caused tremendous confusion in the child and contributed in his later development to uncontrollable temper tantrums. In this example one can also see how there is also a denial on the part of the parent of the developing sexual awareness and sexual identity of the child.

Toilet training

Toilet training is another area in which parents may find that they enter a battleground about who is in control. The very term toilet training suggests that somehow there is a training that one can impose from outside, rather than relying on the fact that the child has an inherent physiological and psychological capacity to become toilet trained. Generally, any attempts at toilet training before the age of two do not meet with much success because the child simply does not have the physiological and neurological capacities to manage this process. The focus on toilet training at an earlier stage would suggest anxiety on the parents' part about the child's bodily products, perhaps an obsession with cleanliness and a need to have everything under control. I return again to the theme of partnership in relation to the child, which is that the child himself will have an expectation that he would like to be clean and dry, and he is ready and willing to co-operate with the process at the right time. If parents can take a relaxed attitude to toilet training and follow the cues that the child will inevitably give them then toilet training becomes an almost imperceptible process so that one can hardly understand how one moment the child was in nappies and the next appears to be able to go to the toilet quite independently. It is important for us to understand as well that there are variations in development and in the achievement of developmental tasks such as toilet training, both among children of the same age and also between boys and girls.

The place of regression

I have stated before that the young child is faced with having to negotiate a number of different developmental tasks simultaneously. Feeding, sleeping and toilet training therefore are all key developmental tasks for the young child which are subject to regression. That is to say that when the child is under stress, through a change in circumstances in the family – such as the arrival of a new baby – it is usually around these points of development that a crisis may take place in negotiating a task. For example, the child may no longer want to eat solid foods or, if there is a new baby, may want to go back to using a bottle; they may no longer wish to sleep in their own bed, or they may regress in the toileting they have achieved. The process of regression is as much a part of the developmental task as the striving for mastery; both in a sense are of a piece. Here the parents' capacity to tolerate uncertainty comes to the fore, as well as their ability not to be critical of the child or have too high expectations.

The development of sexual identity

The period of early childhood from approximately the age of two years old to the age of four years old is a time of intense curiosity and discovery about the nature of sexual differences. Children at this stage, from the time they are able to walk, begin a much more active exploration of their own genitals and become aware of the genitals and different body shapes of the opposite sex. The idea of sexuality and sexual curiosity in relation to children is one which faces many people with embarrassment to the point where they may deny its very existence, despite the fact that we see ourselves as a highly sexually liberated society. Freud's first writings on childhood sexuality provoked furore and shock as though he was suggesting that childhood sexuality was the same as adult sexuality.

This, of course, is not the case. At this very early stage of development, young children are preoccupied with what one might call questions about 'which orifice does what'. Young children may describe a confusion between, for example, their genitals, penis, vagina and their anus. When parents are having a second baby, these researches and questions will be very much to the fore. Young children may have intense speculation about how the baby got into Mummy's tummy – through which orifice, and from which orifice it will come out. Will it be pooed out in the toilet, for example?

It is also at this point that children begin the first main definition of their sexuality and gender identity in relation to the way in which parents and others respond to them. The choice of clothing which is so specific to boys and girls, the toys they are given, the activities they are taken to, already begin to identify and separate the gender-specific attributes of male and female. If we can understand how intense the bodily and mental preoccupations are for the young child, as well as these beginnings of specific gender identification, then we can see how confusing and baffling it must have been for the little boy I described above who was taken alternately into his mother's bed to be a companion to her, to snuggle up to her body, and perhaps become quite warm and excited at this experience, but then to be banished into the cold when his father returned.

I am not suggesting that parents should never have their children in their bed. And of course all children will come to the parents' bed at some stage if they have nightmares, are frightened, or are feeling ill. Cuddling up to Mum and Dad in the morning on the weekend is a normal part of happy family life. What I am referring to rather is the long-term specific confusion about the sexual awakening and curiosity of the child coupled with a denial of the reality of the child's development. I am also referring to issues where the sleep problem of the child may mask a deeper problem between the parents. For example, it is not unusual when a child continually finds it difficult to sleep and comes into the parents' bedroom, that one parent may, in desperation, retreat into the child's bed, leaving 'the couple' of mother and child in the bed. At times this has been referred to as an effective form of contraception. It may also point to some difficulty in the parental relationship. Almost always it is an unhelpful way of dealing with the problem. It activates the child's feelings of omnipotence, by the child believing he has displaced his parent in the marital bed. It may also exacerbate the anxiety that the child feels about the sleep problem and his parents' inability to solve it.

Going backwards, going forwards

This early period of development in the child is sometimes referred to as 'the terrible twos'. I think this is an unfortunate title as it suggests that there is something problematic and destructive about a particular phase of development, and that the child is somehow to blame. It seems to me rather that what we need to understand is that the transition from infancy to childhood is a dramatic one, and that different parents either relish it or are dismayed by it for various and different reasons. These reasons are almost always connected with the past history of parents themselves. We all go into parenting with our own history of childhood. This is a history that needs to be valued and recognised. It has positive as well as negative aspects but, since it belongs to us, it is an area of our experience that we should try to be curious about.

For some parents the transition into early childhood where the baby becomes more of a personality may be a source of regret and they may wish to keep the child in an infantile state for as long as possible. This may have something to do with the fact that they genuinely believe that the child is not capable of independent growth and thought. Here the parents do not really have any faith in the innate strength and thrust towards health and integration of their child. We may see young children dressed in an infantile way, responded to as though they are tiny babies. Occasionally they may still be breastfed. Toilet training for these children is something that has been left to the distant future. The parents descend into a panic at the point at which they decide that their child should go to kindergarten but realise that she is not able to manage the appropriate tasks for her age. I have noticed that mothers in this situation will talk as though they are absolutely and totally indispensable to the child to the point where it is not possible for them to leave the child even for a short period. In some cases, the young child may become quite tyrannical and not allow her mother to venture forth too far. She both wishes to exert her power over her mother but genuinely feels that, since she has not had any opportunity to utilise her own internal resources, she really has none, so that her mother's absence really does invoke a tremendous panic inside of her.

In this type of relationship one may talk of a kind of 'fusion between the mother and the child' which is not helpful to the process of separation and individuation, and usually suggests that there is a poor marital or sexual relationship between the parents. In these situations the father has not succeeded in re-establishing a sexual relationship with his wife in the sense in which Robin Skynner has described. In this way we can see what a delicate and intricate balance there is in the variety of relationships that surround the young child. These give it either coherence or confusion. The child may be enabled to move forward in her development or she may be left in a fused and dependent relationship with her mother where she is not able to begin to tackle the normal developmental tasks of this phase of development. Thus, as Winnicott has said, there is no such thing as a baby. We continue to see, through the various developmental phases, that there is no such thing as a young child existing in isolation, since the formation and development of personality is so interdependent with the intimate and powerful relationships the child has with parents and other caregivers.

 ## HELPING YOUNG CHILDREN COPE WITH DEPRESSION AND ANXIETY

I have said before that the developmental tasks of early childhood are extremely intense and set a tremendous pace for the child. Recognition of the child's feelings and his emotional experience is in this connection an integral part of helping him to negotiate these tasks. I have found it useful to talk about the place of depression and anxiety in relation to child development because both represent important paradoxes in healthy development. Depression and anxiety are emotions and experiences which as adults we struggle to deny or overcome in one way or another. We tend not to want to feel miserable and we want to avoid stressful and difficult situations. However, if we explore these two emotions and experiences from a different perspective, we can see that they contain within them very positive aspects that are also an important part of our internal intrapsychic development and are a way of satisfactorily negotiating a link between the inner world and the outer world. For example, depression can be seen as a way of understanding a need at times for things to slow down, in order for us to be able to be in a more reflective mode and integrate our experiences and be able to digest what we have heard and learnt. The world at large is quick to deny that children may ever feel sad or lonely, or even depressed, when this is clearly not the case. I have already mentioned the complex repertoire of skills with which the baby comes into the world. This will include the capacity for sadness and depression. The same can be said of anxiety: that it is important for the developing child to feel that there is a sufficient challenge to prompt him to move into the next stage of his development. By this I don't mean challenging the child to do things before he is ready; rather I refer to the parents' need to be able to tolerate uncertainty and to be able to allow the child to be frustrated at times.

In our society the advertising consumerist, almost merchandising view of childhood suggests a bland emotional state where nothing much is really allowed to happen internally. Children and parents are exhorted to acquire status both through looking right and learning how to do the right thing. As a society we pay little attention to the need to help children to handle their deeper and more complex emotions, which is vital and will stand them in good stead as they move into the school years and in their social relationships. At times there appears to be a schism between this bland advertising consumer view of childhood and the concerns which spring up in the general community about the way children are turning out when they become adolescents. We are concerned about aggression, violence towards women and children, and lack of respect and what is commonly referred to as a lack of values. However, it is unfair and unrealistic to imagine that these can be developed by children out of thin air. They can only be developed through relationships. Most importantly, they have to take place as part of the negotiation between the inner and outer world. A respect and recognition for the child's capacity to be really sad and depressed, and also at times to need to be able to be sad and reflective about his actions and his relationship to others, is a vitally important part of developing internal values which can be used in later life. The ability to face challenges without too much parental anxiety is also a part of reasonable achievement.

One of the most common refrains one hears from parents about their child's experience is that 'they don't know what is going on'. This is a sad reflection of parents' inability to validate what the child really knows and to recognise how sensitive and curious they really are about the world.

When parents separate or divorce, the idea of children 'not knowing what is going on' can be used as a way of denying the painful experience for adults.

Talking about divorce

Two parents about to separate came to talk about how they might discuss this with their children, then aged five and two. It emerged from their discussion that they could see themselves sitting down with the five-year-old and explaining what had happened, but had not given any thought about including the two-year-old in the discussion or talking to that child in a similar way. I asked them together about what the two-year-old would feel the day after one of the parents had left, and how this would be explained to her. It was almost as if they had decided that this child did not understand what was going on and had no real sense of engagement with the most important people in her life, her mother and father. I explained that the denial of their two-year-old's feelings could lead her to have a profound sense of betrayal. She might feel that not only had one of her parents left the family home, which was bad enough, but that they had not thought it was sufficiently important to mention it to her.

Sometimes parents say that they are at a loss to know how to talk to young children, almost as though they are members of a different species. My usual advice in this regard is to suggest that they talk in ordinary language and to tell the truth about the situation. Children are far more baffled, confused and angry about that which is hidden and not said rather than by hearing the truth, even though it may make the child feel appropriately sad. I refer here to the importance of *validating the child's experience* and not denying a real content to the child's experience. When parents deny that there is a real content to the child's experience or deny that the child is capable of understanding the truth about events or capable of digesting and making sense of it for themselves, then they may be struggling with an idealised perspective of childhood. In this idealised, rosy view, childhood is a time of carefree experience where there is no realisation or recognition of the realities of any aspect of life and where the child is suspended from having to take any responsibility for her actions or for any of the events surrounding her. This type of idealised response to childhood in which reality is not supposed to impinge on children until a much later stage is actually a false view and denies the reality of children's experience. This does not mean that we must overwhelm children with realities to the point where they are not able to make any sense or digest what is going on. However, we must acknowledge the contradiction we impose on children; on the one hand, denying that they understand the reality of day-to-day changes in the family such as separation and divorce, but on the other hand, exposing them to bombardment of information and traumatic scenes which they may witness on television.

THE IMPORTANCE OF PLAY

As stated earlier, play is very important at this stage in the child's development to help him make sense of the world in all its aspects – physical, emotional and social.

The place of creativity in play

I mentioned at the start of this chapter that Selma Fraiberg has described this period of early childhood as 'the magic years', a time when the child is preoccupied with play and fantasy. It can be a time of magic and delight for parents as well, who can enter this world of make-believe with their child, if they can feel relaxed enough. Many parents report that this phase is a particularly pleasurable time of being with their children because it takes them back to experiences in their own childhood. For some parents who did not have many opportunities for play, it can open new possibilities for exploration of the child part of themselves.

Play as language – the meaning of play

I have mentioned earlier in this chapter that Donald Winnicott has used the term 'transitional object' for the little blanket or soft toy that reminds the child of his mother and the relationship with him. Here the child is able to play with the toy or blanket in such a way as to create an opportunity for a transitional space between his own experience and development and the safe link with his mother.

Play is important as a form of communication for children and always has meaning. I have stated that children are always aware of what is going on in the relationships around them. They have a far better understanding of what is told them than adults may realise, although their specific capacity to put things into words may be limited. The child's play, in many senses, is an opportunity for communication. It is also an insight into some of his deeper preoccupations. At this stage of early childhood there is little sense on the part of the child of being self-conscious or wanting to put up a barrier to conceal his feelings. Part of the pleasure for parents at this time is that young children are so open and available. I have said before that Freud has talked about how, in adults, the dreams that adults report constitute what he calls 'the royal road to the unconscious'. By this he meant that our dreams are able to describe events and concerns for us that have an important logic and sequence and can also enable us to use this information as data to be able to think about the concerns that we may have during our more rational daytime activities. For the child *play* is the royal road to the unconscious and can give us important insights into his anxieties and concerns.

Keeping Mother in mind

Catherine, a three-year-old girl, was referred for therapy at a point at which her parents had separated. What made this particularly painful was that her mother had decided to leave the family home and abandon all rights to her. Her mother had left the town in which she was living but maintained a rather tantalising relationship with her by phoning her occasionally, sending her presents or arranging visits rather out of the blue. Despite the pain of this rejection, Catherine valued her relationship with her mother and struggled to retain a place for her in her mind despite her father's resentment and anger about the actions of her mother.

When Catherine's mother telephoned the home she did not speak to Catherine's father, but spoke only to Catherine so that she had a rather special private conversation with her mother, totally excluding her father. While during her daily life Catherine struggled to keep her mother good in her mind, some of her deeper feelings towards her mother were allowed to surface in the course of her weekly psychotherapy. As part of her therapy sessions, Catherine had a set of family dolls which included a mother doll. Her therapist reported how, for weeks on end, Catherine would attack this mother doll, fling her around the room, try to smash her against the wall, stamp on her and almost tear her limb from limb. In the therapy through her play Catherine felt that it was safe enough to show her therapist what a struggle she had in maintaining her positive feelings for her mother and how these were so threatened by her overwhelming hatred and disappointment with her at the same time. In this case we can see how the therapy, with its focus on play, provided Catherine with an important opportunity to be able to bring together these different aspects of her experience. It is related to the question I have raised before about the nature of depression and anxiety, and how it is important to validate the child's experience. In this example it was important to validate Catherine's experience of both loving her mother and hating her. However, it would become dangerous for Catherine if these two experiences became split off from each other; if she became too frightened to show her rage and anger but kept it hidden when it would indeed become dangerous and explosive at a later stage. By communicating her preoccupation through play Catherine was able to enlist her psychotherapist to assist and make sense of these opposing emotions and help her to be able to contain them both in a safe and integrated way.

The healing nature of play

The important function of play for the young child exists in creating a bridge between the child's internal and inner experience and the reality of the outside world. We can see this very dramatically in the example I have given of Catherine above. Play almost always has a strong reparative and integrative function. Donald Winnicott, in the many years in which he saw children for consultation, reported that the capacity for play, even in a child who had experienced great deprivation or abuse or distress, was always a sign of hope and health. The opposite, of course, holds true as well, which is that a child who has no capacity for play or an imaginative life may show signs of the beginnings of disturbance. The reason for this is that play acts as a healing and 'making-sense' process for a child. For example, as I have stated before, in war-torn areas adults may be very disquieted by the fact that children appear to act out and repeat some of the violence that they have seen. Some people may see this as a bloodthirsty and unnatural interest on the part of the child or group of children. However, the contrary is in fact true. The children have been bombarded with an intolerable experience and their need to act it out and repeat it, with all the accompanying detail, is a healthy way of trying to make sense of the experience and in fact to digest it, so that it can allow them to go forward in their development. In the course of acting out the horror they have witnessed, they are also able to allocate roles of 'doing to' and 'being done to', which enables them to introduce a degree of control, as opposed to feeling small and vulnerable to outside events.

The use of fantasy and daydreaming

An essential part of the whole process of play for the young child, and indeed for the adult, is the use of fantasy and daydreaming. I have described how, for the young child, it is difficult to make a distinct separation between 'what is me and what is not me', between the world of what is imagined and what is real. Being able to be imaginative and make fantastical arrangements for play are part of this process. One of the requirements for the development of children's fantasy is that there is a need for an appropriate time frame to allow the fantasy to be explored. Regrettably, this is not always possible. Bruno Bettelheim has commented that the one word he found most commonly used in relation to young children is 'come on'. Here the time frame and urgency of the adult world is imposed on the child, and fantasy is given extremely short shrift.

Play as learning and preparation for life

Play operates across a variety of boundaries, particularly emotional, and is always family and relationship-oriented. It is also strongly related to cognitive development and mastery. Another aspect of play which is often overlooked is that if the child can be allowed to use their fantasy, imagination and daydreaming, and this is seen as offering them creative opportunities, they are then able to develop the capacity to be alone. This 'capacity to be alone', which Winnicott has particularly described, is the precursor for the ability to learn to read and to take in information at school. It is vital, for example, that children are able to develop this capacity at the point at which they enter school, otherwise it becomes impossible for any learning to take place. The child who has had little opportunity for play and imaginative activity may find it extremely difficult to transfer on to the difficult task of learning. Play and learning at this stage go hand in hand. Indeed, even in adult life the language of learning is couched in terms such as 'playing with ideas', as a precursor to formal thinking and research.

Play as problem solving

I have mentioned before that play crosses a number of bound-aries, that it is part of imagination, fantasy and the internal world and at the same time is connected with purposeful, cognitive activity. We can see that, for the young child, play is a serious activity and should be validated. Obviously, it is not something to be taken seriously in the sense of taking all the fun out of play and trying to control and direct it too much. When I talk about play as an opportunity for the child to engage on some problem solving I do not mean this in the adult rational sense, but rather that the problem which the child wants to sort out for themselves may be very different from what we, as adults, might see as the problem. For example, a child who has been to hospital and has had a painful or frightening procedure in the course of his treatment may, on return, re-enact the experience he has just gone through. Invariably, he is likely to take on the role of the doctor or the nurse and may involve a younger sibling or friend in becoming the patient. Sometimes parents are surprised to see how this re-enactment involves a doctor or nurse who is very punitive, insists on jabbing injections into the body of the young patient, or is very cross about the patient getting out of bed. It is important for adults and parents to understand that the child here is not re-enacting exactly what has happened to him; rather he is re-enact-ing with a sense of relief the anxieties that may have preceded his going into hospital, and also the anxieties that were associated with the various procedures. This does not mean that people were actually cruel or unkind to him, but that the child felt himself to be small and powerless, and had a fantasy or a worry that he might be hurt. Of course, we cannot deny the fact that some med-ical procedures are very painful or, in some cases, quite humiliat-ing, so that the child's re-enactment as well has a ring of accuracy about it. The child's ability to re-enact this painful or frightening procedure offers an opportunity to solve the problem of feeling small and powerless by reversing roles and inventing or imagin-ing what it might be like to be the powerful doctor or nurse.

Play and the parental partnership

I have referred to the healing quality of play for children. In adult life it may take the form of having a sense of humour, and in both acting in comedy and appreciating comedy as adults. We recognise, as adults, that very painful, difficult or traumatic experiences can become transmuted through comedy or satire. Often this can help us to come to terms with the difficulty, or essentially allow ourselves to hear it when we might not be able to tolerate the particular communication or piece of information if it were communicated in a more straightforward way. The fact that a serious communication can be made in a playful way enables it to be received by an audience and paradoxically taken seriously. A similar process is at work between children and parents when playfulness, particularly on the part of parents, can be a major factor in facilitating communication. It is striking, for example, how often adults recall with great pleasure and delight the sometimes, perhaps rare, occasions when parents played with them or were playful, particularly if life was a bit stressful at home or if parents were not normally playful. This does not mean that parents have to be able to get down on the floor with their young child and constantly play with them, or that they have to be exactly like the child. Rather, they need to appreciate what the child is producing through her play and, at the same time, have some capacity for playfulness and humour themselves.

 # THE IMPORTANCE OF SETTING LIMITS AND BOUNDARIES

I have referred to the need for parents to take the child's experience seriously in the form of acknowledging depression and anxiety, and trying to work with it in a positive way. The same can be said about the need to establish and set limits and boundaries for young children right from the outset. This is one of the areas that parents often have greatest difficulty with in our contemporary society where we have, on the one hand, abandoned a rigid form of control and perhaps arbitrary discipline, but have not found a comfortable way of asserting parental authority. One of the difficulties that parents find is that it is difficult to know how to use appropriate authority without being authoritarian. We do not wish to live in a world in which children are seen and not heard and are at the mercy of adult arbitrary control, but we also feel uneasy about encouraging omnipotent 'boundarylessness' in young people. In many ways today, parents feel themselves to be in a state of transition. As parents we have experienced so many changes in our own lives since our own childhood, and this degree of change appears to be accelerating rather than slowing down. Because of these rapid changes, it is even more important for children to feel that there is a secure anchor within the home. In this regard Bion's concept of 'the container and the contained' is much to the fore. It is vitally important for parents to set limits, to have ideas about what they feel is right and wrong, and to be able to communicate this in a fair and reasonable way to their children. The setting of limits offers containment to the child and establishes a clear boundary which makes the child feel safe and secure. It also makes the child feel that the parent actually has taken the trouble to think this through and holds the child in mind. The child who feels that there are no boundaries, or that his parents can never say 'no' to him, does not actually feel contained or cared about. In a situation such as this the young child's omnipotent fantasies of wanting to take control and be the centre of the world becomes fact. This, however, does not make the child feel happier, but actually makes the child feel much more anxious. This experience of the child wanting to feel in some way in control always needs to be counteracted by the parental assertion of their authority, not in an over-controlling way but in a way in which the child can feel safe and contained.

No containers in the home

A family were referred to the clinic because of difficulties in the behaviour of their four-year-old son Nigel, the second youngest in the family. The parents reported that Nigel at times behaved in a very difficult way and flew into uncontrolled rages. What was most worrying for them was that he refused to go to bed at the same time as his siblings and would roam around the house, up until all hours. He would turn on videos when it suited him and seemed to be totally immune to any kind of control or discipline.

It was clear from our discussions with the parents that their own troubled childhoods had made it hard for them to know how to set boundaries. They had both had to 'grow out' of their childhoods in order to look after their own parents. A complicating factor was that the mother's grandmother, who had cared for her for most of her childhood, was now resident in her home and in fact competed with the mother for maternal control in the family. The children were even at the best of times confused about who held the parental authority. Most confused, however, was Nigel, who would run between his mother and his great-grandmother whenever it suited him. Nigel's mother had become reduced to a child in her own home. At times it seemed as if the squabbles between the mother and the child were almost the squabbles of two siblings. The parents admitted that they often gave in to Nigel for the sake of peace and quiet. Nigel had omnipotent fantasies about controlling all these adults and parental figures but it did not make him a contented child.

Living with negative as well as positive feelings

In trying to set reasonable limits and boundaries for children, parents have to be able to deal with their own negative feelings as well as their positive feelings. I have talked of the need of parents to say 'no'. This may mean temporarily that the parent is construed by the child as a hateful person. Here parents have to be able to contain their own feelings or the emotions that are aroused in them in relation to what the child provokes or how the child sees them. With the newborn baby, I have described the process of how the parents have to contain not only their own uncertainty of what is happening to the baby, but also at times their feeling that the baby has indicated by her crying or discomfort or lack of contentment in one way or another that what the parents have provided is not satisfactory. How can parents take this in and digest it without wanting to retaliate in anger or a feeling of not being 'good enough'. For some parents who are able to manage the infantile period, the point at which a child becomes more of an individual in terms of asserting themselves can be difficult. Parents who have difficulty in engaging with a child as he grows older may have difficulties with their own hostility and aggression. The hostility and aggression in their child may provoke in them either memories of their own inhibited hostility or a sense that they were not allowed to feel as free to express what they felt; or it may remind them of aggression that they did in fact experience and blocked out. Either way, this may be a frightening prospect and they may seek to either inhibit these feelings in the child or go to lengths to placate the child so that she will not be in a position to react negatively to them. There may also be situations in which parents have misguided ideas about the child's capacity to respond to limit setting. They may believe that any limit setting causes a diminishing of the child's personality or spirit. They may believe that the child should never be in a position to be deprived, or that one should never have to say no to the child. The problem here is that the child may soon feel very anxious and boundaryless about the extent of her omnipotent powers and may become more angry and attacking towards the parent for not setting appropriate limits, as we can see from Nigel's experience.

The process of setting limits and having appropriate boundaries in early childhood also enables this process to become internalised by the child, so that she is also able to develop skills of her own in this area and to develop real inner resources for herself.

How we can avoid setting the scene for later problems

In my clinical experience, adolescents are often referred for help and present with difficulties at the critical age of around 12 or 13, at the onset of adolescence and when they are about to start secondary school. Their presenting problems are often related to the early childhood stage of development I have just described which has not been resolved. The problems very often have to do with the absence of limit setting and boundaries and appropriate structures for the developing child. It is not uncommon for mothers particularly to complain of difficulties in their son's behaviour which they feel has become disrespectful and contemptuous of them. Often the boys complain of feeling very stuck in their development and unable to move forward, either educationally or emotionally. I will describe some of these examples in more detail in the chapter on adolescence. However, we can see, as the development of the young child unfolds, that the stage may already be set for some of the potential difficulties which can develop later on. We can speculate that a child who has no boundaries, or whose parents are very anxious about being construed negatively, develops a sense of unreality. This means that the child really never has a solid structure against which to test himself or his experiences. He may develop very unreal expectations of himself and the outside world. This may result in a child who is very vulnerable to criticism and who has limited internal resources to be able to manage some of the challenges of learning and social interaction, particularly in the school environment. In a sense there is a kind of shared fantasy here with a parent who perhaps believes in the possibility of a perfect child, or creating the perfect child who never needs to be reprimanded and who has no limits. This instils in the child a sense of their own perfection. This problem is sometimes described as a 'narcissistic' state, where the parents' belief in having created a perfect child is enacted by the child who believes himself to be without blemish or unchallengeable.

Breaking through this type of narcissistic barrier is often very painful for both the child and the parents. It is extremely important for these problems to be recognised at an early stage so that young children and their parents can be assisted when the child is still a pre-schooler. The painful and negative aspect of this problem is that invariably the parent, particularly the mother, begins to feel very persecuted and at times denigrated in relation to her son. She may find herself putting up with her son's behaviour and excusing it endlessly, but then when she does feel she has had enough her own retaliation is often extreme and may end in the child feeling that he has been totally excluded from her affections. We can see that this problem reflects difficulties which have not been worked through or understood by the parents themselves. For example, a woman who may have had a bad or difficult relationship with her own father finds that she idealises her son and feels that he can do no wrong, and has great difficulty setting any limits or boundaries for him. However, when this backfires and he unleashes his aggression on her, she feels that, once more, she has become the victim of a man who is aggressive towards her.

I go into more detail in discussing these specific interrelationships between mothers and sons, and fathers and daughters, in a subsequent chapter. However, here I would like to emphasise the critical importance of these internal-external interrelationships and the fundamental impact they have on the course of a child's development.

CHAPTER 5

Children in Child Care and Kindergarten

SUMMARY

How can our understanding of child development help us to provide better facilities for children in child care and kindergarten? In this chapter, we put ourselves in the young child's shoes and imagine what it is like to live in an open plan world for long hours each day. The following issues are considered.

- The importance of providing separate age appropriate spaces for children.
- How staff and parents manage 'coming over the threshold' in the morning and leaving in the evening – this is important for the child's sense of containment.
- Children in child care and kindergarten extend their affections and love to significant others, namely the staff – it is vital for parents to accept and respect that their child needs these significant relationships if he is going to flourish in the child-care or kindergarten setting
- The *core consistent relationship* between the child and her caregivers in a child-care centre or kindergarten is more important to the child than attention to routine or expensive equipment.

It has become a fact of our times that a large number of children from an early age are placed in child care. This change has a considerable amount to do with major changes in family structures, financial difficulties, female emancipation, as well as the rising number of single parents.

It is not my brief here to state whether I agree or disagree with the prevalence of child care. Rather, I accept that child care for young children is one of the options available and that we need to be able to understand its impact on the child's development. In my talks and lectures to child-care workers, nursery workers and kindergarten teachers, I always emphasise that their task in caring for children is second only to the important task of parenting. It is one of the most important tasks of life and as such should be valued. Regrettably, this is not always the case, and the arrangements surrounding child care, both in terms of the physical circumstances and the training of staff, as well as the numbers of staff available, leave a great deal to be desired.

PUTTING OURSELVES IN THE CHILD'S SHOES

Let us, for a moment, put ourselves in the shoes of the two-year-old entering a child-care facility for the first time. The noise and the activity that greets him may be very different from the quiet of his own family home. He is suddenly confronted with a large number of children, some of his own age, some slightly older, some babies, none of whom he has met before. He will also be confronted by the caregivers or workers at the centre, all of whom will be strange to him. How will this first day at a child-care centre be negotiated? How long will he have to remain there? Has he been prepared for this change by his parents? Child-care facilities vary enormously in their understanding of how a child needs to be received at the door, what kind of help he may need in being literally helped over the threshold. The child who enters child care, particularly a very intensive child-care program, needs to be prepared in a very careful way by his family, and will also need opportunities to visit the child-care centre so that he can become acquainted with this new environment.

It is particularly important for young children that their parents are able to be available to stay with them for the first days or even first weeks of settling in. Often this may not be possible for the parents. It is not unusual for parents to start a new job on a Monday and at the same time bring a child into child care for hours ranging from eight in the morning until six in the evening. This kind of experience for the young child introduces an unprecedented change in child rearing practices, because in a situation such as this it will be the child-care workers who will be witness to the child's emotional and physical milestones of development and not the parents. *Child-care workers will literally stand in the place of parents.* If we consider the complexity of the child's development that I have described thus far, it is an awesome task and burden that we place on child-care workers. Perhaps, because of this, it is understandable that in some centres these critical areas of emotional development and emotional experience are denied. They may simply be too much to bear for the staff concerned who would, if they have to be in touch with the child's anxiety about separation and loss and changing circumstances, have to be in touch with these feelings themselves. They may also feel worried or guilty or feel blamed, and may in turn want to blame the parents for leaving the child in their care in the first place. More often than not a compromise is found where lip service is paid to the child's needs.

How can I be heard?

A student on a child development course was carrying out a young child observation at a local child-care centre. His task was not dissimilar to the task of the observer I have described previously in infant observation. The task of the observer in the nursery was to observe the activities of one child and his relationship with other children and the staff, to take a sympathetic attitude but not to feel under pressure to intervene or take charge of events as they occur.

During the course of one particular day of observation the student noted the distress of a little boy aged three who was finding difficulty settling into the routine of the nursery and was obviously missing his mother. He would rush backwards and forwards to the gate, peering out into the road, in the hope that she would return. It was obvious that he was unable to engage with the other children or the staff. After a time it seemed that he had given up in despair and was sitting on the floor crying. The staff at this point were very preoccupied with routines and, while a number of them attempted to attend to this little boy at various times, they did so in the form of wanting to stop the crying or wiping his nose or trying to persuade him to join in other activities. They had difficulty being in touch with the extent of his distress. His need at that moment was not to be distracted, but rather to have help from the staff to support him in his anxiety about the separation from his parents and from home. Here we can speculate that the staff may have wanted to deny the real problem, because it would have made it harder for them to cope.

Living in an open-plan world

If we stay with the image of putting ourselves into the child's shoes for a moment, we can speculate what it might be like for us as adults to be in the company of other adults in a large open-plan area for up to ten hours a day, where there is no privacy, where all meals are taken together, where sleeps are taken together, and where toileting is also very much available to public view. Understandably, we would find a situation like this quite intolerable, but it is one which we feel is acceptable for young children.

Of course, young children are supremely adaptable and it is this capacity to be adaptable, to please parents, to fit in with situations, that we may take too much for granted. The majority of children will adapt to long hours of child care with little protest, but this kind of adaptation is always made at a price. It is adaptation of a particular kind of independence, of struggling to co-exist with a large number of children making considerable demands. The price invariably that is paid is that the child has to deny her infantile needs and the baby part of herself. This is particularly poignant and disturbing considering that a child of two or three who enters a child-care centre has barely passed out of her infantile period. It is important for parents to validate the child's experience and needs. If she is faced with having to be independent from a very early stage, and struggles to deny her infantile, dependent needs, she may learn to develop a facade which becomes something of a false self because it denies her original real experience of separation.

A high staff turnover in a centre or staff rostered in an unhelpful way does not allow the child to identify with or relate to one particular person. Again, if we can put ourselves into the child's situation and imagine ourselves in a series of relationships where people come and go, we may eventually decide that it is not worth forming very deep emotional attachments to people because they will depart. Young children, in the same way, may draw this conclusion very rapidly and may, as a result, develop fairly affable but rather low-level, shallow relationships, both with the adults and the children around them. Now some people may suggest that this can make for a much easier life because the lack of intensity around emotional relationships and attachments may make for easier day-to-day management and care. However, we may wish to consider what type of personalities we want to develop in children, and also what particular vision we have for the children of the next generation.

I have referred in the example above to the little boy whose anxiety about separating from his mother could not be acknowledged by the child-care staff. Instead the child was responded to in terms of the day-to-day routine of the nursery which seemed to take precedence over the individual needs of the child. I have said that it is understandable for staff to become focused on routine as a way of avoiding the overwhelming emotional realities of coping with the needs of young children. In Chapter 3 on early infancy, I mentioned how mothers from time to time may find it easier to rely on a routine, particularly if it is imposed from outside, rather than getting to know their baby and learning from the baby, because they may feel too overwhelmed by the emotional intimacy or they may feel that the infant may place demands on them they will be unable to meet.

Discontinuities of experience

An interesting piece of research which highlights this problem was carried out by Lynn Barnett, a child psychotherapist who has made videos on infant observation, and Alistair Bain, a group and organisational consultant. They were involved in an action research study of a child-care centre in England which enabled them to be able to spend considerable periods of time observing how the children interacted, the routines of the staff, how the programs were set up, and the particular problems that arose in day-to-day experience.

In the course of their research, Bain and Barnett (1980) came to identify what they called 'discontinuities of experience' in the day-to-day lives of the children in the child-care centre. What they meant by this was that the staff tended to place a high precedence on routine, such as the preparation of meals and of moving the children from one activity to another. This meant that, on occasions, the children who were engaged in one particular kind of play or task would be suddenly interrupted and have to move on to another activity. Bain and Barnett referred to these experiences as discontinuities which had the effect of disrupting the behaviour of the children. They found, for example, that children who already tended to be shy and withdrawn tended to be more so, while children who tended to be aggressive became even more aggressive and out of control. If we put ourselves in the place of the child, we can see that there are important parallels in how adults are able to work successfully. It is very difficult for us, for instance, to feel able to complete a task when we cannot see it as a whole or when it is removed before we can complete it.

HOW CAN WE RELATE AN UNDERSTANDING OF THIS EARLY PHASE OF CHILD DEVELOPMENT TO PROVIDING GOOD CHILD CARE?

I would not like to suggest, in the light of my observations and comments, that I am totally against the idea of child care for young children. Rather, I believe it is important that an understanding of child development and the needs of the child inform the way in which child-care centres are established and run. What then can be changed, and what do we need to be mindful about?

Putting relationships first: sharing the love for the child

We need to put relationships right at the centre of any child-care facility. The capacity of the young child to relate and to form an attachment to a consistent caregiving figure is of primary importance and informs all the other activities that the child is able to engage in at the child-care centre. In this sense the smartness of the centre or the availability of elaborate toys and equipment is secondary to the availability of a strong emotional relationship with a consistent carer. This strong emotional relationship provides the containment for the child in a new and different setting, which is not his home setting and which will facilitate the possibility of his continuing development.

It is vitally important for child-care centres to be aware that frequent turnover of staff and rostering on of different child-care staff at different times of the day has a detrimental and undermining effect on this capacity to establish a relationship. It is the antithesis of containment and will cause inevitable chaos and uncertainty in the child's mind and life.

A corollary to the need for the child to attach to his caregiver in the child-care centre is that this necessarily involves strong positive feelings on both the part of the caregiver and the child, so love is very much involved. This means that the parent who is keen for the child to participate in child care for reasons of work or other reasons must be able to allow the child to have another love relationship. This love relationship will not undermine or diminish the relationship that the child has with his parent or parents. However, sometimes it may be construed by the parents as a rivalrous experience. Because of the anxiety surrounding this type of rivalry, child-care staff may collude with this so that the child ends up not having any opportunity for a really intense love relationship with either the parent who is not physically available or the child-care provider who may have to become a rather frag-mented person in the child's mind if the question of rivalry is seen as important. However, in the best of circumstances, we can see that if the parent can allow a good enough child-care provider to have a special relationship with their child, they can in turn work in a partnership with the provider to create the all-important net-work and facilitation of development that the child needs. The child thus recognises that both people have his interests in mind, which means he can grow and thrive.

This problem of being emotionally available for the child and of allowing the child to become attached and in turn becoming attached to the child, of handling potential rivalries, of working in a partnership with parents, requires great sensitivity and tact. It reinforces even more the importance of the work that we entrust to child-care workers and how vital it is that they should have both sufficient and appropriate training and support to carry out this task.

What kind of physical surroundings do children need?

Differing age groups

Another factor that is of importance in enabling the child to feel appropriately contained within the child-care centre is the type of physical arrangements which are made. For example, it is very important for the head of the child-care centre and the staff to recognise that children of varying ages have extremely varying needs and cannot be lumped together. It is enormously stressful for children to have to relate to very large groups at any one time or for long stretches at a time. There is an optimum number of children that can be managed and related to in a group, and that the child-care worker can actually 'hold in mind'. Ideally, a child, whether of two or three or four, should always be able to spend the day with other children within their particular age group and with the same worker. There also needs to be reasonable physical space between these groups so that they can actually operate in different rooms, rather than in one open space in which there is at times a clamouring and competition for attention. Young children, just like adults, also need quiet time in which to contemplate and think and gather their thoughts together. Mealtimes ideally should also be taken separately for children in their specific age groups. This supports the idea that feeding and relationships go hand in hand and enables the young child not to feel totally overwhelmed. Imagine, by contrast, the situation in which a large group of children are all fed at the same time, banging their plates and spoons on the table. Who would want to feel like eating amid such a clamour and clatter? Certainly, the staff themselves would want to rush to clear everything up as quickly as possible to get away from the demanding, noisy exchange.

A need for the child to have a quiet time and an opportunity to withdraw is also of great importance. This is more than just sleep time for the child to physically rest. Instead there needs to be a recognition that children from time to time simply may want to withdraw without doing anything. They should not have to be forced into constant activity all of the time. The capacity to be alone, to be reflective, needs to be nurtured within the child-care setting if that is where the child is going to spend the majority of his time.

Coming and going – arrivals and departures

The question of how the child comes to the child-care centre each day and how she leaves is also one of central importance. Coming and going, arrivals and departures, remain very much a feature of our lives as we grow up. The way these are handled at the earliest stages of our development are very crucial to our experience later on. No matter how settled a child may be in the child-care centre, the initial personal meeting and greeting enables her to cross the threshold and find a focus for the day. It gives a depth and meaning to her relationship with her particular caregiver and allows her to have a differentiating relationship with the caregiver, one that is different from the other children. Although she will share the caregiver, hopefully with a small number of children, she and the others in her group can be identified as being particularly linked to one individual.

The way in which children leave the child-care centre is also of importance. Many parents remark that this can be a very fraught time when, as they are going out of the door, the child plays up or sometimes becomes irritating or difficult to control.

On other occasions parents report that their children behave very well, but the minute they get into the car they turn into little wild monsters and appear almost irreconcilable with their earlier selves.

If we return to one of the tenets of the psychodynamic approach, which is that all behaviour has meaning, we can see that this form of behaviour on the part of the child is a very fundamental communication. It represents the confusion and difficulty the child may have on making the transition from the relationships she has established as part of her child-care experience to resuming her relationship with her mother or father. The child may be telling us that in order to move from the one physical experience, mental and personal experience, to the other she needs a period of time in which to internally reorganise her feelings and thoughts. Most often, when parents collect their children from the child-care centre they are in a hurry. It is often the end of a tiring day for the staff and there may be insufficient acknowledgement of how demanding it has been for the child to be part of a group for nearly ten hours that day. Can we allow then for children to be able to gather their thoughts together quite literally at this time and also to have an appropriate time frame in which to be able to orient themselves from one situation to another?

I have mentioned the importance of allowing time for some of these processes to take place in the context of all aspects of development, particularly the process of maternal and paternal reverie. Something similar is required here when the child needs to be able to say goodbye properly and have the time to do so. Sometimes the tension that is created when the child moves from the caregiver with whom she has been all day back to her mother's care may be connected with the child's anxiety about having formed an attachment to the child-care worker. The child may feel that her mother may not approve of the love or affection she has for the worker and she may also feel confused about her feelings for both at this time. The parents' understanding of the child's dependence and need for affection can play an important part in making these leavetakings less traumatic. It is important for the parent at this stage to be able to recognise the value of the child's relationship and acknowledge the validity of the child's experience during the day. When parents are in a hurry and the child is snatched away from the activity she has just been involved in, as well as her caregiver, it may seem to the child that her world is invalidated and not of great importance in the scheme of things.

Limit setting and discipline within the child-care setting: acknowledging differences between boys and girls

I have talked about the importance of setting limits and boundaries for children as they move into toddlerhood and early childhood. For children who spend their toddlerhood and early childhood in a child-care setting the situation becomes more complex. What role does the child-care staff play in relation to disciplining and setting limits and boundaries for the children? I have mentioned before the misuse of routines. We can see that a routine can be used as a buffer between the staff and the child, and can also be used inappropriately as a way of creating a disciplinary structure.

A world of women

One of the things that is noteworthy about the way in which child-care centres are established and staffed is that they are run almost entirely by women, and that men are significant by their absence. Nevertheless the children who attend the child-care centres comprise equal numbers of boys as well as girls. The absence of men in the lives of young children is a significant factor which we cannot overlook. It affects the way in which boundaries are constructed in which limit settings take place and is of particular significance to the experience of boys in their development. I reiterate throughout this book that the presence and involvement of men and fathers is as vital to the development of positive mental health in children as is the presence of women and mothers. The absence of men for young children, particularly young boys, has a depleting effect on the opportunities for identification with a member of the same sex and opportunities for appropriate modelling. We could say in this regard that the young boy in child care may be particularly vulnerable because of this total exclusion of male figures. A preponderance of female staff can also cause confusion and misunderstanding at times about what behaviour means and how it is construed. For example, if we observe three-year-old-girls and three-year-old-boys we can see that they use their bodies differently in relation to their immediate physical environment and use the space around them in a different way. They also interact differently with children of the same age. It seems clear that boys interact in a more vigorous, physical way with their environment, while girls tend to be more focused inwards both towards the physical environment of their bodies and towards relationships and verbal activity.

While I would not want to suggest that we prolong stereotypes, I think there are certain factors about the differences between boys and girls that are critical to their development and should be taken into account to inform the way in which they are responded to at this early stage of their development. Sadly, in child-care settings, it is not uncommon to hear complaints from staff about how to contain or discipline the boys in their care. For example, I knew of one nursery that provided outstanding care and support for its young children. However, for a very long period there were only women employed on the staff. Over the years, within the groups of children one child, almost always a boy, tended to become identified as the 'problem child or the aggressor'. It was obvious that the staff were more skilled in facilitating the girls than they were the boys. At home time, when the parents came to collect their children, it was striking to see how the boys, particularly the ones who had been identified as having 'a problem', would hurl themselves at available fathers, to engage in physical jousting. If the fathers were generous enough to pick up these cues and become playful with the child – for instance, picking them up on their shoulders or carrying them aloft – this would result in a quite delirious happiness which indicated something of their need for a different kind of physical expression. It is a sad reflection indeed if we so misunderstand the meaning of behaviour that we can misinterpret what is vigorous, interactive seeking behaviour in boys as problematic and aggressive. This particular nursery had the fortunate experience of hiring a young male member of staff whose engagement with both the boys and the girls was highly sensitive and facilitating. It was striking to note that the incidence of having to identify 'a naughty boy in time out' totally disappeared at this point. Here we can see how the presence of the father and the male offers another important dimension in the whole process of containment that is necessary for the development of the child.

BABIES IN CHILD CARE

It is not uncommon in Australia for babies of three months old and upwards to be placed in child care, for long periods of time. There may be many complex reasons which force mothers to be separated from their babies in this way, but an automatic assumption about placing a baby in a child-care centre is one that we should definitely question. I have attempted to describe how the infant's relationship with the outside world has its starting point in the positive psychosomatic experience with the mother. For the baby the mother's body *is* her world. Through the mutual interaction of touching, smelling and feeling, the baby begins to build up a picture of her own body and her identity. We may wonder how this process can be substituted for in a child-care centre. For staff looking after babies the day-to-day care of a group of babies is excessively demanding. One young woman in a child-care centre recently told me that she had 12 babies to look after. It is simply not possible for someone in this situation to give more than fundamental physical care to each baby. There can be very little time for the development of intimacy of the personal relationship that is characterised by one person's voice and manner.

I have talked about Winnicott's comment that the baby looks at the mother and sees himself, which is a way of developing personhood for the child. How can this take place in a setting in which there are other babies clamouring for attention, and possibly staff who may be rostered on at different times. The reality is that the child's development cannot be rostered on and off. It is a flowing experience which is based on connectedness and the centrality of a relationship with the caregiver who, above all, has the baby's interests at heart and can hold the baby in mind. I have mentioned that the capacity of young children to adapt to a variety of different situations is considerable. The capacity of even the young infant to adapt is also impressive. From a very young age the infant may learn that it is not worth making particular demands because they simply will not be met. The infant will reorganise himself internally and externally to adjust to the immediate surroundings, demands and what is available. The baby who has learnt that it is not worth protesting, because nothing will be forthcoming or he will have to wait in a queue with other babies, may take this experience into a later phase of development. Again, to reiterate the theme of containment: who will be available in the child-care centre for a young baby to help him digest or metabolise his experiences along with his food? How can his own individual needs be considered in such a group context?

What kind of attention do young children need? Preventing deficits of attention

The problem of a lack of attention has achieved prominence most recently in the publicity surrounding Attention Deficit Disorder. The symptoms of this disorder are described as intense over-activity in children, an inability to concentrate, short attention and memory span, with resultant upheaval in family relationships and in the classroom. A higher proportion of boys than girls are diagnosed with this problem.

We may pause for a moment to consider why this problem has become so manifest and ask ourselves the question: 'Is this an illness for our time?' My concern about identifying a blanket syndrome is that it can become a catch-all for much more complex behaviour. It represents a passive way of viewing the problem as if something from outside has happened to the child, rather than looking at the process of interaction which underlies the problem.

We have seen how from the beginning of life specific patterns of attachment and attention are already established between the infant and his parents; the idea of the parent holding the baby and young child 'in mind' paves the way for the child in turn to feel sufficiently contained to begin to organise his thoughts for subsequent cognitive activity and learning. The quality of the external environment also has an impact on the quality of attention which children can bring to a task be it playing, learning or relating to others.

Finally, we can see how the absence of men and fathers in the day-to-day lives of young boys can create a deficit of attention in which boys' physical attempts at emotional contact may be mis-interpreted as aggression.

Taking a developmental view which assumes that the child's behaviour always has meaning and is a communication poses challenges for those professionals working in the field of early childhood. However these challenges, if met, can lead to far greater rewards and enjoyment in the vital task of caring for young children.

CHAPTER 6

Early Childhood and the Transition to School

SUMMARY

This chapter discusses school readiness and the child's emotional ability to make the transition into the school setting, covering the following areas.

- The way in which relationships have developed thus far within the family are seen as a prototype – these will affect the child's capacity to learn and form relationships with his teachers and peers.
- Play and learning need to be viewed as part of a continuous process.
- How the child and parent can manage separation as the child starts school will also depend on the child's capacity to be alone.
- Some children are not free to learn because of problems at home, which may take the form of needing to support the parent; or a crisis in the family, such as divorce and separation.
- The 'language of learning' is described as having a close affinity with the relationship of the child to his mother's body and his own bodily functions, when we talk of 'taking in' information, 'digesting' what we have heard and 'producing' work – acknowledging this developmental process enables educationalists to provide the right setting for young children to learn.

n exploring the emotional milestones of development, we need to keep in mind that these milestones do not take place in a tidy way. The child does not neatly go through each phase of development, master it and then move on to the next. While there are indeed key emotional tasks that have to be negotiated both for the child and the parent at different stages, these tasks are never totally complete and aspects from the previous stage will continue into the next phase of development: some of them not at all resolved, others not entirely satisfactorily resolved.

The transition to school for the young child represents a momentous experience for both the child and the parents. It also represents the end of early childhood and the transition to a new phase of development, one in which learning and mastery will gain increasing prominence.

The learning and mastery that will be expected of the child as she moves through this transition into school will be of a more formal nature than the kind I have referred to before. Happily, though, schools and the education system increasingly recognise that play really is learning and there are far greater opportunities for children in the early years of schooling to be able to make a more gradual transition between the state of play and formal learning.

In describing the basic tenets of the psychodynamic approach I have referred to the idea of the child in the parents, and the parents in the child. There are very few parents when their child first starts school who are not brought in touch with the deep emotional experience of their own first days at school. Parents' hopes and expectations for their child at school thus are bound to be mixed with their own school and learning experiences, both positive and negative.

For some parents the start of school for their child may represent a period of anxiety. They may feel that this is indeed the end of early childhood and that their child should have overcome particular problems, such as bed-wetting or separation anxiety. Their fear of how acceptable their child will appear to the outside world is also very much to the fore.

SCHOOL READINESS

School readiness is an important factor in this regard and points to the recognition of the fact that children do not all develop at the same rate, and that we need to acknowledge the differences between children and their readiness for the school experience. In considering the transition to school there are a number of factors which we may want to take into account. Firstly, the child, to be ready to enter school, needs to have what Winnicott has called a certain capacity to be alone, that is to say to begin to be alone with his own thoughts. In the first year of school, children are generally introduced to the process of reading and of carrying out pieces of work within particular periods of time. There is a different structure to the day. Bells are rung to define the end of lessons, and the end of particular sessions. There are fixed times for playtime. Children are expected to take responsibility for themselves, to eat their lunches and mind their possessions.

The centrality of relationships that I have referred to throughout this book, from the beginning of life, is a significant feature in the whole learning process and the child's capacity to learn, since we can say that all learning at this early stage particularly takes place in a relationship. The type of relationship that the child is able to form with his teacher, to enable him to learn from him or her, will depend on his history of relationships within the family and outside of the family.

Allowing others to be good enough

Earlier I have described Winnicott's idea of the good enough parent, which refers to the fact that the parent does not need to be perfect or wonderful, or get everything right all the time. Being good enough also suggests that the child is able to make a great deal out of what is available; since the child has resources within herself. We can extend this idea of a good enough parent to include the good enough others. The good enough others may be other members of the family or friends, who can be allowed by the parent to relate to the young child, and perhaps also have an important place in her life. This enables the child to generalise the intensity of her relationships from her parents towards significant others and to learn to trust people outside of the immediate parental environment.

The good enough others may also be represented by other children in the child's life. While I have described above some of the shortcomings of a 10-hour child-care schedule for the young child, it is certainly important for her to be able to have some experience of playing and relating to children before she goes to school. Thus kindergartens, playgroups and well run child-care centres can provide an important foundation for the learning experience. Within this context children are able to learn to share, to recognise the needs of other children and also to begin to recognise their differences.

Some families may have a particular culture which encourages a very closed series of relationships. Here the child may be cloistered with his parents to the exclusion of the outside world. The parents may convey through their actions and communications that the outside world cannot be trusted or relied upon, and there may be little opportunity for the child to test himself out in relation to other children of the same age. Children in this situation may find themselves completely overwhelmed once they start school. They will have had little transition or preparation for the social demands of the school setting, and possibly the learning demands as well. Often these children become very timid and withdrawn, while being superficially compliant. The rough-and-tumble experiences that they experience within the school setting may further reinforce the parents' view that the outside world is unsafe and not to be trusted.

The language of learning

It is significant that the language we use to describe learning is related so closely to feeding, and also to bodily processes which in turn are associated with the close relationship of the infant and young child, most particularly to the mother's body. For example we use expressions such as 'taking in', 'absorbing', 'digesting' and 'producing'. At the point of transition to school the child, of course, has absorbed and digested not only the food that the mother has produced, but also her emotional state of mind and his father's emotional state of mind. This will set the scene for the way in which the child is able to cope with the transition to school and with his readiness for learning.

I have mentioned before that development does not move forward in a tidy way, and that children develop at very different levels and in different ways. Happily, there is an increased recognition of this both among parents and early childhood educators, who may, for example, suggest that a child spend a second year in a kindergarten. This is very encouraging as it indicates there is a growing awareness of the need for children to be able to explore and enjoy their infancy and early childhood, and not to be rushed into the next stage for which they may not be ready.

We should not underestimate the significance of starting school for the young child. I was reminded of how my daughter, in the first few weeks of starting school in Prep, seemed to enjoy it while she was there but at home became very controlling and fretful with us. She would insist on things being done in a certain way or within a certain time frame. We tried to overcome our irritation at this by recognising that the new school experience for her at this stage appeared a controlling one in parts, where bells would ring without any notice and where it may have seemed to her that she was losing control and that others, like the teachers around her, were assuming control over her life and daily activities. Thus she in turn had to play out the control with us.

The capacity to be alone

I have mentioned that one of the key factors in the child's ability to learn is the child's need to have achieved more or less a capacity to be alone with their own thoughts. Some children may find this very difficult because of the stage of earlier development that they are still attached to, others may find it difficult to have the capacity to be alone for different reasons. This may have more to do with the fact that they can literally not be alone with their own thoughts because they are so very busy and preoccupied with their parents' thoughts and anxieties. For some children the start of school may coincide with a time of major change or disruption within the family. Their parents may have decided to separate or divorce. There may be longstanding difficulties in the family related to abusive relationships. In this context one could say that the child literally cannot think his own thoughts and is not free to do so because he is kept so very busy being worried or preoccupied by the events around him. In later school life we can see how children with school phobia, that is children who are apparently anxious about coming to school, are in fact very anxious about leaving home. They may be worried to leave a vulnerable parent, or the parent in turn may give them a mixed message about wanting them to go to school but, at the same time, hope that the child will stay at home and be a companion to them.

Thus, in order to be able to manage the transition to school, the child, and indeed the parent, needs to be free enough of conflicting thoughts and experiences. This will enable the child to feel that he will be both safe and contained within the school environment, that his parents will be able to manage without him, and that there will not be any major distractions and serious dislocations in the home environment to fill up his mind in such a way as to make him literally not free to take in anything new or to be curious about learning and play and engagement with his peers.

ISSUES OF SEPARATION IN THE TRANSITION TO SCHOOL

The negotiation of separation in assisting the child's transition to school is one which very much calls forth the need for a partnership between the child and parents. At its most basic the child cannot tolerate a separation if the parents cannot. The parent needs to feel confident about literally handing over the child to the care of someone else, in this case the school and the teacher. In the process of doing so they need to feel that the teacher can be 'good enough', and that they can tolerate the idea of the teacher perhaps being very special to the child. At times the parents' focus on his or her exclusivity of a relationship with a child can impede the child in being able to reach out to others and feel confident about being able to make relationships with other adults and peers.

The start of school very much represents a focus on the establishment and consolidation of separation and individuation for the young child. In the course of the school experience the child will make relationships on her own which will be less and less dependent on those that are chosen by the parent. The relationship that she makes with the teacher will also be independent of the parents. Can parents tolerate this experience? Some parents may find that it is very difficult to avoid speaking disparagingly of the teacher in the child's presence, as a means perhaps of ensuring their supremacy in the child's affections. The problem of separation that the parent may have may also find its way into an over-concern and over-preoccupation with what the child is doing at school or what the child brings home from school, to the point where the child is not able to have her own individual separate experience. The parents' potential intrusiveness in this regard can have the effect of making the child uncertain about her loyalties between home and school, and also uncertain about whether she should be preoccupied with home while at school. All of these factors contribute to problems in concentration and learning.

IDENTIFICATION WITH THE GROUP

The transition to school involves for both the child and the parents a major transition in the types of identification that the child develops. Up to the point of going to school, the child is in total identification with his parents. At the point of starting school, the child widens his social repertoire of identification. It is important, in order for learning to take place, that the child is able to identify with his teacher as well as with other children. The child not only learns academically about specific subjects but also learns about how to socialise. It is the child's observation of what other children do, how they behave and how they relate that is all-important at this stage. Thus the key issue of a partnership between the child and the parents, and indeed the school, is central to facilitating this whole process. Parents need to feel they are ready to allow the child to develop other identifications. The school in turn needs to be sensitive to the social and family context from which the child comes into the school. Research would suggest that learning and education is at its most productive where the school can achieve a partnership with the parents, in which parents are knowledgeable about what the school is trying to do and do not feel excluded from the process. At the same time, it is important for both the parents and the staff at the school to be clear about their respective boundaries. Here we can see how the concept of a partnership, which I described from the moment of the child's birth and before, extends to include a partnership with a teacher and with a school. The other concept that I have referred to, namely the idea of containment, is also very much to the fore in the transition to school in terms of the containment that the school as an organisation is able to provide for the parents, who can in turn feel confident about providing containment for the child to enable him to feel free enough to learn.

PLAY AND LEARNING

In describing the importance of play in early childhood, I have referred to the fact that play can be seen as a very serious business indeed because it is about the child learning to make sense of her life, linking a variety of different events together, making sense of her internal fantasy world and dreams and her relationship with the outside world. I have also stated that play is intimately connected with cognitive development. The preparatory school setting for children therefore needs to be a place which can understand and acknowledge this aspect of the child's development. When we talk about the transition to school we really do mean a transition, rather than a radical change in which the child is suddenly expected to be grown up. The structure of the schoolroom and the way it is set up in the preparatory classroom is just as crucial as the structure of rooms and the way they are set up for children in a child-care or kindergarten setting. Until relatively recently, children were expected to start school and enter a room with rows of desks all facing to the front. Some schools may still be very much like that. Here a message was conveyed to the child in no uncertain terms that she had left her childhood and play behind, and that there would be no room or space for those experiences within the classroom. I would like to emphasise at this point that play and childhood are not simply processes and aspects of development that need to be 'grown out of' and put aside. The capacity to play, and therefore to learn, and an understanding of the child part of ourselves remains with us throughout our development and well into adulthood. The psychodynamic approach focuses on striving to integrate these different aspects of the personality, rather than to chop them off and throw them away.

The following example describes the long-term effects of a bad transition to school.

Hiding from school

A man in his late thirties came to see me for psychotherapeutic help because of a crisis he was undergoing. The crisis, which concerned the ending of a relationship with a woman, represented the tip of the iceberg of numerous other problems which had developed in early childhood. This man had grown up from infancy torn between his warring parents. His father had been rejecting of him, while his mother tended to over-protect him and to draw him into an identification with her so that it was difficult for him to make contact with his father. Over several sessions of the therapy he returned time and time again to an incident in his childhood, when he had just started school, at the age of five or six years. For reasons that he could not recall he found the experience overwhelming and begged his mother not to let him continue. When she refused to do so he tried to hide under the table when it was time to go to school in the morning. He recalled the sense of panic and total abandonment that he could not convey to his mother. His mother, feeling bewildered and angry about what he was doing, responded by telling him that if he did not go to school he would grow up to be no better than a dustman. He had been haunted by this remark from his mother, and in fact had found great difficulty in educational achievements at school and subsequent employment. He described how he had been extremely withdrawn and anxious while at primary school, while at secondary school he attempted to compensate for this by becoming disruptive and aggressive.

My patient's difficulties obviously were not limited or caused solely by this experience. However, we can see in this example how an important opportunity for growth and development was actually lost or in fact destroyed. Had my patient been able to effect a successful transition into the school environment at this early stage it could have provided a suitably containing experience for him, which could have mitigated against the disruption and marital warfare of his parents. One might wonder whether his mother, although on the one hand very identified with him and wanting to keep him very close, also used him in a merciless way to express her aggression, perhaps the aggression she was unable to express towards her husband.

In conclusion, the transition to school represents the end of early childhood for the developing child. The beginning of school life represents a significant emotional milestone for the child and his family. If events have progressed in a reasonably good enough way, he will be able to master separation from his parents and the family home; he will have the capacity to be alone with his thoughts to enable learning to take place. He will feel sufficiently engaged with others to begin identification with a peer group and with other adults. He will be able to ally a capacity for play with a capacity for learning and curiosity. Listed like this, these requirements may seem formidable indeed, and of course some children may find that they are not in a position to master all of these different areas at the point at which they make the transition to school. For many children, the preparatory year is often the year in which they are able to complete or work towards integrating those aspects of their development which seem to lag slightly behind or which may inhibit them. The likelihood of this happening depends of course on the emotional awareness and understanding of the teacher, who needs to recognise that the child's development is in progress rather than in a static state. I return to the theme of containment, so crucial to all of the developmental tasks and processes of life, and the specific tasks for the school as a containing institution. Central to the idea of transition is the notion of a crossing of a boundary from one stage to another, which I have described at the very beginning of life when the mother becomes pregnant. For the child the step into school represents a major crossing of a boundary. The extent to which this can be recognised and worked with will facilitate the transition for all concerned.

SUMMARY

This chapter describes the impact on the child of the birth of siblings and the need for the family to acknowledge and handle the resulting mixed feelings. The advantages of a sibling group and the dilemma of the only child are also discussed. The points are made that:

- The feelings of ambivalence a child may have following the birth of siblings are natural ones.
- The handling of positive and negative feelings in these intense relationships are part of the family task.
- A sibling group can offer a healthy opportunity for children to 'gang up' against their parents, to define the generation boundary between children and parents, and an opportunity for identity testing and sharing.
- Expanding horizons for the only child through opening up the child's contact with friends and peers is important so the child can compare and contrast experience outside and within her own family.

Sibling relationships within the family lay the foundations for the continuing intrapsychic, interpersonal and social experiences that are part of the development of the child's personality.

Winnicott has described this as a unique experience for the first child who discovers with a powerful realisation that his mother's body and the milk from her breasts can be shared and given to another child, and do not exclusively belong to him. The pain of this realisation can be profound and is often recalled by adults in later life with an extraordinary vividness. How these processes of sharing and rivalry can be assimilated and negotiated constitutes the very core of development and, as I have mentioned at the outset, carries within it the opportunity for development to take place on a number of different levels: intrapsychically, that is internally within the child in terms of his dreams, fantasies and nightmares; interpersonally in relation to his mother and father in the sense perhaps of surprise or shock that they could ever have contemplated having a second child (was he not enough for them?); and interpersonally again, in relation to the new sibling who is seen as taking up space that once only belonged to him, but also holds the potential for sharing games, fun, even the possibility of ganging up against the parents, which I will refer to later.

SIBLINGS AROUSE AMBIVALENCE

I have stated earlier, in describing the birth of the first child, that birth arouses ambivalence in everyone concerned in the form of very strong mixed feelings. In the same way the birth of a second child will arouse strong ambivalence, leaning towards negative and aggressive feelings, particularly on the part of the first child. The displacement from being the only one, and the centre of the parents' universe for a time, to being one of two children presents an enormous upheaval for the child. It may also present a similar upheaval or anxiety for the parents. For example, a woman remarked, before she decided to have her second child, that she found it difficult to contemplate how one could love a second child if one loved the first so much. The fear that parents may sometimes have of not knowing whether there will be enough love and affection and commitment on their part may sometimes be echoed in the anxiety of the first child, who will be asking exactly the same questions.

Generally, it is hard for parents to acknowledge the full extent of their child's rivalry and anger towards the newcomer. They may believe that, because they have told the child about the impending birth and tried to involve him, it will not come as quite such a shock. Very often parents will talk about the first few weeks or even months of the newborn's arrival and how their first child reacts with such sweet concern, showering kisses on the baby's head. It is only later that they may report that the older child perhaps hits the baby or deprives it of a toy in a rather sly way, or has shown other signs of distress, usually through regressing – bed-wetting and soiling themselves if they have been toilet trained, talking like a baby, wanting to have a bottle.

A woman who had given birth to a baby when her first child was nearly three years old commented that feeding times were the worst. It made her feel very guilty to breast feed her baby girl while her little three-year-old boy sat close by and looked rather longingly at the baby sucking contentedly from his mother's breast. It had crossed her mind that she could actually offer the three-year-old the breast as well, even though he had been long weaned and was clearly in a different phase of his development. This need on the part of the mother suggests how pressured parents can feel to try to deny the strength of the first child's feelings of being left out. They may also be fearful of the child's negative feelings towards them when hitherto they may have experienced a positive relationship, and fear that this will be spoiled. The difficulty in this example of giving in to the wish to offer the three-year-old the breast is that it denies these complicated but nevertheless important anxieties of the three-year-old. He would be left with no way of having his angry feelings and rivalry acknowledged in a way that would be constructive.

If parents can acknowledge the reality of their child's anger and not feel too overwhelmed or frightened by it, they can in turn talk to him about it so that it becomes part of ordinary, everyday experience and behaviour, rather than something that has to be kept hidden from view. We can see as well, for the three-year-old, that one way of helping him to negotiate the birth of a sibling is to acknowledge his angry and rivalrous feelings and his feelings of displacement, and of course to reassure him that he will still remain a loved child. However, as well, it is important to recognise that the three-year-old is in a different place developmentally from the newborn baby. There are a number of things that he has managed to master, such as his various achievements in talking, probably in toilet training and perhaps attending playschool. These are all things he would not really want to give up in order to revert back to being a baby.

If the parents are able to recognise and be reasonably accepting of the child's rivalry and negative feelings towards the newborn baby, they will also be more aware of and able to acknowledge the child's wishes to make some sort of reparation in this regard. For example, it is not unusual when the family goes out to visit that, when the family leaves, the older child may panic about the possibility of 'leaving the baby behind'. Sometimes it is this older sibling who busies around making sure that the parents have not been forgetful. This is a beautiful example of how the young child struggles to master her own feelings of genuinely wanting to leave the baby behind and hoping that the baby will fall out of her parents' mind combined with anxiety and guilt that her thoughts might actually make this happen. At the same time the young child is aware that, if the parents are able to forget the baby, they may also forget her. So it is in her interests to ensure that the baby is kept in mind and brought home!

I have mentioned the importance of acknowledging ambivalence during pregnancy. A woman may not be totally thrilled with the idea of becoming a mother and needs time to gradually adjust herself to the prospect of maternity. So we should not expect a first-born child to be totally thrilled with the arrival of a brother or sister and force her straight away into showering kisses and love. The child, as much as the adult, needs time to form an acquaintanceship, particularly when it is based more on her own terms rather than exclusively on one that is there to please the family.

The inclusion of second and subsequent children in a family obviously creates a totally different dynamic within the family. Just as with the birth of the first child life for the two parents will never be the same again, similarly it will never be the same again for the threesome once the fourth person is included. All the relationships within the family will change, whether imperceptibly or not. These adjustments can of course go both ways. They have tremendous potential to enable children who grow up as siblings within a family to develop depth and maturity. They can also of course become deadly rivals, but this will be very dependent on the parental relationship as I describe below.

THE ROLE OF THE FATHER

The role of the father continues to be of high significance throughout the child's development, and the partnership between both parents will be crucial in defining the success or not of the sibling bonding relationship that ensues. At the time of the new baby's birth fathers have a particularly important role to play in offering an appropriate space, potentially for the older child, and of creating a space for their partner and the new baby. They may also find, because they are less, perhaps, intensively physically involved with the baby, that they can defuse some of the intensity of this emotional time. Going off to do something special with Daddy while Mummy is with the baby acknowledges both a separate, different relationship and different activities.

THE DEVELOPMENT OF THE SIBLING GROUP

There are many advantages inherent in being one of siblings in a family, not the least of which is the ability for children to form a group which defines their own status i.e. that of children which is different to that of the adult world. This gives children a sense of identity and clarifies a particular boundary around them. It also helps them in the important task of 'ganging up' on their parents from time to time. In a family, adults are perceived by children to always know best or are the ones who lead or take the initiative and make all the decisions. It is very important for children as well to feel that they have some degree of control. For siblings this can often take the form of ganging up, not necessarily in a destructive way, but rather in a way which suggests that the sibling group have their own secrets, and their own dynamic. It can often release tension in the household and make the atmosphere seem to be less hothouse and intense than it otherwise might be. The capacity of parents to allow children occasionally to get the upper hand, or to recognise that the siblings may be forming a little group of their own, depends very much as well on their own experience of being siblings. They may feel, in a narcissistic sort of way, that they need to know all the details of their children's lives and that nothing should be kept separate or secret from them.

The establishment of positive sibling relationships can be of enormous benefit to children in their future childhood and later adult life. In many families, of course, the extent to which this happens varies enormously. Some families may err on the side of almost cloistering the children with them and of creating a boundary between the family and the outside world. In this situation the family is seen as very closed and the children urged to trust only each other and not the friends that they may make for example. Always putting family first and only putting your trust in family may cause difficulties in later life. Often these difficulties emerge when the various siblings enter into relationships and marriages, and the respective spouses feel themselves to be excluded from this charmed inner circle. At the other extreme, the difficulties that parents may be experiencing in their marital relationship have far-reaching consequences for the atmosphere in the family and the war between the parents may be carried on by the children. For example, Lisa, a young woman of 18 whom I had treated for several years for obsessional anxieties, came from a family in which almost all expressions of emotion were highly sanitised. For example, both parents had great difficulty expressing their anger or differences of opinion; instead they resorted to illness and would withdraw from each other with a whole succession of symptoms. Part of the anger that my patient's parents felt was also towards her grandparents who controlled and infantilised her parents. Thus the tensions that existed across three generations. Lisa's memory of her younger brother was that of a sickly baby who developed into a sickly boy and who for many years dominated the household with his own physical illnesses, some real and some, it seemed to my patient, imagined in order to attract the family's attention. The result of this was that Lisa and her brother had very little opportunity to develop a sibling relationship. In fact, it seemed almost as though her parents actively discouraged it. They were thus not able to form a little gang and gang up on their parents, and in this way find a small space of normality and everyday activity.

The difficulties that Lisa and her brother had in engaging with each other and sharing activities were echoed in the difficulties they experienced in establishing social relationships at school and in later life. After many years of ignoring her brother, Lisa remarked rather wistfully that it seemed as though she had lost an opportunity to create a friendship with her brother, and the divide was now so great between them that she despaired of ever being able to get close again.

SIBLING ORDER IN THE FAMILY

Clinical observation and family therapy suggest that where we come in the family influences the dynamic of family life and will affect how our parents relate to us, which in turn is linked with our future relationships and achievements. It is generally acknowledged that first-born children carry a particular responsibility in a family. We must be mindful of the danger of imposing too much responsibility on older children at too early an age. While this may fit in with their omnipotent wishes on the one hand, it also places them in a situation of responsibility for which they have no corresponding maturity.

I have come across a number of mothers in my clinical practice who have traced some of the difficulties in their relationship with their children back to the fact that they were the oldest of large families and were given responsibilities that they were absolutely not ready for. Sometimes these women have acted in a rather delinquent way with regard to their own children, neglecting them slightly or being grossly unaware of some difficulties they may be experiencing. This may suggest that these women commit the delinquency with their own children that they had actually wanted to commit with the siblings that they were forced to look after. The illness, separation and death of parents can exacerbate the problem for an older child who is already in the position of responsibility for younger siblings.

Younger siblings, for their part, may be seen as the baby of the family. The price they may have to pay for this is that they may feel that they are not taken seriously or listened to, and that parents do not have as high expectations of them as they do of the elder siblings. The position that parents themselves have occupied in the family will obviously affect how they interpret and repeat experiences with their own children.

 # THE EXPERIENCE OF THE ONLY CHILD

The experience of the only child in a family is a different one from that of having siblings, and the demands placed on an only child are correspondingly different as well. I have referred to the fact that siblings have a naturally made group, whether of two or more, and can set themselves apart from their parents with a particular boundary around them. Thus there is a clearly defined space between the children and the parents. For the only child this is a more difficult process, for of course there is no one else with whom to form a group.

Thus the creation of a separate space between child and parents is something that has to be actively negotiated in a much more conscious and determined way by the parents themselves. It is all too easy for an only child to become one with the adults, where there are no boundaries between the child world and the adult world. It may at times seem convenient, for example, just to include the child in a variety of discussions and decision making because there is no one else around.

For the child himself there may be a fantasy that he has really succeeded in some way in preventing his parents from having another child. This may fulfil his wishes for omnipotence but, at the same time, may make him feel guilty or worried about what he perceives to be his powerful position. The child may believe that his natural fantasies and wishes to keep the parents apart sexually may actually have worked in that they were not able to get together to produce another child. For their part, the parents may find themselves over-investing in their only child and placing him at the very centre of their lives.

Only children may also feel that, if anything happens to them, their parents are left with nothing.

 # MANAGING DISTANCE AND INTIMACY

In all families there has to be negotiation around issues of distance and intimacy. This involves the creation of space between each member of the family and particularly the space between the child and her parents. Only children may necessarily have to be allowed to be in a position where they can reasonably negotiate some space with their parents. Since they have no one to gang up with they run the risk of feeling constantly overwhelmed by the superior forces of the parent group. Only children will need both reassurance and support about this, and regular discussions which can enable these issues to come out into the open. Sometimes when these issues are dealt with, with humour, it can create a sense of enormous relief for the child.

As with many situations, there are a number of stereotypes which surround the parenting of an only child. These usually revolve around the notion that the parents are selfish for only having one child. For parents struggling to deal with rivalrous siblings this may seem a state of almost unimaginable luxury. There may be an anticipation of selfishness in the behaviour of the single child which may or may not be justified in reality. What is particularly important, however, is that parents of only children need to acknowledge how very small their circle is. Family conflicts, issues and concerns reverberate within a very small space indeed in terms of numbers, and there is a danger of the small unit becoming rather inward looking and enclosed. For this reason it is particularly important for parents of only children to encourage an open and relaxed relationship between their family and the outside world. Parents of only children require possibly even more flexibility in being able to facilitate their child making friendships and allowing for the presence of other adult relationships, whether family or friends, and generally widening the social and familial network in as supportive and vibrant a way as possible.

THE USE OF SIBLINGS AND PEERS TO TEST REALITY

I have mentioned before that the growing child requires a sense of a boundary around herself where she can form identifications with children of roughly the same age, in order to be able to carry out various researches on a small scale into how things operate and why people relate in the way they do. These areas of inquiry, as I have indicated above, must be conducted away from the parental group. For example, my daughter and a friend from school of the same age were talking quite intensely together as we were walking across a car-park after an outing. I caught occasional phrases such as 'And then they do things sometimes that they say they won't do' and 'Sometimes they tell you, you absolutely can't have a pet and then suddenly they agree that you can'. Various other words and phrases to this effect floated upwards. The two girls were engaged in such an intense exchange that it was almost as though they were concentrating their energies and observations to try to make sense of this adult world of grown-ups who one minute might say one thing to you, and be adamant about it, and the next minute change their mind. The nature of the discussion almost had the air of an anthropologist discussing the particular rituals of a tribe. Both girls at this point seemed quite oblivious of my walking a few paces behind them. It is this kind of discussion and research that children require in order to help them test out reality, make sense of the world, and feel they are part of a broad group called 'children' with whom they can check out these important matters. The following example also illustrates this process.

Daniel in the lion's den

Daniel, an only child, had a father who was extremely intrusive into his son's activities. This intrusiveness also hampered his son's ability to form relationships with other children. For example, if Daniel managed to get a few local friends to come around to the house his father would comment on the fact that his son's ability to play was so much more sophisticated and advanced than that of other children. He seemed in effect to be quite rivalrous with Daniel's friends and extended his intrusions to the point of listing boys who were satisfactory and acceptable and those who were not. For his part, Daniel found his contacts with other children very important in helping him with his researches about the nature of his own anger. He commented, for example, that two local boys had come to play with him over a period of days during the holidays. These boys had also been close friends. He was fascinated to see how they would at times argue with each other, even punch each other, but that once the argument was over they would settle back to play with each other and the fight did not appear to damage their relationship. This was information that Daniel could not possibly have gleaned from his father or mother. It was essentially a peer sibling experience which enabled him to develop this insight.

CHAPTER 8

The Middle Years of Childhood from Five to Twelve

SUMMARY

This chapter focuses on the following aspects of child development in the middle years of childhood.

- The difficulties which may arise where parents' anxieties and expectations are out of touch with the child's needs and capacities – parents may be motivated by the pressure of success and achievement to involve their child in myriad activities which serve no particular purpose.

- The need to help growing children to cope with depression and anxiety and to get to know themselves better. This is seen as the precursor for a later capacity to tolerate boredom and uncertainty, develop inner resources and be more sensitive and interactive in relationships with members of the same and the opposite sex.

- The particular role of the school and teacher, emphasising the strong emotional component to learning and teaching, the need for containment to be continued within the school setting and the partnership between child, parent and school on which the success of school and learning depends.

Psychodynamic theorists have traditionally described this phase of middle childhood from the age of five to twelve years old as 'the latency period'. By this they mean that the more urgent developmental tasks and thrusts of the early childhood period which are so associated with the child's discovery of his own bodily processes such as urinating and defecating, the child's exploration of his genitals, his gender identity and his relationship with the parent of the same and opposite sex – these urgent developmental issues and concerns – are temporarily laid to rest. That is that they are perceived by the child as less urgent and are certainly less exposed. Another way of describing this process is to say that these intense sexual bodily preoccupations become 'sublimated' or transformed into other activities. The continuing consolidation of learning and mastery for the child of middle years is one example of this process. This process of sublimation or transformation leads to the development of skills, interests and hobbies which can become the pleasures of a life time.

However, it is very important that we should not stereotype this phase of development as a kind of emotional waiting room between the intensity of early childhood and the drama of adolescence, since this period of childhood brings with it its own particular characteristics and intensities.

THE PRESSURE OF SUCCESS

One of the new factors that perhaps characterises this phase of development more than any other is the competitive urge and anxiety which surrounds parents' hopes and intentions for their children. Whereas perhaps a generation ago it was considered good enough for the adolescent to knuckle down to work towards the end of their schooling in order to achieve reasonable marks, for many families and communities today this no longer holds true. Family life, of course, is substantially influenced by the economic, social and cultural attributes of the community and society. We can say that Western society is itself at a major point of transition in terms of how we view employment, unemployment and leisure time, and how we value skills. The skills and professions which may have seemed appropriate for even a generation ago may no longer be seen as relevant or may not even exist for the new generation. These pressures and worries inevitably filter down through the educational system and into family life, and we may find that children in this middle childhood period are probably placed under pressure in a way their parents may never have experienced themselves.

Many parents are anxious that if they do not give their child a good start educationally then the child will miss out at a later stage. Whether this will happen or not we do not know. However, we do know that a high level of anxiety and pressure will not facilitate learning and ultimate success.

At its most extreme in our consumer-driven mechanistic society we may have an expectation of children that, once they are in the school system, we have the right to apply 'the manual'. That is to say that if we only knew which buttons to press or which type of school would have the best results, then we would be assured of the child as an excellent product at the end of this process.

In our society many children in this middle childhood period embark on an astonishing number of activities which many of their parents would not have dreamt about when they were children. It is not unusual for quite young children to have every afternoon at school marked off for different activities, whether it is to develop sporting prowess, computer know-how, play several musical instruments or attend extra classes of one kind or another. Many children have their time thoroughly made up for them by the family and people in the outside world. We may wonder how often the children actually ask to be involved in these myriad activities or whether the competitiveness and anxiety of parents sets them on a cycle of activity from which there appears to be no escape. They are making sure that the child's every waking moment is accounted for and that the child is kept busy and involved in purposeful activity. In doing so, parents may inadvertently be depriving their child of the capacity to be alone, which is such a prerequisite for real learning to take place.

REVISITING DEPRESSION AND ANXIETY

In describing the development of the toddler and young child, I refer to the importance of negotiating depression and anxiety. These two areas of our experience remain very critical throughout our lives. They come into particular prominence in this phase of middle childhood, and one can say that if the child is able to negotiate these two aspects of her experience satisfactorily, this will stand her in very good stead when she faces some of the turbulence of adolescence.

I have mentioned the capacity to be alone as a precursor for the young child to be able to be alone with his own thoughts and to master the task of learning. The capacity to be alone with one's thoughts of course is vital to being able to negotiate sad, unhappy and difficult experiences. For the child who is shunted from activity to activity it is as though there is a fear that he must never be alone with his own thoughts, and never face any notion of sadness or depression. Indeed this idea of a fear of being alone with our own thoughts is echoed in our communal surroundings, for example in shops and supermarkets where continual music is played as though silence itself has become something of an obscenity.

The ubiquitous Walkman radio and earphones seem to suggest as well that people need to have some sound in their head to avoid being alone and to be alone with their own thoughts. This suggests that one cannot be discriminating about silence or thinking one's own thoughts, perhaps to produce something positive in the form of an idea. There is a parallel here for me in observing how indiscriminately dummies are used for babies. I have said before that it appears as though the child's crying has to be stopped, literally stopped up. The ubiquitous dummy denies the fact that all cries of the baby have different meanings. The dummy suggests that every cry has the same meaning and that the baby should be stopped from giving voice. However, the baby does need to cry and give voice in order to find out who she is and who she is in relation to the people in her world who respond to her. In the same way, it is vitally important for the child, particularly in the middle years of childhood to be able to have her own thoughts, as opposed to having thoughts, ideas and expectations imposed on her. This may mean for a time that the child may find herself bored or irritated or at a loss. What is important here is that the parents should not rush in and feel that they always have to fill the gap. The reality is that they will not always be available to 'fill the gap' and the child must learn to struggle to find her own inner resources.

In many families the child's cry of 'Mummy, Daddy, I'm bored' is one they may dread more than any other. I have spoken earlier, in relation to the development of the toddler, of parents' need to tolerate the hatred or intense feelings that the child may provoke in them. In the same way, it is very important for parents to be able to contain what may be their panic at the recognition of the older child's boredom or the child's inability to know what to do with himself at a particular time. If parents can contain some of this anxiety and panic, and not rush in and suggest various activities, then the child has the opportunity to learn to develop some resources within himself. He can begin the important task of developing mastery in this area. Thus, just as it is important for even a very young child to be able to have some time he can enjoy playing by himself, so the older child can feel a sense of growing achievement in being able to manage times in his life when nothing is immediately to hand in the form of activities or friends. He will begin to feel more reassured to know that he can rely on himself. If left to some extent to their own devices in this way, children can find remarkable capacities and also opportunities for creativity which may surprise their parents.

Where this process has not been allowed to take place, parents may complain that their child never seems satisfied. They may feel very attacked for the lack of gratitude that they perceive in the child and talk about the many activities and opportunities that they have given the child. They may complain of their child being continually unhappy, not knowing what to do with his time, complaining that life is so boring and attacking his parents for not making it more interesting. In this situation we can see that the child has not had an opportunity to make an experience his own. He has not been able to speak with his own voice or literally *own his own experience*. If parents can step back a little and allow the child to own his experience they will be facilitating the process of development and maturity for the child, because he will then be able to get to know himself better and understand both his limitations and also his unexpected capacities.

EXPECTING THE CHILD TO FULFIL PARENTS' FANTASIES

As parents we all have the best intentions for our children, particularly when it comes to attainment. We hope that opportunities for their development will be at least as good, but usually better, than our own. Where we believe we have failed in a particular area such as sport or academic prowess, we hope that our children will somehow make up for this failing in ourselves and excel in this particular area. Sometimes it is depressing for parents to recognise that their child may have a similar difficulty in the same area that they as parents had when they were children.

In most families where there is enough give and take and where children's needs are actually listened to, children are able to maintain a reasonable boundary around parental expectations and their own capacities and interests. For example, they may be able to resist their parents' insistence to learn a musical instrument when they have no musical interest or capacity whatsoever. For their part, parents can accept that their child's attainment at school is good enough and feel pleased that their children are settling in well and enjoying a wide range of interests and friendships without necessarily feeling that they have to focus too much on academic ability.

In some instances, however, the child's attainment has a meaning that goes beyond his or her own life and experience, but can be seen as a way of operating as a substitute or compensation for parents' own disappointment. A psychotherapy colleague of mine mentioned a remark which a patient of hers had made in the course of her therapy which aptly sums up this predicament. She said to my colleague: 'My parents did not have me in mind, rather they had things in mind for me.' This suggests that somehow the scene has already been set for the child, the future that is intended for her is carved out at a very early stage. This problem is very much to the fore in the following example.

Doing things right for Dad

A boy of eight was referred because of temper tantrums and outbursts at school which appeared to be inexplicable to the staff. Stephen was described as a highly intelligent boy and also gifted musically. It seemed to the teachers at the school that a very small event might trigger off a huge outburst from Stephen in which, though a small child, he would suddenly develop enormous strength, punch other children, overturn chairs and desks, and even intimidate the teachers. The problem had been going on for some time in this school and the parents were motivated to receive help for this difficulty because Stephen had been threatened with expulsion.

At our first meeting, Stephen's father, a man in his sixties, appeared overbearing and totally consumed by his identification with Stephen. Stephen's mother, a woman in her forties, tended to hang back and leave most of the discussion to her husband. She talked of deferring to him because she believed he had more experience in these areas. She appeared, on the surface, to be rather passive and uninvolved with Stephen and made various suggestions to the effect that he should pull himself together and not cause so much trouble to everyone concerned. In this meeting Stephen's father spoke almost non-stop. He presented a detailed scenario of almost every situation in which Stephen could have found himself in the school in relation to his teachers, in various classes, on the sports field, and in relation to other children. These scenarios all concluded with the fact that various people did not understand Stephen sufficiently or had overreacted, or had not handled the situation properly. His identification with Stephen was one of extreme idealisation in which Stephen was clearly the apple of his eye, a child who, as he put it, had given him enormous pleasure. He described Stephen as a particularly sensitive and intelligent child from the moment of birth, and it was clear that he saw Stephen as innately superior to the other children and therefore somehow immune from criticism or the setting of reasonable limits.

Stephen himself appeared a charming and attractive boy. He was clearly devoted to his father but felt under enormous pressure to fulfil his father's ambition and hopes and fantasies. His father's consistent talk of 'learning to win' and 'playing to win' had an air of such a powerful intrusiveness that one could understand how Stephen might well explode. Stephen, for his part, was acting in the only way that seemed reasonable, which was to take his explosion to the school situation where perhaps it could be seen as a cry for help. It would not have been possible for him to explode in his father's presence, since his loyalty and devotion to him was too intense. It transpired that Stephen's father had been made redundant in his work and so had a particularly painful disappointment to bear. He clearly invested all his hopes and longings in his son.

As part of his strategy to get his son to 'win on the playing field and in the classroom' he had enrolled him for innumerable activities at the school, so that Stephen was in effect kept busy virtually from six in the morning until eight in the evening. Some co-operative discussions with the parents and school enabled us to persuade Stephen's father to lessen some of these activities and to allow Stephen to have some time 'to just mess around'.

I have mentioned earlier that the child's ability to settle at school depends very much on his 'availability for a new experience'. He needs to be in a position to not feel impeded or full of worries and anxieties that connect him with his home in such a way that it makes it difficult for him to operate outside. In the following example the freedom to learn and explore was not available.

I don't feel free to learn

Martin, a boy of six, was referred because of his general state of unhappiness at home and at school. He had started school that year but did not seem, according to his parents, to be able to make the best of the experience. He tended to hang back from various activities and not fully participate. At the first consultation it was striking that Martin refused even to leave the car and come into the building to see me. This seemed to suggest that he was a child who was suffering from considerable anxiety and perhaps had built up a fantasy of the horrible lady he might see, or felt that he might be punished for something. His parents and I managed to coax him out of the car and I tried to suggest to him that it was perfectly reasonable for him to feel rather worried because he didn't know where he was coming and had never met me before. In the course of the consultation with Martin and his parents, it became clear that the problem that Martin presented was in a sense part of his parents' own unresolved experience. The parents were going through a particularly tense time in their marriage. The tension and difficulties had begun at the birth of their second child, just over two years before. The birth of this child coincided with the sudden violent death of Martin's uncle. Martin's mother had never allowed herself to mourn her brother or the circumstances of his death and the events surrounding this experience had hardly been discussed by Martin's parents. However, the non-verbal communication in the family had obviously been very powerful in the form of Martin's mother's depression and the tension between the parents. We could see that by the time Martin entered his schooling he was not really free to fully participate and engage with this new experience, since he was preoccupied and filled up with the unspoken dread and unhappiness which had pervaded the household.

In an example such as this we can see how the parents and child share a belief or a fantasy about the status quo, which in a sense paralyses them both. Here the unresolved mourning caused both parents to get rather stuck in their marriage and in their communication with each other. This in turn led Martin to feel inhibited about engaging with his new school and with social and intellectual challenges.

BUILDING UP A REPERTOIRE

I mentioned at the start of this chapter that psychodynamic understanding of this middle period of childhood suggests that the young child's preoccupations with the discovery of his own body, including his genitals, and the intensity surrounding the relationships with his parents become transmuted as he grows older. These activities may carry within them some way of either transferring these preoccupations or converting them into forms which are more accessible and indeed acceptable within the family and community. The term that has been used for this form of behaviour is 'sublimation'. Sublimation enables the child, through exposure to other adults and children and a wider range of activities, to develop opportunities for literally widening his repertoire to find other outlets for some of these original emotional processes and experiences in relation to the bodies of his parents, his own exploration of his own body, and the intensity of his early developmental experiences. In the process of widening his repertoire the child may develop skills and interests, hobbies, sports activities and musical activities which are of lasting importance in his life.

In extending himself and mastering these new skills, we must remember, however, that the child still has one foot in the camp of childhood and the other moving towards independence and autonomy. The particular interests and hobbies which children develop at this stage may characterise some of the internal conflicts they may be experiencing and often form a productive way of struggling to work through particular issues. For example, one might suggest that a child who is very interested in stamp collecting needs to feel that he can put order into things. This is also a way of attending to detail and maintaining some sort of control which is not always possible in everyday life as a child.

THE LINKS BETWEEN HOME AND SCHOOL

In the last few years there has been an increasing emphasis on the need for a partnership between the home and school. Educationalists realise that, in order to provide the optimum conditions for learning for children, there needs to be a strong bond between the school and the parents, so that the parents need to be involved in knowing what is going on in their child's daily school life. This goes a long way beyond a small coterie of parents supporting the school as part of a Parents Association. It looks towards a different engagement with parents on an everyday level. A link between home and school is of particular importance for the developing child. Throughout this book I return to the theme of partnerships and of containment. I have stated that learning always takes place as part of a relationship. The child moves from her relationship with her parents to a relationship with her teachers. The learning process is at all times influenced by these emotional experiences and the capacity for relatedness, not only of the child but also of the teacher.

If we stop for a moment to consider that most classes these days in primary schools have groups of around 28 to 30 children per class, we can see that each child brings into the classroom her own history and, in particular, her experience of relatedness with her family. We can thus see that the average classroom abounds with emotion in terms of what the child brings from home, how the child projects these feelings onto the teacher, how each child may project feelings onto other children. Thus the task of the teacher is a challenging one, to respond both to the individual needs of each child, but also to be able to see how the children are able to work effectively in groups. The single demand for children as they enter primary school is the testing of the child's capacity to live and work effectively in the group. The capacity to do so has been described as a paradigm for the future since it will enable children to be able to deal with interpersonal tensions and conflicts in later life and to develop interpersonal skills. However, the capacity to do so depends on more than glib rhetoric.

Writers on this subject have talked about the provision of the facilitating 'school climate', one which provides empathy and reciprocity. It enables the child to feel that she has some affiliation within the classroom and indeed the school, which can assist her towards mastery and achievement in learning social and other skills. We can see how the provision of the right kind of school climate to enable learning to take place echoes the need for what Winnicott has described as the 'facilitating environment' in the earliest infant and parent relationship.

THE ROLE OF TEACHERS

It is important to emphasise that the task of the teacher is of course to teach, and not to be a psychotherapist or counsellor. Some teachers may find themselves drawn into these roles when they become anxious or concerned about the difficulties that a child may be encountering. The way in which these problems are handled will depend very much on the policy of the school and whether the school structure is able to contain the anxiety of the individual teacher, who in turn can contain some of the anxiety and problems which the child possesses. We can thus see that, just as with family life, the model of containment runs throughout the system.

The British child psychotherapist Isca Wittenberg (1983) has written most interestingly on what she calls 'the emotional experience of learning and teaching'. What she finds critical is the development of an *emotional awareness* on the part of the teacher to enable them to be able in turn to be in tune with what is happening in the classroom. I have said earlier that the average classroom abounds with emotion and that it is a false position to assume that one can separate ideas about learning and teaching from emotional feelings, and indeed even the emotions that are attributed to a particular subject that is learnt. This does not mean of course that the teacher should only be in touch with the emotional aspects of the learning experience, rather it means that the teacher needs to be aware of the boundary between the way children learn and how they feel about it. The emotional experience that the teacher brings to bear on the situation is also an important part of this configuration. Wittenberg has described the process as a tightrope which the teacher is expected to walk. For the school to be able to recognise emotional experience as legitimate and not to try to push it to the outer edges as irrelevant is part of the task of working with the experience in a creative way. Wittenberg outlines some of the particular anxieties that the teacher may face in interaction with children. Some of these anxieties of course have their counterpart in the anxiety that the child may present within the classroom situation, such as fear of criticism where teacher and pupil may be anxious both about giving criticism and being the recipient of criticism. This links in with the fear of hostility, which again both the teacher and the child can experience in different ways. It is important for children to know that their teacher can help them with their angry feelings without retaliating.

I have mentioned earlier that development is not a neat and tidy affair, and that tolerating a degree of anxiety and frustration is part of the process of growing up. This particularly comes to the fore in helping the child to cope with the fact that there is always some frustration inherent in learning.

Wittenberg describes the ability to tolerate hostile and negative feelings as an actual part of the learning process. She also refers to the experience of envy which may cloud the relationship between the child and the teacher. The child who has not been able to establish some degree of mastery in his own world, and in particular in relation to his parents, can feel that grown-ups and parents always seem to know what to do and have a vastly superior array of knowledge and information at their fingertips. Teachers for their part may sometimes be anxious about an alert and curious child and call them 'a know-all' or make comments such as 'you're so sharp you're going to cut yourself'. This may also suggest that the teacher is anxious for the child to know his or her place.

For professionals working with children, adolescents and parents, we must always be aware that this work puts us in touch with our own infantile and childhood and family experiences. On many occasions this can offer a positive resource for us. On other occasions it may have negative repercussions where, for example, we identify with a particular child or a parent. Some teachers' propensity towards identifying one child in a classroom who they feel has special attributes and becomes a favourite is a typical example of this process.

Wittenberg talks of the danger of the teacher feeling that they need to indulge children in the sense of spoon-feeding them, so that they deny in effect the inevitable frustration involved in the learning process. One may see this as an example also of the teacher's potential anxiety about coping with the anger of the classroom. The capacity of the teacher to handle differences, set appropriate limits and manage some of the inevitable anger and frustration that is inherent in the learning situation is similar to the developmental processes within the family. We can thus see how closely intertwined are the relationships that the child develops in relation to their parents and primary caretakers, and their experiences at school.

Wittenberg has described those children whom she sees at risk as they attempt to negotiate what she calls the 'psychosocial transition of entering the school environment'. These are children who have not been able to negotiate the normal emotional milestones of development that I have described above for a variety of reasons which result both from internal factors as well as external factors. Wittenberg sees these as:

1. Children who have had frequent changes of mothering or fathering in infancy and early childhood, thus undermining the child's capacity for trust in the teacher.
2. Children who have experienced traumatic separation through illness and death of a parent in early childhood.
3. Children who have not been able to what she calls 'internalise' or take into themselves a picture of a 'good enough mother', either because their mothers were unable to provide a sufficiently containing environment or the child was particularly sensitive to any frustration or separation from the mother.
4. Children who have more recently experienced loss and separation and who may be what Wittenberg calls 'psychically overloaded' at the point of starting school or as they progress through the primary school years.

In concluding this chapter, we may be reminded of one of the basic tenets of the psychodynamic approach, which is that behaviour is dynamic and not static. It changes all the time. The school environment, school structure and curriculum need to take this into account and adapt to the changing needs of children and society. The child at school, particularly at primary school, is in the full thrust of her development. Thus, for example, a year at school in which a child may experience a miserable relationship with her teacher, or where there are problems of classroom tension, will have a significant effect on the development of the child and may indeed colour her view of future learning. The school as an institution and individual teachers do indeed carry considerable responsibility for the development of the future generation, and this should be appropriately acknowledged. However, it is also important to ensure that, because this responsibility is so awesome, it should not be carried solely by the school. Rather, the ideal conditions for learning and development are those in which the teacher engages with the parents, and the school environment is able to develop a correspondingly dynamic partnership with the community of parents of the children who it teaches.

SUMMARY

This chapter describes the need to encourage the child's imaginative play and world as well as interests outside of the immediate family and home, looking at the following areas.

- Children's literature – this can provide a lively and helpful way to 'translate' and confirm the experience the child is going through and help him to make sense of what is happening.
- The impact of television, with an emphasis on assisting the child to discuss and digest what she has seen, rather than imposing arbitrary censorship.
- The possibility of the 'erosion of childhood', through an over-concern with a consumer-oriented technological society in which parents strive to produce the child as a perfect product.

Expectation which surrounds children's achievement virtually from the moment they start school has changed beyond recognition even in one generation. There is now a general acceptance that a school must offer a broad curriculum, that other activities such as sport, music, drama and art must play a part in ordinary school life.

THE CHILD'S NATURAL INCLINATION TO DEVELOP DIFFERENT INTERESTS

I described earlier the process of sublimation for children at this particular stage of their development where some of the more urgent infantile expressions and preoccupations become converted into activities relating to learning, mastery and interest of various kinds. It is not unusual for children at this stage to become very preoccupied and fascinated by a particular area, such as sport, ballet or horse-riding. At times these interests may take on something of an obsessive quality which is in itself a hallmark of this particular phase of development. Children's literature gives us particular insights into this form of development, often in an amusing and indirect way. For example, in *Angelina Ballerina*, a book about a mouse by Helen Craig and Katherine Holabird, the obsessive quality of Angelina's interest is beautifully described. 'She danced all the time and she danced everywhere, and often she was so busy dancing that she forgot about the other things she was supposed to do.' Angelina's chaotic room is a testimony to her obsession, with dancing pictures everywhere and dolls dressed up in ballerina clothes. Angelina even dances in her dreams. Most annoyingly, she dances in her mother's kitchen and does 'a beautiful arabesque and knocks over a jug of milk and a plate of her mother's best cheddar cheese pies'. However, Angelina's parents, Mr and Mrs Mousling, are wise parents and they decide to invest in a pink ballet dress and a pair of pink ballet slippers for Angelina, and agree that she is ready to take ballet lessons. At the end of the book Angelina does brilliantly well at Miss Liddy's dancing class and becomes a famous ballerina, thus fulfilling her earliest dreams and hopes.

The book sums up exactly the mood of younger school-age children, in particular, who, for the first time, encounter experiences that take them outside of the home and immediate family relationships. This may be in the form of a particular school activity or preparation for a school concert. The endless practising of cartwheels in the living room, for example, shows the child at once oblivious to the needs of the rest of the family and yet, at the same time, wanting the family to notice him. For boys and girls there may be an intense preoccupation with the new sport they are playing or a developing detailed knowledge about the particular teams. These experiences enable children to feel that there is life outside of the family and that they can water down the intensity or emotional impact of family life from time to time. They find themselves referring to other adults in authority, and this gives children a necessary breathing space in order to be able to step back from their own family and consider themselves and their families in relation to other children and other families. I have said before that children at this middle stage of development still have a foot in the camp of early childhood. However, they do not always want to be reminded of this fact.

The older child's need to distance herself from infantile preoccupations is beautifully captured as well in Roald Dahl's *Revolting Rhymes*, in which all the traditional children's stories – Cinderella, Jack in the Beanstalk, Snow White, Goldilocks, Little Red Riding Hood, The Three Little Pigs – are given a rather different version of events which borders on the bloodcurdling. The Cinderella story starts: 'I guess you think you know the story. You don't. The real one's much more gory. The phoney one, the one you know, was cooked up years and years ago, and made to sound all soft and sappy, just to keep the children happy.' This approach suggests that children are able to take on a more realistic, challenging view of their favourite tales.

THE IMPACT OF TELEVISION AND KNOWLEDGE OF THE NATURE OF THE WORLD

It has become virtually impossible for parents in contemporary life to be able to exclude the impact of the world we live in today from the experience of their children. The impact of television and other forms of communication are now so powerful and potentially intrusive that it behoves us to try to understand how we can live with them, rather than struggle to eliminate them. Some parents may say proudly that they do not have a television in their home, as though by doing so they have the power to control these experiences.

Of course television can be used as a babysitter and as an anaesthetic within the family, and neither of these is particularly helpful for the child's development. What many parents find anxiety-provoking is that their children have access to information and are, in some cases, overwhelmed by news about atrocities and difficult events which they cannot really digest properly. The problem is exacerbated by the fact that this is still a relatively new medium. There is a whole generation of people who did not grow up with television when they were children.

It is therefore important for parents to be vigilant about what their child watches and the hours of television watched. What experience suggests, however, is that we cannot protect children and pretend that they inhabit a totally different world from that of adults. Some adults will, for example, fondly recall their own childhoods which they saw as an opportunity of the child group or little gang to have an opportunity to be totally separated from the adult world. This kind of experience is reported particularly by parents who grew up in country areas. Increasing urbanisation of family life has introduced corresponding restrictions and has created a very different form of experience for all concerned. It is rare for the majority of children, for example, to be able to travel to and from primary school on their own. Parents are involved in far more supervision of day-to-day activities. How can we then help children make sense of this less safe, fast-paced world where they are bombarded with information from a wide range of sources? I would suggest that it is important to help children to be selective about what they watch on television. Most of all, it is important to be able to take seriously children's questions about what it is they have seen or read or heard about. Children need to be given an opportunity to air their views and concerns, for example, about a famine they may have seen reported in another part of the world. How can they be helped to make a connection with their own experience?

The need to take children's experience seriously has its parallel at this stage of development in the earliest experience of the infant-parent relationship. For example, staff at a primary school were faced with the sudden death of a parent of one of the children attending the school. The staff were anxious that rumours should not spread about the details of the death and tried to discourage the children from tittle-tailing. However, it would have been wrong to have assumed that the children's interest was purely to tell tales. Their concern was very much focused on their own experience: 'If another child's mummy can die suddenly, then maybe this can happen to my mummy as well?'. It was important for the school to be able to open up discussions about this event with the children most closely involved and to take seriously their fears, as well as their wishes to help their bereaved classmate. In this context, teachers can learn from their pupils in the same way that parents can learn from their children. Children's capacity for understanding and tolerance is greater than we give them credit for, as indeed is their capacity for forgiveness.

THE EROSION OF CHILDHOOD

I have stated how important it is for children to be able to be involved in activities outside of the home. However, this can be taken to extreme degrees by parents whose vision of childhood is imbued with competitiveness and anxiety that their child will not succeed in a harsh and demanding world. They therefore enrol their child, from the start of school, in every conceivable learning activity in the hope that they will be able to develop an edge over other children. At present, understanding about computer technology seems to have taken some parents by storm. The problem with this amount of activity is that it can literally leave children without breath or space or time for simple and ordinary pleasures. The majority of children go along with these projects and lessons to appease their parents and to comply with them, but they may be denied access to other important experiences, for example just having time to think, and 'just being', just messing around.

Some parents become disappointed that, after a time, their child ceases to want to play the instrument or practise at the sport or continue with the particular project. Alternatively, they may find that all their investment has resulted in producing just a very ordinary child and not the exceptional gifted person that they had hoped for. This suggests again that the experience needs to be one that the child can own and identify with, rather than one which is imposed by his parents.

Parents talk of giving their children opportunities when they may in fact be taking these opportunities from them and making them very dependent on the idea of activity which is organised from without, rather than assisting them to develop their own internal resources.

Another aspect which threatens us with the erosion of child-hood is the problem of living in an extremely consumer-oriented technological society in which parenting may be viewed as a package which produces the child as the 'perfect product'. Parents in this regard may falsely believe that the more they do for their child the better the outcome will be.

Parents are naturally concerned about the spectre of unem-ployment which looms so large for many young people today. They believe that they need to take the necessary steps to ensure that their children are equipped in the best possible way for a role in society. However, there is a danger that the child's develop-ment in this regard can become subservient to economic rational-ism and we must be mindful at all times of what the child really needs and wants and is capable of digesting. Information tech-nology presents us with unprecedented access to information of all kinds. This is very new territory for parents and can appear to present the child with unlimited choice and almost unlimited mastery over this environment of information. However, infor-mation is only as useful as it can be understood and applied. The task of parents in this regard, as with so many other areas of experience for children, is to be able to assist them to compre-hend and make use of the information in a way which is mean-ingful to them rather than to believe it to be an alternative to real life experience.

SUMMARY

- The difference between boys and girls is acknowledged as well as their specific and different needs in relation to parents of the same and opposite sexes. How parents 'model' masculinity, femininity, mothering and fathering will have a crucial influence on children.
- Core developmental tasks which are negotiated within the family are addressed, including identification, separation, rivalry, potency, testing out sexuality, the drawing of generational boundaries and the place of assertion and aggression.
- The vital importance of the father's role and interaction is emphasised, as well as the problem of families repeating a negative inheritance, of 'lack of relatedness' and a limiting notion of masculinity.
- It is noted that the parents' own sexual and marital relationship will have an impact on how they relate to their children of the same and opposite sex and also what 'unfinished business' is introduced from previous generations.
- The transforming influence of both parents is important in being able to facilitate gender and sexual identity and the widest opportunities for personality development for boys and girls, sons and daughters.

The subtleties surrounding the interactions between children and their parents, and how they relate to the development of gender and sexual identity, are frequently overlooked but are a crucial part of intrapsychic and interpersonal development. Serious attention to this area has been superseded in some ways by the focus on gender and sexual issues as purely social constructs. In the push towards a more egalitarian society in which men and women, and boys and girls, have equal access to opportunities, the important role that feminism and feminist politics have played in this area has been of great value. However, we must be mindful of the fact that our social construction of reality and gender and social issues does not take the place of intrapsychic and interpersonal issues. Rather it must be complementary to them. For this reason we need to be vigilant about the way in which social constructs may be turned into prejudices which find their way into policy making about child development. One example of this is the politically correct notion that there is no difference between boys and girls. The current concern about boys slipping back in academic achievement and their greater involvement in violence and antisocial behaviour points to the fact that this type of glib denial of difference inhibits the need for a proper form of inquiry and understanding into the nature of both the similarities between boys and girls and also their crucial differences. It is vitally important for the development of the future generation that policies are made, with regard to educational and child-care arrangements particularly, on the basis of a real understanding about children's developmental needs, rather than as a response to political rhetoric.

The following identification of some of the developmental issues with regard to gender and sexual identification of boys and girls in relation to parents of the same and opposite sex is not intended as a comprehensive analysis of the subject. Rather, I would like to point out some key elements in the developmental process and show that there are differences in the relationship of boys and girls to the same sex parent and parent of the opposite sex. These differences, if they are understood and handled creatively, can enhance the development of the child and create a sound foundation for their intrapsychic, interpersonal and social development.

▓ GIRLS AND THEIR MOTHERS

Some mothers talk quite openly about how much easier it is to bring up a girl than to bring up a boy. At first glance it would seem that the opportunity for identification for mother and daughter makes things so much simpler but, in reality, the picture is much more complex. One can say that the relationship between a girl and her mother stands as a precursor for all subsequent maternal relationships and will foreshadow the type of relationship that the girl will have in turn with her children when she grows up and becomes a mother herself. One could thus postulate that the mothering relationship between the mother and her daughter is particularly critical in terms of the transmission of this value or entity that we identify as the mothering capacity.

The psychosomatic connection

I have described earlier the relationship between the infant and the mother as having a strong psychosomatic component. The cuing in of the mother to the baby's body, the baby's state of mind, and emotions is at once a physical as well as a psychological experience. One could suggest that the girl's development continues in a more psychosomatic way than the boy's. By this I don't mean psychosomatic as a reference to the development of illness. If we take Winnicott's view of the psychosomatic state as one which naturally focuses on an interrelationship between the body and the mind, we can see how the girl needs to identify with her mother in a way which at the earliest stage enables her to view herself, even as a little girl, as a potential mother. Another way of looking at it is to suggest that the little girl views her body differently from that of the boy. She is preoccupied with the inner spaces of her body, the knowledge that her breasts will develop, that she will begin menstrual periods, and that her body will also contain, develop and nurture a child. This is information that I believe is on some level passed on almost subliminally between a mother and her daughter. In the best of circumstances, it becomes a confirmation of femininity and gender identity from infancy through the early years of life and into subsequent development. The developing girl, in a sense, can check out her mother's body and see it as a reference point for her own subsequent development. The way in which the mother herself feels about femininity and sexuality will, of course, determine how easily she allows herself to be made available as this kind of reference point.

I have wondered, for example, about the prevalence of the illness anorexia nervosa among girls and how one can view it as fundamentally a psychosomatic illness. Anorexia presents us with anti-development, a kind of body and mind clash which grinds everything to a halt, particularly the development of a sexual and feminine identity. One may speculate about how much this illness has its origins in the earliest infant young child and mother relationship, which is the crucible for the development of these personality identifications.

A positive development of sexual and gender identification depends on what I would call 'appropriate narcissism' in the relationship between mother and daughter as part of their psychosomatic relationship, particularly at the earliest stage of development. By appropriate narcissism I mean that the mother takes pride in her own appearance and enjoys being a woman and feels comfortable about her status. She can take pleasure in the similarities between herself and her developing little girl, and can enjoy the idea of the child resembling her and promoting a sense of continuity into the next generation. This state of narcissism, however, must find its place together with all the other components of development, rather than take precedence over them. So, for example, a focus on a narcissistic notion of how wonderful little girls are carries within it an idealisation that is unrealistic. For example, a mother who had had three boys, all of whom were a disappointment to her in one way or another because they were either too aggressive or too passive, gave birth to a little girl whom she idealised. She kept referring to how feminine the little girl was and how her dear sweet behaviour was so different to the aggression and boisterousness of boys. The little girl also tended to be dressed up in lots of bows and frilly dresses. This saccharine sweet image of femininity denies the reality and need for the girl to also be able to express her aggression. One could anticipate that, at a later stage, once the aggression in this little girl had come out from under her frills it would equally disappoint her mother as her brothers' aggression had done.

The role of narcissism changes again as the girl grows and develops in her own right. The kind of intertwined psychosomatic necessary narcissistic stage I have described as the sine qua non of the infant child relationship changes as the child grows up to include both the components of difference and of rivalry. One could say that one of the tasks of development for the girl, particularly in relation to her mother, is to be able to negotiate a close identification with her mother and her mother's body and to reconcile this with the rivalry that this arouses in both the mother and the daughter. For example, in adolescence mothers may complain of their daughters borrowing garments of theirs and not returning them. This suggests that the developing child, in trying to establish her own identity, still needs to have an opportunity to borrow a bit of her mother's identity for herself. If we keep in mind that there is always a paradox involved in development, then we can see that running alongside this thread of the girl wanting to identify with her mother and be the same is another thread of needing to assert her own individuality, independence and difference. It may naturally be difficult for a mother to comprehend that these apparently contradictory processes are in action simultaneously and need to be patiently comprehended and contained. This later rivalry between mother and daughter is a natural part of this process. One can therefore talk about the 'process of natural rivalry'. The task of the mother is to be able to contain this process and not to feel too personally attacked or denigrated by it, so that it does not become pernicious rivalry. For example, a girl of eight or nine may look in the mirror, press her cheek next to her mother's and the contrast between the rosy peach complexion of the child and the more wrinkled aspect of the mother may be only too obvious. At times the child, with scrupulous honesty, may point this out to the mother. How the mother is able to react to this without feeling narcissistically attacked is of crucial importance. The little girl is actually truthfully stating that she is going to move on to the next generation and will indeed supersede her mother. Her mother may have narcissistic fears about the waning of her own beauty and sexuality and she may turn on the little girl and get very angry with her, which will in turn have the effect of developing a sense of anxiety in the child about a critical area to do with how one looks and how one appears as a sexual and feminine being that may become too dangerous to talk about.

I have said before that the delicate developmental task for the girl and her mother is to develop these somewhat paradoxical processes at the same time. This involves an intense identification on a critical and emotional level with the necessity for the girl also to feel free to be separate and individuated from her mother. Thus she needs to be able to have the kind of psychosomatic identification with her mother which brings together mind, body, emotions and physical experiences and which will lay the foundations for her own capacity to be a mother. At the same time she needs to be able to do this in a way which will identify her own identity as a woman and a mother. Thus she has to bring to the task of mothering her own sexual and feminine identity and the characteristics of her own personality and choices.

Finding a breathing space

Rebecca, a girl aged seven years, was referred because of extreme anxiety about separating from her mother. Her mother Jane was a single parent who had never been married to Rebecca's father. Her relationship with him was an extremely complex one. He was a married man with a family of his own but continued to have sporadic contact with Rebecca and her mother, of a tantalising and frustrating kind. Rebecca was an attractive, intelligent little girl who was doing well at school and in her friendships and her social relationships. Her problems were very specifically focused on her mother, and the separation anxiety that she experienced was particularly acute at night. For example, Rebecca would refuse to go to her own room to sleep. She would insist on coming into her mother's bed. Since her mother did not want to go to bed at an early hour, she would set up a little bed of pillows and blankets on the floor behind the sofa in the living-room where Rebecca would doze off and then later join her mother in her bed when they were ready to go to sleep. This state of affairs had gone on for many months and Rebecca's mother had got so used to it that she had even entertained occasional friends in this way, with Rebecca snoozing behind the sofa. Rebecca, for her part, felt that she wanted to be privy to all her mother's activities. Rebecca's mother appeared a depressed woman who gave the impression of not sufficiently standing up for herself in life. It was as though she had not allowed herself to believe that she could have real expectations of people and had a somewhat self-effacing manner. I could imagine that her lack of assertiveness might make Rebecca quite anxious about standing up for her needs. One could speculate that Rebecca perhaps felt that she had to be quite vigilant about her mother's activities and check up on what she was doing. In the course of the sessions it was striking how Rebecca sucked one of her fingers constantly as though she felt impelled to fill up an empty space. She was very angry at the suggestion that she might need to sleep in her own room. In the course of the sessions she drew a picture of herself and her mother. Figure 2 on page 186 represents the fusion between Rebecca and her mother. Rebecca is shown as the little girl right inside of her mother's body. It suggests that she is at once the little baby who is contained in her mother's body in a safe way. However, it also has a sense of claustrophobia and captures the claustrophobic quality of the relationship between Rebecca and her mother. It was as though they were in what has been described as an 'adhesive identification' – stuck to each other – rather than a constructive identification in which they could also be separate. For Rebecca this seemed to mean that to be close to her mother was synonymous with being stuck to her, with the very real fear that, without her mother's presence at night, she would fall apart. I wondered whether her mother, for her part, in her loneliness had also begun to use Rebecca as a partner-companion. This may have resulted in a total confusion and blurring of boundaries about who was the mother and who was the child, which would further exacerbate both their anxieties. A subsequent session enabled Rebecca's mother to begin to feel that she had a right to a separate space for herself which could be an adult space in which she was able to think her own thoughts and entertain her friends. She was also able to make contact with Rebecca's father in such a way as to ensure that his visits to Rebecca took place on a more regular basis which was more satisfactory for both herself and Rebecca. Rebecca was able to make the transition to her own room and her own bed, and we worked out a good-night preparation story time which also included the presence of the family dog. Rebecca could thus feel safer in her own space, acknowledging the difference and separateness between her mother and herself without feeling overwhelmed by anxiety and loss.

As the sessions progressed Rebecca did a second drawing. Figure 3 (p. 187) shows two figures, herself and her mother, going to the hairdresser to have their hair cut. However, this time they are sitting next to each other, indicating that she has acknowledged an internal as well as an external space between herself and her mother, and she literally herself now has more space and room to operate as a developing child.

A place for assertion and aggression

It has often occurred to me, in contemplating the development of young boys and girls, that they could each take a leaf out of the characteristics that at times seem to typify each group. For example, boys could benefit from reconciling notions of sexual prowess with tenderness and concern, and become more inclined towards negotiating and listening; and girls, for their part, need to learn to infuse their sexuality not just with being a receptacle but to include a more assertive stance. I use the terms assertion and aggression not in their usual negative sense of being violent and unpleasant, but rather as part of development and life. The idea of a developing daughter who has a sense of assertion and aggression in a positive sense may seem anathema to a mother who may have had difficulty in expressing these feelings herself. It is, however, a critical part of asserting a difference and a separate identification. In my work in London child guidance clinics over many years, I was struck by the number of cases of what I would call 'adhesive identifications' between mothers and daughters. These are types of identifications which spring up in highly dysfunctional families where the father is often identified as the aggressive or violent man or totally unresponsive to the emotional needs of his wife and children. The mothers in these families would tend to draw their brood around them, particularly their girl children who would end up in close identification with them, in some cases sleeping in bed with them. Here one could see the total denial of assertion and aggression on the part of the mother and a projection of all her aggression into the husband, to add to his own existing aggression. By taking her daughter into her bed with her the mother would be giving a very clear message to her husband about the cessation of sexual activity. At the same time she would be giving a confused and bewildering message to her daughter, who would need to be seen as her mother's protector. In many cases, girls in this predicament would move into repetitive family experiences by becoming pregnant at a young age or becoming the partners of equally unsatisfactory men.

The conclusion of such a family drama often took the form of the daughter coming back into the family with her own baby for her mother to look after. One could wonder about this being both the gift for the mother as well as the wish on the part of the daughter to rework some of her own infantile experiences with her mother through the next generation.

Identifying with the mother to become a mother

The sight of a little girl playing with dolls, tenderly putting them to bed, wheeling them around in a pram, playing elaborate games with other little girls, is an immensely familiar sight to all of us. I do not wish to enter here into a description about gender-appropriate play, and I assume as a given that girls will have access to a variety of play experience and materials. However, the politically correct notion that playing with dolls for girls forces them into gender stereotypes totally confuses the issue and points

Figure 2: Rebecca represents the fusion with her mother

Figure 3: Rebecca represents the transition from fusion to
some degree of separateness

to a misunderstanding about the developmental task. I have referred previously to the idea that play for the young child is work. For the little girl playing with her dolls and family and pretending to be mother the task is highly specific and the child plays it with all the energy at her disposal. She is involved at every level, both emotionally and physically, thinking about what it is like to have babies of her own, how they might need to be looked after, how sometimes they get forgotten about and thrown into corners and need to be rescued. If one observes young children at home or in a child-care setting, one can only be impressed by the intensity and commitment of their activity. It is through this form of play that the little girl acts out in a safe and appropriate way her preoccupation with the fact that her mother may have babies in her tummy or has had a baby in her tummy, and she has not. We could say that the relationship between the mother and her daughter is always underscored by this fact, which in turn leads to the stage of natural rivalry between the mother and her daughter. As I have mentioned above, this state of rivalry in relation to the child preparing herself for a mothering role needs to be handled with tact and recognition of its particular meaning. It is very important for the mother not to flaunt her superior fertility and superior forces in a sense in the face of the little girl as though to set up some competition between them which may give the little girl the impression that she will never be able to be as successful as her mother and produce a baby.

Sometimes in her attention to her dolls, the little girl may try to demonstrate how she is a much better mummy than her own mummy and take so much better care of her babies than she may feel her mother is doing at that moment in time. This more challenging behaviour also needs to be understood within the total context of the child working and playing at the development of her sexual and gender identity. At times this may become confused, as illustrated in the following example.

Somewhere in between

Helen, a little girl of seven, was referred by her mother because of her concern that Helen was very identified with being a boy and would insist on wearing only boys' clothes. This had gone on for a few years and her mother wondered if she should talk to someone about it. At our first session it was striking to see how Helen walked and used her body in relation to the furniture in the room. She swaggered in with a boy's walk and slung her legs over the side of the chair. She appeared in the first session to be entirely dressed in boys' clothes of the unisex kind – t-shirt and tracksuit pants. Her mother indicated that these were specifically boys' clothes and that she had also begun to buy her boys' underwear because Helen did not want to wear girls' knickers with flowers on them. Helen's hair was cut almost painfully short in a gamin style. Beneath the swaggering walk my impression was of a rather pinched, deprived little girl who seemed not to have a proper identity for herself. Her older sister, by contrast, was dressed in more typically feminine clothes and looked entirely more comfortable with her own body and identity.

In my subsequent meetings with Helen's mother it transpired that Helen's father had left shortly after her birth and the separation and subsequent divorce had been extremely traumatic for the whole family. However, Helen's sister, because she was a bit older, had managed to have more of a relationship with her father and had held on to a notion of both a mother and a father, male and female. By contrast, Helen's mother described situations in which it appeared as though Helen had dropped out of her father's mind. So, during access arrangements, for example, Helen's older sister might visit her father while Helen stayed behind, and it seemed that she had not developed a separate relationship with her father. What appeared to have happened instead was that, as though to compensate, Helen had been drawn into a very close relationship with her mother. Over time it emerged that Helen's mother was not so perturbed about Helen's attachment to a masculine stance and dress. In fact, she partly encouraged it and I wondered why this was the case.

Over our several discussions it emerged that her own mother had suffered a longstanding psychiatric disorder so severe that she had on occasions been hospitalised. Helen's mother had in effect received very little mothering herself and relied heavily on her father. They had themselves formed a close alliance within the family. Helen's mother confessed that her greatest fear was that Helen in fact resembled her mother, both physically and, she thought, emotionally. She saw Helen's rather scatterbrain personality, her lack of concentration at times, as similar to that of her mother and had both a sense of foreboding and helplessness about being able to change anything. It appeared from our discussions that Helen's attachment to a masculine way of behaving and dressing could be understood on a number of levels. It appeared most of all to represent an alternative personality for Helen which, in her mother's mind, rescued her from becoming like her grandmother. In a sense she was saying: 'It's better for Helen to be like a boy than like my mother'. We could understand another aspect of Helen's need to be like a boy as a way of compensating for her absent father. My initial work with Helen's mother was followed by some individual therapy to clarify the issues for Helen herself. At first Helen was very timid and unforthcoming. However, quite soon she took to racing into the room ahead of me, closing the door firmly and immediately beginning to play. It was evident that she used the therapy with me as an opportunity to create a different kind of space for herself. On one occasion her older sister had to come to the sessions because she had a cold and was waiting in the waiting room. When her sister tried to come into the consulting room to see what was happening at the end of the session Helen closed the door on her face, shouting 'No, no'. She desperately wanted to preserve a special place for herself and also our relationship, in contrast to her pinched and deprived experience of falling out of her father's mind during access visits.

Shortly after the start of the therapy, Helen brought a new toy to the sessions, a bright yellow lion called Leo. Leo doubled as a hot-water bottle and this dual function made him the perfect toy for Helen at this moment in time. Leo truly represented what Winnicott has described as the transitional object. Helen had not, according to her mother, had any significant soft toys in her life before. She had lighted upon Leo in a shop window and had become enormously attached to him. In our sessions Leo would sit either on the chair or on the table. At various times during the sessions he would be taken up and cuddled, and Helen would curl up in a chair with him. Helen's attachment to Leo enabled her to work through a period of transition connected with her need to take on a masculine stance. Her swaggering walk melted away. In its place she was able to show me a little girl whose strong infantile wishes and needs had not properly been met. The masculine stance was truly a swagger, something like a protective cover to keep at bay her hurt and rejected feelings. While Helen was not a little girl who would immediately turn to frilly dresses and bows, her whole appearance underwent a transformation. Her hair began to grow, her sweatshirts and trousers were of a more feminine variety. I had also suggested to her mother that it was not helpful to buy boys' underwear as this would only serve to confuse her further and consolidate her defences. The therapy progressed to the point where Helen felt much more able to make a contribution in her class and to begin the actual task of learning, which had been difficult for her until that point because she had obviously been so preoccupied with loss and separation. Her father, who had initially thought the whole idea of counselling was ludicrous, made a special arrangement to come and see me and we had a very positive communication about Helen's future and the need for a supportive relationship between the two parents in their parenting task.

BOYS AND THEIR FATHERS

One of the themes of this book is that fathers matter. They matter enormously to the development of their children and they have a very specific and vital role to play in the unfolding personality of their sons and daughters. In view of the importance of the father's role, it is particularly tragic that men either view themselves or are viewed by society as being of less importance or of little importance in their children's development. The idea that 'bringing up children is the wife's business' may represent a traditional attitude, but unfortunately one which can only deplete family life and development.

Women, for their part, may also have to consider their role in excluding fathers from contributing substantially to their children's development. An inherent rivalry in terms of what belongs to the world of men and what belongs to the world of women is not helpful for the bringing up of children in our present time. For example, I recall that at the first Exploring Parenthood workshop we ran in London some years ago there was a complaint about the small number of men who attended. When we inquired of the participants why this was so and whether in fact they had invited their partners, one woman mentioned that she had told her husband that morning that she was going to a day on parenting and had added, in the same breath, 'You don't want to come, do you?'. While this aroused gales of laughter and recognition among the participants, it also pointed to the collusion between men and women in excluding each other from valuable aspects of family life and the task of parenting. I have already stated that the presence of the father and his full interrelationship with the family is a good indicator of positive mental health and development.

For the young boy the presence of his father acts as a reference point for sexual and gender identification in the same way as the mother does for the girl. Fathers play a particular part in helping boys to be in touch with and use their bodies. A boy's experience of his genitals and his reproductive capacity is an external one, contrary to the more internal development of girls which is focused on the inside of their bodies and their mother's bodies. Fathers play an important role in helping both with the external and internal manifestations of this external genital. They can assist their sons, for example, with the practical task of showing them how to urinate correctly. At the same time there is an opportunity to deal with the rivalry or anxiety which may surround the little boy's worry about not having a penis as big as daddy has.

The problem of inheritance

One of the most difficult aspects about bringing up boys in our society may refer to the issue of what we expect boys to be. Our expectations of girls generally tend to be more fluid and accepting, which in turn facilitates the development of a more flexible personality. The cultural idea of inheritance being passed on through the male offspring may seem at times to have a corresponding internal psychological life in which fathers believe that certain characteristics or ways of doing things or ways in which boys should be must be passed on through the generations from grandfather to father to son. The problem with this inheritance approach to psychological development is that it can seriously impede the development of the child's own personality and lays down rigid structures which diminish the possibility of growth. For example, I was struck in Britain by the way in which men who had had a particularly painful and difficult experience at a public (i.e. private) school when they were children would sign their children in for the same public school at the point of their birth. This suggests the need to repeat the pain or the sadism experienced with the next generation. It is vital for the development of boys that a wider range of options in terms of what is expected is made available to them. The idea that an unhappy school experience will somehow create a strong personality is echoed in the accounts some men give of having received physical punishment from their fathers. They will talk about how this did them no harm and in fact helped to build up the strength of their characters. This insistence on strength of character, on denial, on tolerating unhappiness and aggression represents an extremely narrow and limited view of masculinity. The acceleration of feminism has left many men uncertain about their role and their own masculine identity. At the opposite extreme they may be anxious to present themselves as highly sensitive, gentle and totally non-aggressive. Sometimes men believe that their current task is to be like women or a different kind of mother. Certainly, it's fair to say that the move from a traditional, more stereotyped version of masculinity towards a new and different way of identifying masculinity requires some trial and error. For children the problem is never that parents make mistakes or that they sometimes get it wrong. Their concern rather is for the presence and the commitment of the parent.

How do we construct masculinity?

I have referred to the problems of a narrow construction of masculinity. For some men a boy is only a boy if he has a total interest in sport and is skilled at playing a range of sports. For some fathers sport may take the place of communication. For them taking part in sport or watching sport is genuinely the only real opportunity they feel they have to make contact with their sons. If their son does not fit into this sporting mould then life may become a problem. We have all heard of examples of grown men who reflect back on their childhoods and how they felt that their fathers indicated to them that they somehow 'didn't rate' as men or didn't qualify because they were not particularly skilled or interested in the sporting world. A man who had experienced a poor relationship with his father and had grown up drawn into an over-close relationship with his mother described a telephone call to his father living overseas. He knew that they had absolutely nothing in common and could find no area of common ground. He was, however, anxious to make some contact with his father and he said: 'So we talked about the cricket test match'.

For some fathers the appearance of a boy in the family who does not like sport and prefers books or music, or who may be more interested in discussions than in racing around a field or in outdoor activity, may arouse considerable anxiety. The reason for this is that these more thoughtful, indoor intellectual activities may be construed as the feminine side of the personality. Fathers who have not allowed themselves to develop this side of their personality may find it difficult or confusing to know how to relate to such a child. The boy may feel that what he is good at is devalued because it doesn't fit in with what his father knows about or can relate to. The father may feel on shaky ground because he has no experience of knowing how to identify maleness with these particular talents.

A different physical interaction

At its best, fathers and boys can develop a camaraderie and understanding, both through talking and doing, which is tremendously important for the whole process of modelling and identification. For example, the opportunity for sons to work alongside their fathers in the shed, learning about using tools, making objects of their own with their father's assistance.

I have already described some of the difficulties that young boys have in child-care settings related to the absence of men. I have referred specifically to the sense in which boys occupy space in a different way from girls. Boys relate their bodies in a more rumbustious, energetic way to the outside world. They both need a space, but they also need an opportunity to be able to grapple with or wrestle with their father. Fathers need to be able to appreciate the boundary between the boy's need to explore the range of his body and physical activity and skills and the point at which this activity descends into flagrant aggression. Some fathers may encourage their sons to become aggressive and believe that, by doing so, they have encouraged a strong form of masculinity in their sons. This is very unhelpful because it denies the task of this particular kind of physical energy which is about finding out about the range and extent of the boy's body in relation to the rest of the world, and a descent into straight aggression cuts the process short and also leaves the boy feeling overwhelmed by the power of his feelings if these are not contained.

The management of narcissism and rivalry plays as important a part in the development of the boy in relation to his father as it does for the girl in relation to her mother. The boy needs to feel that his own father feels confident and happy about being a man, and his son can in turn identify with this. However, it is important that this necessary state of narcissism does not become a focus for idealisation of the father particularly. Some men talk about their experience of growing up with their fathers as one in which they were full of admiration for their fathers but felt that they could never reach the same position or were never allowed to. Their relationship with their father existed on good terms as long as they did not present themselves as rivals. If the task for mothers is to help their girls into womanhood, then the task for fathers is to help their sons into manhood. This is a job which requires the suspension of rivalry and an investment in the boy as a separate individual.

The writings of psychoanalysis and of Greek tragedy explore the particular vicissitudes for the young boy growing up in the family and of how he has to negotiate both his love attachment and the intensity of his feelings towards his mother, as well as a positive identification with his father. The handling of this delicate state of affairs will vary from family to family. It may largely be denied or it may lead to lifelong antipathy and rivalry between father and son and become acted out in subsequent relationships. In its essence the little boy feels naturally strongly attached to his mother. His bodily and emotional feelings are all directed towards her and can take the form of his conviction, for example, expressed to her that they will one day get married. This excludes the idea of a father who also has to be taken into account and may be perceived as a rival for his mother's affections. I have mentioned that there are various ways in which families negotiate this particular triangle and the tensions and emotions it produces. Even where its existence is totally denied the repercussions will have an impact on day-to-day development and on subsequent experience. The resolution of this triangular intensity depends upon the awareness and tact of both parents. There is also of course the point at which these issues which are connected with attachment and sexuality and sexual identification become bound up with how power and control are handled in the family. If the father presents himself as a particularly aggressive and authoritarian figure, then the opportunity for resolution of this phase becomes more difficult and may never in fact take place. The father may see the son as a potential aggressor and misunderstand the nature of the developmental task and the boy's need to find an identification with him. His rejection of his son may push the boy into an over-intense relationship with his mother in which they both join forces as the victims of the father's aggression.

One way in which some families deal with the triangular task that I have described above is to create rigid divisions along sexual and gender lines which are also incompatible with the possibilities of resolution. Here the father may invite the son into a close identification with him, but at the cost of denigrating the mother. This may also include denigrating what women do and how they think. Here the boy can identify with the aggressor and feel at least temporarily protected by him, but it is a relationship that starts on shaky ground and is also of little assistance to the boy in his subsequent relationships with women.

If we return to my earlier statement that mothers sometimes find boys more complex to rear than girls, I would suggest that this is partly due to the fact that the developing structure of the boy's personality is so dependent on the critical resolution of this three-person interaction and the particular identifications it produces. Where this does not take place satisfactorily, boys can become hopelessly enmeshed in the types of emotional tangles I have described above.

In my clinical work I have become absolutely convinced of the need for fathers to facilitate boys in their development and into a positive idea of manhood. Their absence physically or their absence psychologically often leads to a paralysis in development in the boy. Typically, it manifests itself in adolescence when young people are confronted by some of their first real challenges within the academic or social spheres of their lives.

Fathers, sons and potency

In the triangular relationship I have described above, the tensions that have to be resolved revolve around the fact that the young child is fearful that his father will take revenge on his passion for his mother and his attachment to her. This revenge will take the form of being castrated, literally losing his penis. We can

understand this idea as a metaphor for the rivalry that can potentially exist between father and son and the struggle for potency
which is often linked to the way issues of power and control are
managed in the family. In order for boys to progress into adolescence and manhood they need to have a sense of their own
potency. While this has its core around sexual activity its impact
is far wider, so that we can talk of potency in work and thinking
as well as in social relationships. We must not confuse potency
with aggression or being authoritarian. Rather, at best it is about
having a sense of authority, of knowing one's self and being
effective. Many boys, because of the vicissitudes of their personal
and family experience, may feel the opposite of this potency,
which is to feel totally impotent and out of control. Thus impo-
tence, which has its core focus in sexual life, can spread to all
other activities.

Peter: saved from death, but unable to live

Peter, a 15-year-old boy, was referred to the clinic because of
excessive anxiety attacks. He appeared a strikingly handsome
and tall boy. His good looks were countered by clothes which
looked as though they had deliberately been put together to
suggest an air of total poverty and raggedness. Peter arrived at
his first session with his parents, a couple in their late thirties who
had espoused an alternative lifestyle, living with their family in a
rural area just outside the city. Peter was the youngest child, the
only boy in a family of three. Peter explained in a vivid way how
his anxiety attacks would overwhelm him to the point where he
believed that he was going to die. He would be flooded with
feelings of anxiety and have a sense of not being able to
breathe. The immediate precipitating factor for these anxiety
attacks was a recent experience at a rock festival where he and
some friends had taken LSD. Prior to this he had a long history of
smoking marijuana, virtually all day. His parents' reaction to my

questioning him about his taking of drugs suggested that this was probably part of the family culture since it had not occurred to them to really challenge Peter in any way.

One of the powerful themes of this first session, when we started to talk about Peter's early history, was the revelation that Peter had, at the age of 18 months, suffered from a very severe attack of meningitis. His parents had been told that he would not survive but he did so against all the odds. This led his parents to perceive him as the delicate child who had miraculously been saved from death. The doctors had mentioned at the time that they wished to do a follow-up medical examination on Peter when he was 15 years old, and it appeared significant that his crisis concerning his anxiety attacks and his fear of dying emerged just at the point that he turned 15. Peter was described as a highly intelligent boy with a particular gift for playing musical instruments. However, he had not been able to fulfil any of his potential and during his school years had experienced difficulty concentrating. He had been disruptive, bored and was threatened with suspension on a number of occasions. He finally left school at the age of 15 and embarked on a job skills program which he attended sporadically.

It was clear that neither parent had been able to set any firm boundaries or goals for Peter, almost as though his rescue from death had put him in a special place in their eyes and they were not able to have the same expectations of him as they had had of their daughters. What was particularly striking from the interaction between Peter and his father was that Peter's father had both idealised Peter and had actually supported his anti-authority attitude throughout his school years. Thus, when the school complained about Peter or when there was a suggestion that they might need to seek some help for him, Peter's father would join with his son in being openly contemptuous of what they called 'the system'. The parents, over the years, had had a particularly stormy and difficult marriage which included a period of separation, and Peter had been particularly drawn into their turmoil. It was as though his life was so busy at home that he had very little space in his mind to attend to school work. However, at 15, Peter had clearly reached a critical stage in his life. He presented as a boy who not only had been unable to develop any substantial learning skills but had very limited inner emotional resources.

As our sessions progressed it became clear to me that it was essential to involve Peter's father in the therapeutic work that lay ahead. However, Peter's father consistently found a range of excuses, mostly focusing on how busy he was at work, which he claimed made it impossible for him to attend. At my persistence, he finally attended one of the sessions and spent a considerable amount of time criticising Peter for his laziness, throwing his clothes around and total lack of concern for other people. He mentioned an incident in which Peter and a friend had broken into a local kindergarten and the police had been called because there was a suspicion that some things might have been taken. Peter's father was very angry when the police came around to his house to make inquiries and challenged his son about this. As the session progressed, it appeared as though Peter's father wanted to take a firm hand and begin to establish some clear boundaries. Peter, surprisingly, did not react by having one of his anxiety attacks. Instead he tried to stand up for himself and spoke to his father in a way which suggested that they could have a meaningful exchange. Since Peter's father had been so challenging of authority over the years he had not in fact been able to assist his son with the development of firm boundaries and his anxiety attacks had their origin in a confusion of roles within the family. At the end of this session, once Peter's father appeared to have established his authority he then announced to us all that he absolutely refused to continue with the sessions and, as he put it, 'I'm out of here'. Here he seemed to be repeating the very problem that lay at the heart of Peter's anxiety: that, on the one hand, he made a stand about the need for authority and boundaries and then, at the crucial point, fell away and abandoned his son. Here one could see how Peter's father reacted in an infantile and narcissistic way to the problem. He also created a tantalising experience in which at one moment he asserted himself as somebody who had insight and would offer some support and containment, and the next announced that he intended to withdraw all support from his son. The overall effect of this would be to keep Peter in a state of developmental paralysis. He could not go forward in his development and therefore challenge his father. By withdrawing his support from his son, and in effect from the family, in such a dramatic way Peter's father was effectively pushing his son into a closer and more intense relationship with his mother, which was also not helpful for him in the struggle to find his own identity.

We can see in this example how parents unwittingly can play a game of emotional ping-pong with their children. In Peter's situation we can see how Peter's development as a boy was impeded by inappropriate narcissism. His father in a sense used him as a challenge to the school authorities. He was praised for his good looks and talents, but was never helped to harness these talents in any disciplined and constructive way. Thus, at 15, his panic was compounded by a sense of overwhelming helplessness and inadequacy in the face of even the smallest challenge.

In conclusion, we can see how fathers play a critical role in facilitating the development of their sons into manhood through modelling ways of offering containment and authority, rather than control and authoritarian behaviour. The need to adapt to a more flexible interpretation of what masculinity represents and how it is characterised by the boy is a major part of this process.

▬ MOTHERS AND SONS

It is commonplace these days to hear women complain about men. They may complain about the lack of emotional companionship, the lack of interest in help with children and, in some cases, problems of aggression and violence. It is striking to note as well that the majority of petitions for divorce are brought by women rather than by men. Clearly, the relationships between the sexes are in a major process of transition and it behoves us to be able to explore this in more detail. In the process, however, it is easy to forget that all men have had mothers and that women have always been men's primary caretakers.

I have mentioned before that it is irresponsible for us to view child development exclusively within the lens of political correctness which makes particular assertions about social constructs and reality, the most striking of which is that there are no differences between the sexes. The acknowledgement of difference is an essential part of understanding the process of what may sometimes go wrong in the relationships between parents and children of the opposite sex.

The birth of a boy child or a girl child has a totally different psychological meaning for the mother and the father. The idea of the special value of giving birth to a boy is embedded in culture and in many different religions. It becomes impossible to segregate the cultural value from the emotional meaning. Thus we may observe, for example, that a woman may treat her first-born boy in a very different way from the way in which she has treated her girl. This does not mean that she has not loved her girl, but that a boy may be treated in a way which suggests that he is of very particular and precious value. This type of over-investment from the outset is a problem that sows particularly disruptive seeds for later experiences. We may find, for example, a woman who has felt devalued herself or has felt that she has not been a particular success in life; may also have an underlying resentment towards men, a sense that perhaps her father did not value her, and that her husband does not take her terribly seriously. The birth of a boy child may represent for her the opportunity to redress this balance. One way of putting it is to say that the boy becomes her golden penis, that she is able through her son to find a way of asserting her own needs and wishes, albeit in a roundabout way. I have mentioned before that there is a state of necessary narcissism in all love between parents and children which is a positive and important part of development. However, narcissism is also a very delicate process and needs to be held in a particularly delicate balance. Difficulties arise where narcissism becomes mixed with idealisation. Here, for example, the mother may put her son on a pedestal and have a sense of over-investment in him of the kind that she may never have had in her daughters. The difficulty with putting people on a pedestal is that they almost invariably fall off; thus one can say that the opposite of idealisation is almost always denigration. The boy child who is invested in this way by his mother cannot fail to eventually become a disappointment to her. One reason for this is that if the boy is to find some separate identity, he needs to be able to separate from his mother. We may see examples of this in the way in which mothers of adolescent sons sometimes describe the extraordinary cruelty of their sons and the cruel way in which they talk to them. We can begin to understand that the son at this stage may have no option but to be cruel to his mother because it represents for him perhaps the only way in which he can create a separation from her. This may leave mothers feeling bereft and confused about how their perfect, loving little boy could turn into such a cruel monster.

One of the particularly complex aspects of this process is that the sense of disappointment at having been let down by men can come full circle. If a woman feels that she has been let down by her father and husband she may try to find a substitute in her son. Here is a boy whom she has given birth to and has created, and therefore has greater hope of being able to shape or perhaps control. The difficulty emerges when the son struggles to separate from this particular identification. He may, as I have suggested above, find that cruelty is the only way to do this, which then leaves his mother feeling disappointed and let down again, thus completing the circle.

Of course, the outcome for mothers and sons is not necessarily always a negative one and there are many examples of excellent and supportive relationships which contribute to growth and health. The critical factor here is most often a satisfying and mutually supportive relationship between the father and the mother, so that the son does not have pressure placed on him to step into the role of a substitute father and is not used by the mother in a rivalrous confrontation with the father.

FATHERS AND DAUGHTERS

I have described above how the task for both parents is to provide for their children of both sexes what we may consider as a wider range of 'psychological possibilities' and behaviour in their development. The task is to provide boys and girls with as wide a social and psychological repertoire as possible so that they do not become fixed and rigid in limiting patterns of behaviour. Andrew Samuels, a Jungian psychotherapist, writes about the father's role as a 'transforming one'. He says most particularly that the father's role has a mediating cultural function in relation to both boys and girls. The father's role is also critical in helping psychological growth. In the relationship between fathers and daughters we are faced with the need for fathers to be able to negotiate the erotic relationship, that is to say the awareness of a developing sexuality of the girl, particularly in adolescence. The father's task in essence is to be able to maximise his daughter's sense of confidence in herself as a developing sexual young woman without compromising her by being himself seductive. For some fathers this may prove a daunting task and many young women describe how an originally close relationship with their father evaporated when they became adolescent, and how betrayed and abandoned they felt. This suggests that fathers in this situation had become overwhelmed with anxiety about the recognition of their daughters as sexual beings and fearful of their own impulses and thoughts in relation to their daughter's developing sexuality.

The place of the parental and marital relationship is always to the fore, as I have mentioned several times. Where parents' own sexual and marital relationship is reasonably satisfying the father may not feel overwhelmed by his inclinations to be seductive or his worries about getting too close to his sexually developing daughter. In some families there is an identification between father and daughter where both are seen to aspire to intellectual activities which may be very different from those of the mother.

In this situation, the daughter may feel that she is triumphing over her mother by forming a special alliance with her father and being a kind of mental wife to him and creating a stimulating and exciting experience for her father. The problem with this type of identification is that it may lead to an idealisation of her father and disappointment in subsequent relationships. It also leaves a permanent black hole where her relationship with her mother should be. The girl may be left with the feeling that she has somehow stolen her father from her mother, as we see from the following example:

Leaving mother behind

A young woman in her mid-twenties referred herself for psychotherapy for anxiety attacks which followed the sudden death of her father. She had grown up in a family that was typified by the types of identifications I have described above in that she had a denigratory relationship with her mother, whom she saw as a rather stupid non-intellectual woman. She herself was very ambitious and concerned with academic achievement. She had been close to her father and they shared an interest in intellectual activities. On the death of her father she had returned to live with her mother and they existed in a mutually rivalrous relationship which had been typical of their earliest experience. Her father had been highly idealised in her mind, although in reality he had not been very supportive of her or the family in real practical terms.

The difficulty for this young woman was that at her father's death she was left, as it were, in no-man's-land: she had lost her highly idealised relationship with her father and she was left with a denigrated mother who also existed as an internal object within herself. This contributed to her feelings of anxiety and to the resulting panic attacks. Her return home represented, at least in part, a wish to make some reparation i.e. make the relationship better between herself and her mother.

In this chapter I have hoped to show, as we see from the following example what a critical effect parents have in helping to facilitate gender and sexual identity and the widest range of opportunities for personality development for children of the same and opposite sex. We can talk about the transforming influence of both parents in this respect and how the capacity to negotiate the specific and different tasks in relation to both boys and girls is dependent fundamentally on the parental partnership.

SUMMARY

This chapter focuses on the specific tasks of adolescence with its primary focus on individuation and separation. Adolescence is seen as:

- A time of 'reworking earlier attachments and relationships within the family'.
- Being characterised by the 'process of regression', where the adolescent is struggling to reconcile the move towards adulthood with one foot still in the camp of childhood.
- A major transition, which involves an irrevocable change with the capacity for reproduction.
- A time where the problem of sex and violence as areas of confrontation, because of the proliferation of HIV/AIDS and drug abuse, are particular concerns.
- A time to confront the problem of unresolved conflict in the family which can inhibit the adolescent from being able to work out paradoxes and conflicts in a relatively safe and contained environment.
- A time of vulnerability for young people – acting out can be a sign of health and a cry for help, but we also must be mindful of their vulnerability.
- A time at which earlier problems can become consolidated, particularly in the period of late adolescence and early adulthood.

Adolescence represents a life's task. It is particularly concerned with the process of transition and involves crossing a boundary from childhood to adulthood. The irreversible crossing of a boundary, which I have described from the point of birth where parents go from being someone's child to being someone's mother, is echoed in the process of adolescence. Here the crossing of a boundary for a young person involves sexual maturity and the capacity for reproduction. Adolescence thus involves a total psychological as well as a physiological and hormonal change.

Another characteristic of the adolescent process is that it inevitably involves a process of regression, that is a recapitulation of earlier infantile experiences. I mentioned earlier that the experience of the pre-school child between the age of three and five has its echo in later adolescent experience. Some psychodynamic theorists have described adolescence as 'the second chance'. They see it as an opportunity to make good at the end of childhood some of the difficulties which may have occurred at an earlier stage of development. Adolescence, above all, is about the work of individuation and separation from parents and the family. Part of this process of individuation and separation may involve a degree of protest and heralds the end of idealisation of the parents.

It is interesting to return to the ideas of Sigmund Freud nearly a century ago and his comments about the specific tasks of adolescence. He mentions these as follows:

- to crystallise sexual identity;
- to find a love object;
- to bring together the two strands of sexuality and tenderness.

These three tasks of adolescence, as Freud sees them, are really no different today from the way they may have presented themselves such a long time ago. We can say that these relational tasks are part of the work of internal development, while of course we would add the need for education and social development and wider social interaction and recognition.

I have mentioned before that difficulties that remain unresolved or undetected in the earlier part of development find a way of emerging during the period of adolescence. This happens for a number of reasons. First of all, it is fair to assume that some of the tolerance and support for the younger child tends to fall away as the young person gets older. There are particular societal and educational demands and expectations on the young adolescent and, of course, the major physiological and hormonal changes in themselves can precipitate a crisis of development. It has often been said that we put tremendous pressure on adolescents in that they are expected to perform optimally from an academic point of view at a time when they are most vulnerable to emotional and physiological changes. The academic performance that they are capable of at this time in their lives may influence the rest of their academic or work lives and we may need to reconsider the types of pressures that we expect adolescents to negotiate.

 ## THE REWORKING OF ATTACHMENT WITHIN THE FAMILY

The psychodynamic approach affirms that behaviour is never static but is always dynamic and changes all the time. This awareness is particularly critical in our understanding of adolescence. The relationship between the adolescent and his parents of the same and opposite sexes changes continuously. As part of the developmental task of adolescence there is a more conscious working out of the job of emotional realignments and adjustments of these fundamental attachments. There are many examples in family life of adolescents and their parents struggling to resist as far as possible the reworking of attachment which is the fundamental task of the adolescent stage. There may be particular investments on the part of both parents to keep the child young or childlike and also, in particular, of maintaining rather fixed or idealised relationships. Parents may be very fearful of this adolescent stage and may be anxious about the potential protest or rebellion of their child and fear that this will lead them to abandon the family. Alternatively, they may be potentially anxious about their own wish to reject the child if he does not continue to conform to their expectations. I have mentioned before that parents may find that they operate better with their children at different stages of their child's developmental experience. This also relates of course to parents' own developmental experience, which is never static but changes as well. Some parents who adore babies may find the challenging toddler too much to cope with. They may also find the rebellious adolescent something of a handful. Some parents may find the process of denigration and contempt of the adolescent too much to bear. They may have reached a point of crisis in their own mid-life when their adolescent is asserting himself and trying to cut them down to size.

THE FLUIDITY THAT SURROUNDS THE DEVELOPMENT OF PERSONALITY AND IDENTITY

Adolescence is a process that needs to be recognised as one which is characterised by the fluidity of personality and identity. It involves the adolescent in being able to launch a ' pilot experiment in independent living'. For this reason we may sometimes observe very extreme behaviour in adolescence or behaviour which in an adult may be described as very disturbed. Time plays a particular part in the adolescent process. We can see how in a relatively short space of time the young person physically changes from the body of a child to the body of an adult, and yet inside this adult body may still be a very small child. The adolescent may thus be faced with a total 'lack of fit' or incongruity between the way in which he appears and the way in which he feels. In classical children's literature we find wonderful examples of understanding this process, for example in Alice in Wonderland where Alice, who is on the verge of puberty, drinks a bottle saying 'Drink me'. She both enlarges and shrinks at different stages and has a sense of being totally out of control.

Many girls display the symptoms of anorexia nervosa or bulimia for the first time at adolescence, which has a close link with the problem of wanting to control growth and sexual development.

Coupled with this idea of how time is controlling them, the adolescent may also have omnipotent ideas of how they might want to control time.

Time moves in different ways

Harry, an Afro-Caribbean adolescent of 15, was referred to a clinic I worked at in London for disruptive behaviour at home. His mother was a single parent, a young, attractive woman who had coped extremely well in bringing up Harry and her daughter. Harry had always had a close and loving relationship with his mother, but at adolescence it was clear that he felt the need to break away. Because of their previous good and positive relationship, his anxiety about wanting to be close to his mother and perhaps being anxious about his wishes to be a potential partner to her motivated his cruel and callous reactions. I attempted to set up some counselling sessions for Harry, but it was very difficult for him to maintain these on any regular basis. He would come for one session and then not appear again for about two months. On one occasion, when I had not seen him for quite a long period, he came to see me out of the blue and started off the session by saying 'This therapy isn't getting anywhere'. At first this seemed an extraordinary remark since he had not in fact been having any therapy but had tended to turn up for these sporadic sessions. However, when I discussed this with my supervisor, he mentioned that, in fact, in Harry's mind the work of the therapy had been continuing. He had in the intervening periods been mulling over what had been going on between us and then, when he had exhausted his own capacity to think about it, came to the conclusion that the therapy wasn't getting anywhere and then came back to see me.

THE EXPLORATION OF SEXUAL IDENTITY

Adolescence offers an opportunity for young people to begin the process of developing a sharper definition of their sexual identity.

It is inevitable that young people experience a sense of uncertainty about this identity as it first begins to emerge. They may feel physically and emotionally drawn to people of the same sex as well as to people of the opposite sex. The recognition that this is an exploratory phase and does involve some confusion requires a corresponding understanding in the adult world. It is vitally important that young people are not prematurely seduced by heterosexuality or homosexuality. We need to be careful not to push young people into sexual definitions of themselves at too early a stage. For this delicate process to take place there is a need on the part of adults to allow adolescents their own voyage of discovery rather than for the parenting and social world to have a major vested interest in pushing them to take up particular roles.

If we refer to Freud's task of reconciling eroticism with tenderness, we can certainly see that, for boys, tenderness has to be introduced where there may be an overriding concern with sexual prowess which is not always person-related. However, it is equally important for girls that their sexual identity and eroticism become reconciled with a view of themselves not only as potential mothers and carers, but also of themselves as independent, assertive personalities.

 # SEX AND VIOLENCE AS AREAS OF CONFRONTATION

Sex and violence have at various times been areas of confrontation for adolescents within the family home. The continuing potential for self-destructiveness, however, is of particular concern today because of the proliferation of HIV/AIDS and of drug abuse. We can see, as the developmental stages unfold, how critical communication is to the development of positive relationships. Communication and openness between children and their parents offer the best possible protective factor against the need for the adolescent to act out in a self-destructive or aggressive way. An essential part of positive communication is the capacity of the parents to be able to tolerate the aggression of the child, that is to be hated by the child at times, and to be able to withstand this in a non-persecutory and containing way. In my clinical work I have come across many examples in families where hate cannot be contained satisfactorily and finds its way into the adolescent's need to impulsively act out the destructive scenario that has its roots within the parental relationships.

Bringing the baby home

Constance was the youngest child of a family of three. She was not a planned baby, but was described by her mother as an accident. Her arrival coincided with her mother's wish and belief that her child-bearing years were well and truly over. Constance's mother had not particularly enjoyed bringing up her other children and found the birth of Constance a terrible chore and trial. With her first two children she felt she had been able to do her duty as a mother. Her own early childhood had been severely affected by the psychiatric breakdown of her own mother which resulted in her being abandoned in a children's home for many years. Constance came into therapy with me as a young woman in her early 20s. She had had a child out of wedlock a few years previously and was living, together with her child, in the parental home. Her whole life had been characterised by trauma of one kind or another, and in the last few years she had developed bulimia. In her sessions with me Constance talked about how, as a young child, she had felt that she had no place in her mother's mind. Her mother had difficulty cuddling her or feeling close to her, and she remembered as a three-year-old wandering out of the house into the next door neighbour's home and going into their bedroom.

As a child at school she had invented an imaginary friend who accompanied her to the classroom, which was very disconcerting to the teacher. Inevitably, at the age of 15, she had her first sexual experience with a boy at a party whom she claimed raped her. It was clear from her memory of the experience that she had placed herself at considerable physical risk and had almost invited the event to happen. The traumatic experience of this sexual event prompted her into a whirlwind of self-destructive behaviour and she eventually became pregnant and gave birth to a little girl. We can see in this example how Constance's sexual confrontation in adolescence had its roots in her earliest difficulties in her relationship with her mother, who too had suffered emotional neglect because of her mother's breakdown. For Constance, a sense of denigration and worthlessness that she carried within her was acted out in a compulsive, destructive way as she placed herself at greater and greater sexual and physical risk, culminating in the anorexic attack on her body.

THE DEVELOPMENTAL DEMANDS AND PARADOXES OF ADOLESCENCE

I have mentioned earlier that adolescence from the developmental perspective represents a recapitulation of some of the earlier developmental milestones from the period of early childhood. The reason for this is that there are many developmental issues in common between early childhood and adolescence, in particular the fact that a number of different developmental changes are taking place simultaneously. For the young child we talk about the need to master toilet training, language, and internalising controls in the form of managing boundaries and aggression. The key areas of sexual and gender identity are also being negotiated at this early stage. In adolescence, the adolescent similarly has to negotiate the demands and challenges evidenced by the physical and hormonal changes of his body, as well as his inner world of compelling sexual fantasies, dreams and passionately held beliefs. The outer world of peer group pressure may deny at times the individuality of the adolescent. At the same time there are expectations from the wider group pressure of educational demands and adherence to social norms. As I have pointed out earlier, we expect young people to be most educationally committed and embark on an examination system and selection system which may influence the rest of their academic lives just at the point when they are going through considerable turbulence in terms of personality and developmental changes.

It is therefore not surprising that we find the process of adolescence throws up many casualties as a result of these apparently contradictory demands. Adolescents may respond in many different ways to attempts to resolve these challenges. For young women, as I have mentioned before, the onset of anorexia and bulimia may be a way of physically denying the physiological changes associated with becoming a woman and bearing children. For both sexes premature sexual experience may represent a way out of the anxiety that is associated with dealing with uncertainty. The young person may tell herself that at least she knows what sex is about. They will then be able to be in some control over their feelings and the experience. Often, because of the circumstances in which the sexual experience is sought out, it may take place within an exploitative and even violent context, such as rape, which serves only to confirm the worst fears of the adolescent, as we can see in the example of Constance.

 ## SEPARATION, INDIVIDUATION, DISINTEGRATION

Adolescence is seen primarily as a time when the young person is struggling to deal with issues of separating from the family through the process of separation and individuation. At its best this requires that they are able to integrate different aspects of their personality and that their family life has been good enough until that point to facilitate this process. It is also dependent on a tolerant and flexible family which can stand some of the challenges of adolescence. For example, I have mentioned some of the essential processes which I see as essential to the development of core sexuality and gender identity for children of the same sex as parents, and opposite sex to parents. The handling of appropriate narcissism, as opposed to unhelpful narcissism, is a key aspect of this process. It comes particularly to the fore during adolescence when parents have to tolerate the sight of their adolescent's burgeoning sexuality when they may feel that their own sexuality is on the wane. Women may be challenged by their daughter's beauty and sexual attractiveness, while fathers may be challenged by their son's physical strength and dominance. In some families where these challenges cannot be negotiated or tolerated, it is not uncommon for adolescent boys to leave the family after a catastrophic row in which they may, for the first time, have physically challenged their father and perhaps attacked him. For girls a similar challenge which cannot be tolerated may take place in relation to sexual confrontation.

We can postulate that, to some extent, the process of disintegration precedes that of separation, individuation and integration. Adolescents may have a sense of being out of control; that their body and their self-image don't quite fit. A young woman may feel that she is really a little girl within a woman's body. Most importantly, boys and girls need an appropriate time frame in which to be able to close the gap between how they once perceived themselves and how they are now.

Adolescence has been described as 'a pilot experiment in living', which suggests that trial and error and experimentation are an essential part of this developmental stage. However, in our current society, experimentation unfortunately is fraught with danger and can become life-threatening. The long-term effects of drug-taking and sexual experimentation which can result in HIV/AIDS are a very real threat to young people. The struggle for both adolescents and their parents is to be able to create a different and safer climate for experimentation.

CONFIRMING THE ADOLESCENT EXPERIENCE

In many traditional societies and religions, adolescence has been marked by a ritual or ceremony which represents, in formal terms, an acknowledgement of the transition from the state of childhood to sexual development and adolescence. These rituals are important in that they acknowledge the mental and the physical attributes relating to crossing this important boundary, which is also an irrecoverable boundary. However, in much of our society today, there is no formal recognition of the transition from childhood into the state of adolescence, and many young people are left floundering in a state of uncertainty that may be compounded by increased anxiety about an adult world which is itself in a state of major change and transition. This is evidenced most particularly in the sphere of employment and the fact that many young people can no longer take for granted the notion that they will find a job. It is probably fair to say that, for most people in our secular society, the move into employment represented for adolescents a move from childhood into an older stage of development. Here the taking on of apprenticeship or getting a job and earning money represented the capitalist, secular alternative to the confirmation more redolent of traditional societies.

The problem today is that many adults find themselves in similar situations. They are often not in a position to hand down advice to the younger generation because the social context for both has changed beyond recognition. I have mentioned before that, in a psychodynamic approach, we take the view that behaviour is always dynamic and constantly changing, it is never static. This perspective is particularly vital within the context of facilitating the adolescent process both in terms of the internal interpersonal and developmental experiences of the adolescent and also in terms of the constant changing social context. The dilemma for many families today is that at the time that their adolescent children are struggling with the loss, change and transition associated with moving into adulthood, their parents, too, are struggling to deal with the same processes which are represented by unemployment and changing work practices due to technological advances.

ADOLESCENCE AS A STATE OF MIND

Adolescence has been described as a state of mind as well as a developmental stage. This refers to the kinds of feelings, attitudes and behaviour that we may observe in ourselves, our friends and our clients which have an adolescent quality to them regardless of chronological age. It has often been said that, for all its pain, adolescence is a necessary process for all of us to go through because, if we do not go through it at the right time, we may find ourselves going through it at a later stage. For example, the beginnings of adolescence in their children may arouse unresolved longings and desires in parents. If parents themselves have not had an appropriate experience of adolescence they may need to relive this through their children or may themselves have to experience adolescence at first hand. For example, a man who had lived an apparently stable life in a relatively happy family changed his life totally at the onset of his daughter's adolescence. He started to have affairs, separated from the family; he totally changed his clothes, which up to that point had been fairly traditional and conservative, and took to dressing in jeans and bright shirts; he changed his car to a sports car. All in all, he appeared to be desperately trying to compete with his adolescent children and also to belatedly recover some vestiges of the adolescent experience for himself, albeit in a tragically inappropriate way.

Similarly, girls may find themselves quite disturbed by the fact that their mothers appear to be wanting to dress in identical styles to theirs.

NEGOTIATING BOUNDARIES BETWEEN THE GENERATIONS

The problem of negotiating boundaries between the different generations at this adolescent stage is a crucial one. With the increase of separation and divorce, and the changing expectations of women, the way in which parents perceive themselves and their sexuality has changed on an unprecedented scale. For example, it is not uncommon for adolescents to be struggling with their own identity and sexuality at the point at which their parents may be bringing their marriage to an end or be involved with new partners. The whole issue of parental sexuality becomes tangible at the point at which one or other parent introduces a new partner. Sexuality within the home may become more explicit where a single parent, for example, brings a new partner home. All these factors in turn have an impact on the space, psychological and physical, which is available for the developing identity of the adolescent.

The status of the parental relationship will have an impact on how adolescents negotiate these boundaries. For example, a single mother had successfully brought up her two children, a boy and a girl. Mother and the two children had spent many years together as the marriage had been very brief. However, during his adolescence the son, Joshua, changed markedly in his behaviour towards his mother. She described how shocked and hurt she was by the change in him. It was as though, she said, one day he was a polite, caring, loving boy and the next had turned into a callous, cold young man, rather reminiscent of his father from whom she had chosen to separate. Here we can see that it is likely that Joshua, in this family situation, was overcome by an anxiety about his close and dependent relationship with his mother. Perhaps this family situation was so cosy that he feared that he would never want to leave. The only way to create a space between himself and his mother was to become callous and cruel so that she would be able to withdraw from him. We can speculate that Joshua may have been something of a compensation for his mother and may have represented the good, kind side of masculinity, as opposed to the way in which she viewed her husband whom she saw as self-centred and selfish. Unfortunately, Joshua had to take on some of his father's attributes in order to be able to create the necessary space that he needed for his continuing development. It would have been preferable if his mother had been able to anticipate this.

REJECTING PARENTAL VALUES

One of the tasks for adolescents is to be able to establish a separate identity. This may require, for a time, that adolescents do not go along with their parents' ideas, political views and values. Parents may become disconcerted at the different views to their own that their children espouse, but this is an essential part of the trial and error and experimentation of building up a different personality. Erik Erikson has written most eloquently about this phase of adolescent development. He believed that it was imperative for the young person to be able to contradict or contrast with his parents as part of the adolescent passage. Where the adolescent has failed to do this, it will represent an unresolved aspect of the adolescent state of mind which may need to be resolved at a later stage. Erikson has described the dilemma of the liberal, emancipated family who create such a helpful and open experience for their children that adolescents may find nothing left to rebel against. Erikson has also emphasised the dangers inherent in limiting the scope for allowing the adolescent to be different from her parents. We may see examples of just such a dilemma in liberal, emancipated families who are dismayed when their children espouse reactionary ideologies or become infatuated with fundamentalist religious groups or even sects.

We may wonder what this process may mean in psychodynamic terms and whether it points to an inherent need for the establishment of a boundary and of a reasonable set of values within which the adolescent and young person can feel safe, and against which they can also rebel in an appropriate way. Here the theme of containment again comes to the fore.

 # THE REWORKING OF ATTACHMENT: FINDING A PARTNER

Freud has described the task of adolescence as the finding of a sexual partnership which also represents the re-finding of it. Here we can see how the developmental process comes full circle through the internalisation of the real mother and father by the adolescent and young person. This 'internalisation of a mother and father', that is to say an idea of a mother and father inside, is what informs our subsequent choice of partners and love relationships.

 # THE CONSOLIDATION OF PERSONALITY AND THE MOVE TOWARDS EARLY ADULTHOOD

The period of middle to late adolescence enables us to see the beginnings of the consolidation of personality. The good enough parenting and family and appropriate containment will hopefully have led to sufficient separation and individuation for the young person, who can happily still feel that he belongs within a warm and loving and trusted family, but can also move towards a separate life and possibly different experiences. This period of middle to late adolescence also enables us to identify problems for the young person which may become consolidated in adult development.

The extent of the severity of an adolescent's disturbance and anxiety will always be related to attempts to reconcile the turbulence he may have experienced within his family and specific difficulties in family relationships, together with his own internal needs, strivings and particular personality. For this reason it can be a delicate and difficult process to sort out 'what belongs where' when one is trying to help adolescents in a crisis. We can say that a 15-year-old adolescent or older has already developed an autonomous set of problems and that he might most benefit by being seen individually in a confidential setting which excludes his parents or family. This way of working may well be helpful but we must also keep in mind that, at the point of referral, so many of these young people are struggling with a sense of being in a state of limbo. They may not have been able to achieve a sense of inner autonomy and their particular intertwinement with their parents then becomes one of the issues that need to be addressed.

The problem of unfinished business

Kevin, a 15-year-old boy, was referred because of his aggressive and difficult behaviour, in particular his outbursts at school in which he was said to have punched other boys. He was described as an intelligent boy who had not been able to reach his potential. Kevin was living with his younger sister, his father and a stepmother whom his father had recently married. His father described the family history at length on the telephone before our first meeting. Kevin's mother had left the family when Kevin was only three years old. Shortly after she left, her child by a previous marriage left to join her in another town. This boy had had a particularly close relationship with Kevin and so the tragic loss of his mother was associated with the loss of the much-loved half-brother. Until very recently Kevin and his sister had lived lives which were in effect hostages to their father's professional ambitions. They had been looked after by a succession of housekeepers. Kevin had formed attachments to a number of these housekeepers and their wider circle of friends, and every time they left his separations increased. His life had been a succession of loss and unresolved mourning, but this had never been fully recognised by anyone and not by his father.

The new stepmother was naturally having difficulties settling into this demanding family and the strain had now become so evident that Kevin's father felt himself to be in a position where he had to choose between his son and his new wife. Kevin arrived at the first session together with his father. It was clear that Kevin's father spoke on his behalf, describing his behaviour and his feelings, and leaving very little space for Kevin to be able to say anything for himself. Kevin, for his part, tended to nod in agreement with his father but it was clear that he did so out of a sense of compliance and probably an overwhelming need to please his father. In the short time that was left to me to be able to see Kevin on his own during the initial consultation, he revealed something of his depression and his feelings of loss and mourning for his mother. He talked of how he was still taunted by his friends at school about his mother, that they tended to call her names, and he was provoked to hit out at them and became involved in fights. It was obvious that Kevin was a boy who needed an opportunity to be able to voice his grief and loss in his own way, and not through the domination of his father. His father agreed to regular sessions for Kevin but on the very first of these sessions, two weeks later, he arrived at the wrong time with Kevin and subsequently rang to say that he felt the whole problem was in the 'too hard basket' and the therapy was abandoned. Here we can see that Kevin's father was not prepared to allow his son to enter into therapy because it probably represented a threat to his total control and his need to define Kevin's experience and beliefs and feelings in his rigid way.

Acting out as a sign of health

We can see in this example that Kevin's aggression in the school in fact represented a cry for help amid his extremely fraught home life and his struggle to make sense of all the losses that he had experienced. Winnicott describes this process in detail in his writings on deprivation and delinquency. He describes the act of a child or adolescent organising antisocial acts in the spirit of hope, that is in the hope of compelling society to go back with him or her to the position where things went wrong and to acknowledge this fact. Thus we can see that acting out or acting in an antisocial way, which is generally negatively construed, can also represent a sign of health and struggle towards integration for the adolescent.

Is there a place in the home for me?

Bradley, a boy of nearly 14, was referred to the clinic after he was suspended from school because of his aggressive behaviour. He was due to appear in the Juvenile Court because of his repeated writing of graffiti and his parents were at their wits end. Bradley was the third child in a family of four. He was the first boy to be born in the family and his parents admitted that they found it easier to bring up the girls than the boys. Bradley's parents had met and married when they were themselves in their late teens. They both had a history of severe deprivation and, in Bradley's mother's case, sexual abuse which had been carried out over a number of years of her childhood. It was striking how, in our first session, both parents pointed to the fact that there had been serious difficulties in their own relationship and the family had nearly fallen apart when Bradley was aged three. We could see that the difficulties he was experiencing now in his adolescence were, to some extent, a recapitulation of these early childhood problems. On his own with me, Bradley soon discarded his tough exterior and wept like a little boy. One of the major causes of concern about Bradley's behaviour was that he would take off away from home without informing his parents. His parents had grown to accept that he would disappear on Friday afternoon and return on Sunday, and that they would not have any idea of where he was. It was striking therefore, in his first meeting with me, that Bradley said that his greatest wish was to be with the family doing things together. Bradley, more than any other child in the family, was experienced by everyone as almost too much to handle and he tended in a sense to fall over the edge. His disappearance at weekends, almost on cue, could be seen as his way of trying to minimise the tension in the family, by excluding himself.

In the course of our sessions, which included family meetings, the issue of Bradley disappearing of his own accord at weekends was one we tackled very strongly. Once Bradley actually stayed at home this meant that there needed to be a jostling for position among the other members of the family and they quite literally had to make physical and psychological space for him in the home. It indicated a realignment of relationships, most particularly between the parents, and this subsequently became the focus of the therapy. Despite their considerable difficulties and deprivation in their early childhood, Bradley's parents were able to tackle the sessions which focused on their parenting and their relationship because of their genuine wish to change. Bradley's behaviour, for his part, settled quite dramatically once the focus of attention shifted and he settled down well at school and also within the family. Here we can see an example of how Bradley's apparently antisocial behaviour also contained within it a spirit of hope, which Winnicott describes as a sign of health and struggle towards integration. Understanding this process and also being able to provide support at this critical time can often help facilitate adolescents and their families into the next stage of development so that they do not literally fall over the precipice.

Adolescent suicide

The statistics for adolescent suicide in Australia are among the highest in the Western world. It points to the need for us to be able to take adolescents and their depression and feelings very seriously, and to be more sensitive to the particular triggers for breakdown that may occur for young people. It is rare indeed for suicide or attempted suicide in a young person to come out of the blue. Almost always it is the end result of developmental problems based on longstanding personal difficulties within the family and usually related to problems within the parenting couple. Marital discord, parental divorce, remarriage or, in some cases, abandonment of the young person may often be the trigger for adolescent suicide. The young person may feel that the act of suicide provides them with an opportunity for control in a situation in which they feel both emotionally and physically out of control. We should also not overlook the fact that, aside from the specific act of suicide or attempted suicide, reckless self-destructive behaviour on the part of young people can also represent an attack upon the self. How can we understand these desperate attacks of self-destruction? One way of trying to understand the problem from the developmental point of view is to ask ourselves the basic question: 'How do people grow? What do children and young people need to assist and nourish them in their development?' In facing some of the vicissitudes and problems of adolescence we come back to the earliest statement by Winnicott about the infant: 'There is no such thing as the baby'.

For the adolescent the development of identity and a sense of coherence is a prerequisite for her mental health. The development of identity is only made possible by the provision of modelling that parents of both sexes are able to make available. This modelling needs to be of a kind which combines a degree of flexibility so that young people are not caught up in definitions of extremely rigid masculine or feminine identity which lead them into an emotional cul-de-sac. For some young people, leaving school at the age of 15 or 16 may represent a particular crisis. They may have longed to leave school and have felt that they obtained very little from their school experience. However, the school institution, which would have represented the last structured experience of their lives, was at least a place that they could kick against. Once they abandon school and find themselves thrown into life with no qualifications and very few prospects, their terror must be quite overwhelming. For young people who have experienced a loss of family and parental support the problem is exacerbated even further, and it is not surprising that depression, despair and suicide set in.

FROM ADOLESCENCE TO ADULTHOOD

It is perhaps an indication of our times that the generation gap appears to be diminishing. The process of late adolescence and the transition to adulthood seems to be one which is becoming more prolonged. This may have something to do with our increasing longevity. It may also be connected with changing values about sexuality, patterns of family life, as well as economic realities. Young adults, for example, feel more comfortable about living in the parental home than they would have done in a previous generation. It is often at this stage in the transition to young adulthood that parents wonder whether their children will ever leave home. However, it can also be a rewarding time for both parents and their young adult children when they may discover each other again after the turbulence of the adolescent period. At its best, young people conceive the parenting relationship as one which is also imbued with friendship. This can add an entirely new dimension to the parenting relationship and can be very rewarding for all concerned. This new dimension of course takes into account that the young adult is a separate person, but their strengths, their resources and their very difference have developed out of the support, love and containment of the family. For some young people who have had a particularly difficult time in their adolescence it can offer an opportunity for reflection. Young people at the age of 18 or 20 may feel more able to embark on therapeutic or counselling help for themselves in their own right than when they are going through the turbulence of their adolescent experience. Young people at this stage can be more realistically responsible for themselves. The problems the young adult presents can be worked through in a more truly autonomous way. I have described before the particular generosity of children which cannot be underestimated. At the point of departure from the family home, young people want their parents to have something for themselves and also need to know that their parents' lives will continue to have direction and interest and be rich and rewarding even in the absence of their children. The worry that the parents' marriage may fall apart or that a mother's life investment in her children is so total that nothing else exists in her life is not conducive to a positive feeling on the part of the young person as they make this last transition into independent life.

As the young person goes on in their development there is no doubt that mistakes will have been made. There will have been trial and error. Some phases of development may have been perceived as more successful than others and there will still be issues from the earliest experience to be negotiated as adult life progresses.

PART THREE

Bringing Up Children in a Changing World

CHAPTER 12

The Impact of Separation and Divorce

SUMMARY

This chapter focuses specifically on the impact of divorce and separation on children and how important it is to acknowledge the real developmental experience of children and parents, rather than received wisdom and political correctness. The following points about divorce and separation are made.

- Separation and loss is a significant and traumatic event which, like all the other emotional milestones, requires to be understood and integrated, rather than ignored or belittled.
- Many marriages break down following the birth of children, which indicates that we must try to understand how society may contribute to making it impossible for parents to parent and to stay together to carry out their important task. In Winnicott's terms, society often fails to provide a 'good enough' or 'facilitating environment' for parenting to take place.
- Parents can respond to and contain the emotional pain of their children, primarily by validating their child's experience and allowing themselves to take the child's experience seriously.

This book thus far has offered an outline of some of the developmental processes that take place from an emotional perspective for the child, her parents and family as they move from infancy to adolescence and young adulthood. Throughout the book I have emphasised that emotional development, parenting and family life all take place within a context. The psychodynamic approach shows us that development is not linear but is multifaceted and essentially dynamic. Intrapsychic processes such as our fantasies, our dreams, our wishes and hopes are influenced in turn by social events and the outside world. There is a constant interdependence and interrelationship between these different levels.

CHANGES IN FAMILY LIFE AND THEIR EFFECTS ON DEVELOPMENT

As we come to the end of the twentieth century, it is no longer possible to talk about a parenting identity with totally predictable tasks and roles for men and women. Our idea of what constitutes family has also changed dramatically. The family can consist of parents parenting on their own through divorce or through choice, step families, including children from previous marriages, people parenting across different cultures, and a variety of combinations, including different sexual orientations. This suggests for many people a brave, new and exciting world. However, we may question where these new models of family life and of relationships between family and society leave those most vulnerable to change, namely children, in the course of their development.

The impact of feminism and the questioning of different roles for men and women has had a significant influence on family life. However, despite increased career opportunities, many women find that they have not advanced very much at all when it comes to their mothering role and, at times, face intolerable strain in trying to reconcile the need to bring up children with work requirements. Similar struggles are faced by men and fathers for whom the balance between work and family priorities evaporates beneath the pressure of heavy workloads and feared redundancies.

The cycle of internal and external pressures faced by many parents today inevitably makes demands on the nature of the core partnership between them. It is therefore not surprising that the parenting partnership may collapse under the strain of these many expectations of change, transitions and inevitable disappointments.

THE IMPACT OF SEPARATION AND DIVORCE ON BRINGING UP CHILDREN

In Australia nearly 50 000 divorces take place each year. The impact of the experience of divorce and separation cannot be underestimated. Almost because of the sheer numbers of divorces and the increasing statistics, there is a tendency to begin to view divorce and separation as a norm rather than a difficult and traumatic event for all concerned. The frequency of the occurrence among people whom we know may almost lull us into a state of complacency. We may assume that because divorce is a matter of choice, the resulting type of family which emerges is almost a question of lifestyle. We may believe that there is really no need to understand the nature of children's response to separation and divorce and that they will get over it in the fullness of time and join the ranks of the many thousands of children who have had a similar experience.

This book on development is written in response to the core question of what do children need to grow, what are the basic requirements for the development of emotional nourishment and maturity? The problem as a clinician who is faced every day with the dilemmas associated with children whose parents have divorced is that the needs of parents cannot always be reconciled with what the child needs to grow emotionally. This book, as I have mentioned before, takes prevention as its starting point. In order to prevent breakdown in family life and of individual children and parents, we need to have a fundamental understanding of the basic requirements of individual development and family life. If we pause for a moment to consider the statistics for separation and divorce, we may wonder what sort of alternative partners people may be seeking. If one married or parenting partner offends, what other type of partnership will be put in its place? Will it really be so different from the first? Unfortunately, the increase in the statistics of breakdown for the second and subsequent marriages suggests that this is not the case.

In the best interests of the child

It is difficult to comment upon the area of divorce and separation without being seen as either pro or anti a particular position. Usually this position is associated with apportioning blame, either to men or to women, or being viewed as reactionary. Of course it is essential that adults and parents should have reasonable choices in their lives and they should not be forced to continue in a marriage which is unsuitable and unlivable for all concerned. However, I would like to put forward the view that I believe that breakdown in marriage is often precipitated by the rearing of children. It is known, for example, that women submit nearly three times as many divorce petitions as men, which may reflect their different perceptions of the fulfilling and intimate relationship, particularly when it comes to the demands of bringing up children. My main contention is that society plays a part in making it impossible for many of these marriages to continue and has a crucial role to play in the support of parents and in the creation of an appropriately facilitating environment for individual and family development. I will come back to this point in more detail later on. For the moment, let us consider the effects of divorce and separation on individual children.

Throughout the book I have commented that we must move away from a notion that children do not know what is going on around them, or that they need to reach a particular age before they fully understand events. I hope I have indicated that even infants and young children are primed to be sensitive to the environment around them and exist in an essential interpersonal relationship with their key parental and other caregivers. In describing the different stages of emotional development I have referred to the way in which the personality and integration of the child is built up through what one could call the 'interpersonal, intrapsychic building blocks of relatedness'. Divorce, separation and loss all interfere with the establishment of these building blocks. Because of our adaptability as human beings, even young children will manage to adapt to separation and loss but, we may ask ourselves, at what cost? The loss of a parent through divorce and separation involves a loss which is both external and internal. Whatever sexual combinations or permutations we ascribe to parenting, the fact is that there are two sexes in the world and the child has to make up an idea of himself, of who he is and where he belongs, which is related to these two parents and his essential beginnings. When parents are in the throes of separation or have made a decision about a divorce they will understandably feel very self-involved and may need to rationalise the effects on the children because of the enormous pressure they feel to get out of a bad relationship, or they may be dealing with rejection by their partners. It may be just at this time that their children need to talk about their feelings and have their feelings recognised. However, parents may find this very difficult because they don't want to be overwhelmed by the strength of the child's reaction. When parents put too much of an emphasis on the matter-of-factness of this experience there may be a tendency on the part of the child to develop a kind of false self to cope with the separation and loss through denial, and basically through pretending that nothing very important is happening. This facade of apparent matter-of-factness has a tendency to break down at a later stage with damaging results. Therefore a recognition of and validation of the child's experience of the separation at the time is vitally important to help with the task of making sense of the experience.

Containing children's pain

The intensity of what the child feels, her distress and disturbance may often, regrettably, be used as a reason to not allow a child to continue a relationship with a parent. For example, when children live with their custodial parent, most often their mother, and visit the non-custodial parent over a weekend, most often their father, mothers may complain that the children return distressed and stirred up and it is difficult to settle them. The conclusion may be drawn about the other parent causing deliberate pain or harm, when in fact in most cases the children are expressing the reality of feeling in a sense torn in two, having to find a way to integrate in their minds a place for both their mother and father. Sometimes one or both parents may conclude that, because of the child's distress, it would be better if these visits were stopped. This is a very unfortunate response because it gives a message to the child that her feelings are too unbearable for one or both parents to stand. The child's feelings of course do not go away; they simply go underground. The non-custodial parent who may already feel peripheral in the child's life may use this as an excuse to disappear altogether, which further exacerbates the loss that the child experiences.

In managing the impact of divorce and separation on children, parents might take note of the comment that 'a marriage may have a beginning, a middle and an end, but children go on forever'.

This suggests that what is required is that the parental partnership, separate from the marriage and personal relationship, is able to continue. This of course makes great demands on both parents, but ultimately will prove to be a positive experience for the children who will be able, through this parental partnership, to identify and locate a space for their experience. Again, we can see how the idea of containment operates where, if parents can maintain even a fragment of a parental partnership after separation or divorce, this can provide the necessary security and boundary for the child.

Processing the events of separation and divorce

Processing of the events of separation and divorce for the child and adolescent takes place over a considerable period of time and at different stages. The way that the child will process being told initially about parents' imminent separation or divorce will be different from the way they will process the same information months or even years later. The relationship both to the custodial parent and the non-custodial parent will ebb and flow, and must change for integration and psychic health to take place at different stages of the child's development. Thus, for example, a boy's perception of his father and his need for his father's presence will be different at the age of nine than at the age of thirteen. A boy of nine may be content to see his father on a weekly basis or during regular visits, while being content to stay with his mother as his main caregiver. At adolescence, however, things may change very rapidly. He may feel a need to be closer to his father, and to spend more time with him. This is a natural and appropriate form of development and suggests that the boy has a need to be with the parent of the same sex in order to explore his masculine identification. This indicates the vital need for the parental relationship, if at all possible, to survive beyond the end of the marriage. Of course it also needs to survive in a reasonably helpful way.

No place to call home

Miles, a 14-year-old boy, was referred because of violent and disruptive behaviour in the home. His parents had divorced when he was only three years old after a stormy and violent marriage. Feelings of animosity continued into the divorce and Miles was used as a go-between. He became the receptacle of his parents' hatred, disappointment and vengeance towards each other. Both his parents remarried and had other children. But, because of the earlier difficulties that Miles had experienced, he was unable to feel settled with either parent. Any attempts at normal limit setting for Miles had been undermined by the difficulties of his parents' relationship and he had a confused sense of boundaries and of his own identity.

It's too frightening to look at

Two brothers – Howard, aged four, and Michael, aged seven – were referred because of their mother's concern about her imminent separation. Both she and the children's father wanted to be able to support their children through this difficult time. Michael, the seven-year-old, had been putting bandaids on all his fingers weeks before his parents told him about their separation. He had no sores or cuts on his fingers, but insisted on elaborately wrapping the bandaids around his fingers as though warding off some kind of terrible cut or injury. Here we can see how alert and sensitive Michael was to the changing circumstances in his parents' life before they had even told him directly about their separation. Howard, the four-year-old, appeared on the surface to be less concerned about his parents' separation. However, shortly after his father left the house, his behaviour changed dramatically in the kindergarten. He would go up to staff in the morning to say 'Hello' and headbutt them. He had also taken to hitting his mother in the stomach as though blaming her for his father's absence. Michael and Howard represented in a sense the opposite sides of the same coin: Michael being so frightened of attack and hurt that he struggled to bandage himself in preparation, while Howard went straight into the attack. In my session with them, Howard and Michael drew a series of pictures with a skull and crossbones. At first Howard screamed: 'I can't let you see that, it's too frightening'. When he finally allowed me to see the pictures he said: 'These are very unhappy pirates who are trying to capture Peter Pan'. We can see in these pictures the two boys struggling to deal with their own aggressive and troubled feelings. (Figure 4)

Where is home? Managing access visits

The vexed question for many parents of young children is how access arrangements should be agreed upon. Sometimes a solution is found which centres on the fact that the child belongs half to the mother and half to the father, and parents settle on an arrangement where the child spends half the week with one parent and half with the other. This results in immense confusion and the feeling of the child being split in half with a set of clothing and furniture in one home and another set in another home. I have often referred to this arrangement as 'rostering the children'. Here the time spent with the child is seen as a slot that has to be fitted into a particular schedule for both parents. It almost invariably ends up in a highly unsatisfactory arrangement for the child, who can only live in one home at any one time.

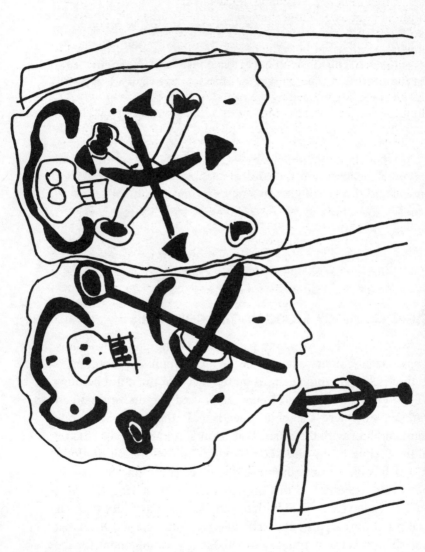

Figure 4: Howard's skull and crossbones

Talking with children

It is always important for children to be told the truth about events or experiences in a way in which they can understand the facts, rather than to pretend that these events are not taking place. Children's fantasies about imminent separation are always worse than the actual experience, and openness about what is actually happening can assist both the parent and the child to manage the vicissitudes of this difficult experience. Sometimes children may feel the need to rescue one parent, particularly if this is a parent who has been abandoned by the other. At times the child may feel a longing for the absent parent out of all proportion to the kind of relationship that existed previously and there may be an idealisation of the absent parent and anger with the one who is present.

Fighting between siblings can also be a way for children to deal with the stress of the parental separation by re-enacting the tension and even the fights between parental partners.

The effects of divorce and separation on children and adolescents have consequences on a number of different levels. Apart from the individual developmental experiences, there are of course the economic and social factors which are related to the status of being brought up by a single parent. It is generally acknowledged that single parents are among the poorest members of the population. Separation and divorce can lead to economic hardship and social isolation for children and their parents, which in turn may limit the kinds of opportunities which may be available for them to fulfil their maximum potential.

Recognising and negotiating loss and disappointment

Central to the whole issue of separation and divorce is the recognition of loss, grief and mourning. However bad or indifferent the previous marriage and parenting relationship may have been, its absence and ending will necessarily involve a period of reflection and sadness. There needs to be some glimmering of understanding of why the relationship has broken down for the partners concerned, rather than a notion of substituting one partner for another as part of a lifestyle change. The problems that children encounter in their subsequent experience after divorce and separation are often not so much to do intrinsically with the fact of separation but of the meaning attributed to it. Where parents can attribute meaning and allow for the recognition of grief, loss and mourning, it is possible for the child and adolescent to be able to come to terms with the experience and work through it. For example, at our Exploring Parenthood workshops on Parenting Alone, in the UK, it was striking that they were attended mainly by women. There was at times a tendency on the part of the women to feel great bitterness towards men, to denigrate them and to shut them out. However, in the course of the workshop, the women's capacity to look at their disappointment with men and nevertheless to keep in mind their absent partner for the sake of the child was a critical part of the work. Almost invariably, at several points during these workshops I had the strong sense of the room being filled with people – all of the absent partners. The recognition of the importance of the absent partner, male or female, and the meaning that this has for the child often results in less fraught arrangements being made for visits and access, and for the way in which the whole process is integrated by both children and parents.

EPILOGUE

Who is Responsible for the Development of Children and Parents?

have referred in the course of this book to the fact that parents
are not born and made at the time of the child's birth; rather
they become parents over time through the process of observing and learning from their child's development as well as from
their own. This process of learning through developmental
experience requires time and a supportive framework for both
children and parents. A theme that I have addressed in the book
is the one of containment and the different levels through which
parents contain their children from infancy right through to adolescence. In this way parents are able to gain knowledge and
experience of the meaning of their child's behaviour and the richness and variety of their child's experience. As adults we all carry
around with us a child part of ourselves that remains as an internal image of our good enough parenting and the way in which we
were parented.

PARENTS AND SOCIETY

Parenting, however, does not take place in a vacuum. The process
of containment is not viable unless parents themselves have a
sense of being contained and held in mind and thought about and
supported. This process of containment of the parents may take
place via their own family, friends and social network. Where this
type of containment for parents does not exist, then the process of
necessary containment that the parent has to carry out in relation
to their own children becomes undermined.

We can thus see that the emotional development and integration for children arises out of a complex emotional ecology. The
social networks of family, school, work, social and support contacts, both formal and informal, provide the broad parameters and
containment within which everyday parenting takes place, and
indeed in which children are socialised. When these networks are
non-existent or break down or change radically, then the quality
of parenting and family life inevitably becomes affected.

Therefore, if we ask the question 'Who is responsible for the
bringing up of children?', the answer must be 'Everybody', most
particularly all adults who are responsible for and have an investment in the development of the next generation. The inclusion of

adults who are not parents themselves must be an important part of this process. We tend to exclude people who do not have children from the whole field of parenting as though their opinions are not of consequence. Many of these adults in turn feel excluded or inhibited about having a say, or indeed feel that they too share an investment in the next generation. The fragmentation of society into those who are entitled to speak on the subject of bringing up children and those who are not encourages a dangerous apathy and indifference which places children at considerable risk. At the same time it is misguided to assume that responsibility for children and children's development, when parents fail, will be taken on exclusively by social services or the courts, or by other institutions which it is hoped will take away responsibility from ordinary individuals and manage the problem somewhere away from their everyday concerns.

 ## PARENTING AS A LIFE TASK AND COMMUNITY TASK

If we view parenting as a life task and community task which involves everyone we can thus begin to create a bridge between the often expressed isolated experience of bringing up children and the way in which everybody can feel that they are able to make a contribution. If we move away from the idea of only biological parents being responsible for bringing up children, it involves us in examining some of the everyday institutions which so shape our very existence and the development of children.

Work and family

One of the most important of course is the world of work. Here, despite the influence of feminism and demands for equal opportunities, very little has in fact changed to ease the tension between the demands of home life and work life for both men and women. Women are as much harried and hurried as men in their need to establish a career and income. Very few allowances are made in the work place or in the professions for the needs of parents. Many companies still control the lives of families and maintain an absolute right to send their staff to work wherever the work is, regardless of the family's needs. The greatest acknowledgement that the work place makes with regard to children is to provide a creche or child-care facility for employees' children, which may make them feel that they have absolved themselves of the limit of their responsibility. However, this creates little opportunity for the development of appropriate relationships. The provision of child care is only one tiny factor in a broad and radical view that has to be taken with regard to future relationship between work and family life. The denial and rejection of any responsibility on the part of important institutions such as the work sector raises questions about the kind of work force we intend to have or hope to develop for the future if we are not prepared to invest in children and parents now.

Inter-generational links

I have mentioned before that parenting and bringing up children is a life's task as well as a community task. As a life's task it also spans successive generations. One of the difficulties associated with the fragmentation of our life today is that there is a danger of splitting off different generations from each other as well as different elements of the developmental process from the rest of society. I have described above the problems which emerge from an artificial split between home and work. We can also observe a split which occurs between generations where we focus on the youth culture or on the productivity and effectiveness of people in the first part of their lives, while denying the rich potential of people in the second part of their lives. It is vitally important for the development of children and for the process of containment which I refer to throughout the book that these different elements and stages of development are not split off and alienated from each other. Thus we need to be mindful of the fact, for example, that when parents divorce, grandparents on both sides may become divorced as well from the children, so that the children lose out not only on their parents but also on their grandparents and the generational input. In the course of their development, children need to be in touch with adults of different generations including older people, so that they become aware of their own position in the life cycle. The contact between children and grandparents can be mutually beneficial and offers a further dimension to the more enclosed nuclear family.

Unfortunately, society increasingly segregates people according to their developmental ages and stages, when it is actually vitally important for development and growth that we encourage greater integration and cohesion. The proliferation of 'retirement villages' for the elderly and 'new towns' for young families is a case in point. In these artificial living environments both groups often experience intense isolation and a sense of being cut off from life

 ## CREATING CHANGE: HELPING PARENTS FIND THEIR OWN VOICE

In writing this book I hope particularly that the knowledge that is currently available about child development and the information about the nature of relationships between parents and children can be taken out of clinic settings and used by parents in the everyday task of bringing up their children. In this sense I hope that specialised knowledge will become common knowledge in order to facilitate greater understanding for all. My approach in this book has been committed first and foremost to the validation of experience, of the emotional world of the infant, young child, older child and adolescent, and the validation of experience for parents who can themselves change and be transformed by what they observe in their children, and find joy and delight in this experience. I would also hope that parents, recognising how important their task is, will be able to find their own voice, to facilitate their child's development and also to be able to make representation to the broader parenting society to provide the appropriate containment and support necessary to carry out their vital task, the most important job in life.

REFERENCES

Ackerman, N. (1966). *Treating the troubled family.* New York: Basic Books.

Ainsworth, S., Blehar, M.C., Waters, E., & Wall, S. (1978). *Patterns of attachment: A psychological study of the strange situation.* Hillsdale NJ: Erlbaum.

Bain, A., & Barnett, L. (1980). *The design of a day care system in a nursery setting for children under five* (Final Report, Tavistock Institute of Human Relations, Doc. No. 2347). London: Tavistock.

Bateson, G. (1973). *Steps to an ecology of mind.* London: Paladin.

Bettelheim, B. (1967). *The empty fortress.* London: Collier Macmillan.

Bettelheim, B. (1988). *A good enough parent.* London: Pan Books.

Bion, W.R. (1962). *Learning from experience.* London: Heinemann.

Bion, W.R. (1993). Container and contained. In *Attention and interpretation* (pp. 72-82). London: Karnac Books. (Article first published 1964)

Bowlby, J. (1951). *Child care and the growth of love* (2nd ed.). Harmondsworth: Penguin.

Bowlby, J. (1973a). *Attachment.* Harmondsworth: Penguin.

Bowlby, J. (1973b). *Separation.* Harmondsworth: Penguin.

Bowlby, J. (1973c). *Loss.* Harmondsworth: Penguin.

Carroll, L. (1956). *Alice in wonderland.* London: The Heirloom Library. (Original work published 1865)

Craig, H., & Holabird, K. (1988). *Angelina ballerina.* London: Puffin Books.

Dahl, R. (1982). *Revolting rhymes.* London: Jonathan Cape.

Erikson, E. (1963). *Childhood and society.* Harmondsworth: Penguin.

Erikson, E. (1968). *Identity.* London: Faber.

Fraiberg, S. (1959). *The magic years: Understanding and handling the problems of early childhood.* New York: Charles Scribner.

Fraiberg, S. (1980). Ghosts in the nursery. In Fraiberg, S. (Ed.), *Clinical studies in infant mental health.* London: Tavistock.

Freud, A. (1974). *Infants without families and reports of the Hampstead Nurseries (1939-1945).* London: Hogarth Press.

Freud, A. (1989). *Normality and pathology in childhood*. London: Karnac Books. (Original work published 1965, London: Hogarth Press and the Institute of Psychoanalysis)

Freud, S. (1961). Beyond the pleasure principle. In J. Strachey (Ed. and Trans.), *The standard edition of the complete psychological works of Sigmund Freud* (Vol. 18, pp. 7-64). London: Hogarth Press. (Original work published in 1920)

Guntrip, H. (1992). The concept of psychodynamic science. In *Schizoid phenomena, object relations and the self* (pp. 384-5). London: Karnac Books. (Article first published in 1967)

Klein, M. (1959). Our adult world and its roots in infancy. In *Human Relations 12*, 291-303.

Klein, M. (1975). The psycho-analysis of children. In *The writings of Melanie Klein, Vol. 2*. London: Hogarth Press and the Institute of Psychoanalysis. (Article first published in 1932)

Luepnitz, D.A. (1988). *The family interpreted: Psychoanalysis, feminism and family therapy*. New York: Basic Books.

Mahler, M., Pine, F., & Bergmann, A. (1967). *The psychological birth of the human infant*. New York: Basic Books.

Main, M., Kaplan, N., & Cassidy, J. (1985). Security in infancy, childhood and adulthood. In I. Bretherton, & E. Waters, *Growing points of attachment: Theory and research*. Monographs of the Society for Research in Child Development, No. 209, 50, 66-104.

Meltzer D., in Astor, J. (1989). A conversation with Donald Meltzer. *Journal of Child Psychotherapy, 15* (1).

Menzies, Lyth I. (1988). The functioning of social systems as a defence against anxiety. In *Containing anxiety in institutions*. London: Free Association Books. (Article first published in 1959)

Miller, L., Rustin, M., & Shuttleworth, J. (1989). *Closely observed infants*. London: Duckworth.

Milne, A.A. (1924). "Disobedience". In *When we were very young*. London: Methuen.

Minuchin, S. (1974). *Families and family therapy*. Cambridge, MA: Harvard University Press.

Polakow, V. (1992). *The erosion of childhood*. (Rev. ed.). Chicago: University of Chicago Press.

Rayner, E. (1990). *The independent mind in British psychoanalysis*. London: Free Association Books.

Robertson, J., & Robertson, J. (1989). *Separation and the very young.* London: Free Association Books.

Sameroff, A., & Emde, R. (Eds.). (1989). *Relationship disturbances in early childhood.* New York: Basic Books.

Samuels, A. (Ed.). (1985). *The father: Contemporary Jungian perspectives.* London: Free Association Press.

Satir, V. (1967). *Conjoint family therapy.* Palo Alto, CA: Science and Behavior Books.

Schmidt Neven, R. (1994). *Exploring parenthood: A psychodynamic approach for a changing society.* Melbourne: Australian Council for Educational Research.

Schmidt Neven, R., Samish, S., Cebon, A., & Dresner, O. (1994). Parents in transition. *Proceedings of three day training workshop, Hebrew University.* Melbourne: Centre for Child and Family Development.

Skynner, A.C.R., & Cleese, J. (1989). *Families and how to survive them.* London: Mandarin Books.

Spitz R. (1965). *The first year of life.* New York: International Universities Press.

Spitz, R., & Wolf, K.M. (1946). Anaclitic depression. In *Psychoanalytic Study of the Child 2,* 313-342.

Stern, D. (1977). *The first relationship: Infant and mother.* Boston, MA: Harvard University Press.

Whitaker, C., & Keith, D. (1981). Symbolic experiential family therapy. In A. Gurman & D. Kniskern (Eds.), *Handbook of family therapy* (pp. 187-225). New York: Brunner/Mazel.

Winnicott, D.W. (1958a). Transitional objects and transitional phenomena. In *Collected papers: Through paediatrics to psychoanalysis.* London: Tavistock. (Article first published in 1951)

Winnicott, D.W. (1958b). Primary maternal preoccupation. In *Collected papers: Through paediatrics to psychoanalysis.* London: Tavistock. (Article first published 1956)

Winnicott, D.W. (1964). *The child, the family and the outside world.* Harmondsworth: Penguin.

Winnicott, D.W. (1965a). The capacity to be alone. In *The maturational processes and the facilitating environment.* London: Hogarth Press. (Article first published in 1958)

Winnicott, D.W. (1965b). The theory of the parent infant relationship. In *The maturational processes and the facilitating environment*. London: Hogarth Press. (Article first published 1960)

Winnicott, D.W. (1988). The human child examined: Soma psyche mind. In *Human nature*. London: Free Association Books.

Wittenberg-Salzberger, I., Henry G., & Osborne, E. (1983). *The emotional experience of learning and teaching*. London: Routledge & Kegan Paul.

■ SUGGESTED FURTHER READING

Background and introduction to psychodynamic ideas and theories

Brown, D., & Pedder, J. (1979). *Introduction to psychotherapy: An outline of psychodynamic principles and practice.* London: Tavistock.

Davis, M., & Walbridge, D. (1981). *Boundary and space: An introduction to the work of D.W. Winnicott.* London: Karnac Books.

Freud, S. (1977). *The Pelican Freud library.* Harmondsworth: Penguin. A paperback collection of Freud's major writings intended for the general reader.

Grosskurth, P. (1987). *Melanie Klein: Her world and her work.* Boston, MA: Harvard University Press.

Kaplan, L.J. (1978). *Oneness and separateness: From infant to individual.* New York: Simon and Schuster. Introduces the theories of Margaret Mahler.

Segal, H. (1973). *An introduction to the work of Melanie Klein.* London: Hogarth Press.

Applying psychodynamic ideas to the broader community

Boston, M., & Szur, R. (Eds.). (1990). *Psychotherapy with severely deprived children.* London: Karnac Books.

Campbell, D., & Draper, R. (Eds.). (1985). *Applications of systemic family therapy.* London: Grune and Stratton.

Daws, D. (1989). *Through the night – Helping parents and sleepless infants.* London: Free Association Books.

Erskine, A., & Judd, D. (1994). *The imaginative body: Psychodynamic therapy in health care.* London: Whurr Publications.

Hornby, S. (1993). *Collaborative care: Interprofessional interagency and interpersonal.* Oxford: Blackwell Scientific Publications.

Marris, P. (1986). *Loss and change* (Rev. ed.). London: Routledge & Kegan Paul.

Sinason, V. (1992). *Mental handicap and the human condition.* London: Free Association Books.

Szur, R., & Miller, S. (Eds.). (1991). *Extending horizons: Psychoanalytic psychotherapy with children, adolescents and families*. London: Karnac Books.

Understanding child and family development

Alvarez, A. (1992). *Live company: Psychoanalytic psychotherapy with autistic borderline deprived & abused children*. London: Routledge.

Brazelton, T.B. (1992). *Touch points*. Harmondsworth: Penguin.

Bruner, J.S., Jolly, A., & Sylva, K. (1985). *Play and its role in development and evolution*. Harmondsworth: Penguin.

Clulow, C.F. (1982). *To have and to hold: Marriage, the first baby and preparing couples for Parenthood*. Aberdeen: Aberdeen University Press.

Cockett, M., & Tripp, J. (1994). *The Exeter Family Study: Family breakdown and its impact on children*. Exeter: University of Exeter Press.

Dicks, H. (1967). *Marital tensions*. New York: Basic Books.

Dowling, E., & Osborne, E. (1985). *The family and school: A joint systems approach to problems with children* (2nd ed.). London: Routledge.

Furman, E. (1974). *A child's parent dies*. New Haven: Yale University Press.

Furman, E. (1987). *The teachers guide to helping young children grow*. New York: International Universities Press.

Furman, E., & Katan, A. (1969). *The therapeutic nursery school*. New York: International Universities Press.

Harris, M. (1975). *Thinking about infants and young children*. London: Clunie Press.

Laufer, M. (1974). *Adolescent disturbance and breakdown*. Harmondsworth: Penguin.

Laufer, M., & Laufer, M.E. (1985). *Adolescence and developmental breakdown*. New Haven: Yale University Press.

Murray Parks, C., & Stevenson, Hinde, J. (Eds.). (1982). *The place of attachment in human behaviour*. London: Tavistock.

Pincus, L. (1976). *Death and the family: The importance of mourning*. London: Faber & Faber.

Pincus, L., & Dare, C. (1978). *Secrets in the family*. London: Faber & Faber.

Raphael Leff, J. (1991). *Psychological processes of childbearing.* London: Chapman Hall.

Rayner, E. (1986). *Human development.* Sydney: Allen & Unwin.

The Tavistock series on child development (1992-5). London: Rosendale Press. (Comprising 16 books, the series is distributed by Australian Council for Educational Research, Camberwell, Melbourne)

Tracey, N. (1993). *Mothers, fathers speak on the drama of pregnancy: Birth and the first year of life.* London: Apollo Books.

Trowell, J. (Ed.) (1995). *The emotional needs of young children and their families.* London: Routledge.

Williams-Harris, M. (Ed.). (1987). *Collected papers of Martha Harris and Esther Bick.* London: Clunie Press.

Wallerstein, J. & Berlin Kelly J. (1980). *Surviving the break-up: How children and parents cope with divorce.* London: Grant McIntyre.

Winnicott, C., Shepherd, R., & Davis, M., (Ed.) (1984) *D.W. Winnicott: Deprivation and delinquency.* London: Routledge.

Gender and sexual identity

Biddulph, S. (1994) *Manhood.* Sydney: Finch Publishing.

Chodorow, N. (1978). *The reproduction of mothering.* Berkeley, CA: University of California Press.

Mitchell, J. (1974). *Psychoanalysis and feminism.* Harmondsworth: Pelican.

Oakley, A. (1979). *Becoming a mother.* Oxford: Martin Robertson.

Samuels, A. (1989) *The plural psyche: Personality, morality and the father.* London: Routledge.

Scharff, D.E. (1988). *The sexual relationship: An object relations view of sex and the family.* London: Routledge.

Silverstein, O. (1995). *The courage to raise good men.* Harmondsworth: Penguin.

A psychodynamic approach to groups and institutions: How we work together

Czander, W.M. (1993). *The psychodynamics of work and organisations: Theory and application.* New York: Guildford Press.

Hinshelwood, R.D. (1987). *What happens in groups – Psychoanalysis, the individual and the community.* London: Free Association Books.

Hirschorn, L. (1988). *The workplace within: Psychodynamics of organisational life.* Cambridge, MA: The MIT Press.

Menzies Lyth, I. (1989). *The dynamics of the social: Selected essays.* London: Free Association Books.

Videos on child development

Barnett, L. (Producer) *The Development of Individuality from Birth to Twelve Years of Age: 'Sunday's' Child – Birth to Two Years.* (Available from Concord Video and Film Council Ltd, 211 Felixstowe Road, Ipswich, Suffolk IP3 9BJ, UK.)

Barnett, L. (Producer) 'Leave them attached': *The importance of good child care for under fives.* A trilogy of videos illustrating principles and practice to enrich day care. (Available from Concord Video and Film Council.)

Robertson, J., & Robertson, J. (Producers) (1967). *Children in Brief Separation* and *A Two Year Old Goes to Hospital.* Concord Films. (Available in Australia from Australian Association for the Welfare of Child Health, University of Western Sydney, Nepean, ph. (02) 685 9318.)

Spitz, R. (1977). 16mm film of last lecture of René Spitz who describes his work. Parents Magazine Films, USA. (Available in Australia from Australian Association for the Welfare of Child Heath.)

GLOSSARY

This glossary offers an understanding of certain psychodynamic concepts used in *Emotional Milestones*. For more precise definitions readers are directed to the original sources found in the References and Further Reading sections.

Words printed in italics in the definitions refer to headwords.

Acting out. The tendency to externalise conflicts and unresolved problems by enacting them in the course of everyday life, often with unhelpful consequences. For example, an adolescent who has a poor relationship with his parents may become involved in the drug culture. The communication problem remains unresolved but is acted out with potentially tragic results.

Adhesive identification. A term that attempts to describe a type of interaction between the mother and her infant or young child – a 'glued on' interaction. The child feels unsafe and vulnerable away from the mother. This leads her to also feel unsafe about being different from the mother, or expressing a separate identity that would include aggression. Term created by the child and adult psychoanalyst Donald Meltzer.

Ambivalence. A term used to indicate that experiences and perceptions are rarely black and white – often they are mixed. We may experience differing emotions about the same event. For example, childbirth may arouse joy, regret and apprehension all at the same time. Allowing children to have mixed feelings helps them to develop greater tolerance and to acknowledge the complexity of events. It helps them build their own inner emotional resources.

Anaclitic depression. A concept used to describe the quality of severe depression suffered by infants and young children in institutional care who were separated for long periods from their mothers. A concept developed by Rene Spitz, who observed these children moving through the phases of protest, withdrawal and despair, accompanied by overall developmental delay and a susceptibility to illness.

Attachment. The experience of emotional dependence of the infant/young child in relation to her parents. This is complemented by *bonding*. Both concepts have been employed in research on infant/parent patterns of attachment, carried out by Mary Main and Mary Ainsworth, amongst others. Theory of attachment developed by John Bowlby.

Behaviourist. An approach based on social and cognitive learning theory and animal behaviour, as in behavioural psychology. The aim of behavioural therapy is to change the behaviour of the patient as it manifests itself. For example, in agoraphobia (fear of going out) or claustrophobia (fear of confined spaces).

Bonding. A term that describes the capacity of the parents to form a close relationship with their child. See also *Attachment*.

Containment. A term that refers to the early infant/mother relationship in which the mother needs to be capable of holding what the child produces in the form of crying, anxiety and discomfort. The mother needs to be able to transform these communications of the child so that they can become reintegrated within the child as a tolerable experience.

This term is used throughout this book to denote the core task of parenting. However, teachers, sports leaders and others who come into regular contact with children may also act as 'containers' from time to time. Here it refers to containing or holding a problem with and for the child rather than blaming the child for it, or rushing to solve it. Containment is modelled by parents and adults to enable children to deal with fear and anxiety. A term derived from the work of Wilfrid Bion.

Defences. A term that refers to the means by which humans protect themselves from being overwhelmed by events and experiences. Defences become less useful when the threat has long since passed but the same defensive behaviour is maintained. Defenses are often used in association with *denial*.

Denial. A term that refers to pretending that events have not taken place. Denial is seen to occur, for example, when parents who are about to separate do not tell their children but rationalise this by saying 'The children don't know what is happening.'

Depressive position. A concept used to describe a phase of the relationship between infant and mother in the first year of life. It refers to the infant's emotional recognition that the mother who leaves her and the mother who feeds her and responds to her are one and the same person. The baby is said to experience sadness and regret about her earlier angry wishes towards the mother.

These ideas can be seen as a metaphor for reconciling good and bad experiences in the course of development. A term developed by Melanie Klein. See also *Paranoid schizoid position*.

Ego psychology. Study of the development and structure of the *ego*, following Freud's earlier work on *id, ego, superego*. An approach taken further by Anna Freud which has taken root predominantly in the USA with a focus on the individual's social, cultural and family context.

False self. A way of presenting one's self which tries to fit in with the requirements of others. May be based on early childhood experience of deprivation, and of giving up and not protesting. Cover for the true self and the real wishes of the child or adult.

Fantasy. A term that refers to personal construction of events the way we would like things to be; similar to a daydream. Fantasies can also be fearful in anticipation of an event. Associated closely with children's play and their experience of living in both their fantasy world and the external world.

Holding environment. A concept that is related to *containment*. Refers to the need for the young child to be held emotionally by his parents in order to flourish. In this book the idea of a 'holding environment' is extended to include all the child's contacts, for example child care centres and schools. A term derived from the work of Donald Winnicott.

Holding in mind. A concept that relates to the task of parenting on a number of different levels, e.g. biological parents, teachers, counsellors. Refers to being able to remember the child and reflect on her experience and needs. The child in turn feels 'held in mind' and can get on with her activities. It is the opposite experience of 'falling out of the parents' minds'. Also, clients in the counselling context fear falling out of their counsellors' minds, for example at a holiday period.

Holding in mind and being held in mind have implications for the way the child is able to organise her own thinking for subsequent cognitive development and learning.

Idealisation. A term that refers to the situation in some families where individual children or the parents are placed on a pedestal. This presupposes an ideal way of how people should behave or be, as opposed to how they really are. Idealisation is often followed closely by denigration when the individuals inevitably fail to live up to these unrealistic expectations.

Individuality. The idea of a separate and autonomous personality. One of the tasks of development is to develop individuality, while at the same time remaining a member of the family.

Integration. A term that refers to the ability of the child to bring together, over time, the wide variety of his experience both positive and negative. This is a key aspect of development, and links with the process of *splitting*.

Internalise. A term used to refer to making an experience one's own; taking it into one's self. Particularly relevant in early infant and child development when we internalise an image of our parents that stays with us for life.

Intrapsychic. A term that refers to the private inner world: to ideas, fantasies, wishes and hopes which may be both conscious and unconscious.

Mourning. The experience of sorrow, loss and melancholy following death or loss of someone close. Mourning is a necessary healing process which enables us to come to terms with loss and grief. The process of mourning is viewed as a necessary part of the experience of divorce, separation from parents, chronic illness and disability, as well as the experience of trauma and migration. In these instances, mourning acknowledges the meaning and value of important relationships.

Narcissistic. A term used to describe the necessary prerequisite for development, particularly of gender and sexual identity. A balance needs to be found in family life between appropriate narcissism and inappropriate narcissism leading to idealisation.

Note the meaning used in this book is quite different from its general use, where it is employed in a pejorative sense to describe individuals consumed by their own beauty or achievements.

Object Relations School. A theory concerning human development with a particular focus on the early infant/parent interactions. Based on Melanie Klein's work, the Object Relations School developed in Britain through Donald Winnicott, Wilfrid Bion and Harry Guntrip amongst others, and is now taking root in the USA.

Paranoid schizoid position. A concept used to describe a stage in the infant's life which precedes the *depressive position*. In the paranoid schizoid position the baby believes that the mother who attends to her and the mother who leaves the room are two separate people. In the course of our development we move between the depressive position (having concern for others, empathy) and the paranoid schizoid position (an anxious, suspicious approach to the world). A term developed by Melanie Klein.

Part-object relationships. A term used to describe the action of splitting of painful aspects of early life experience which cannot be made sense of or integrated. Different parts of the personality may seem split off from each other. We may, for example, observe the need in some adults to split loving and sexual feelings and to engage in promiscuous relationships without much pleasure. The opposite of an internalised whole-person relationship.

Persecution. The experience of feeling attacked or denigrated when this may not necessarily be the case. Feelings of persecution in the baby are associated with the *paranoid schizoid position*. In clinical work one may see people whose early experience of abuse or physical violence leads them to have an almost permanent sense of persecution. In turn this may lead them to repeat similar experiences with their own children.

Projection. The tendency to place unwanted, often unacceptable feelings and attributes about one's self on to others.

Psychoanalysis. A psychological method of treatment based upon an understanding of conscious as well as unconscious processes of the human mind and its development Originally developed by Sigmund Freud in the 1890s, psychoanalysis has evolved considerably since that time.

An intense form of treatment which attempts to bring about significant changes in the patient's life. Central to the process of treatment is the *transference* relationship between the analyst and the patient. Psychotherapists who wish to work with children, parents and adults are required as part of their training to undergo their own personal analysis. This is in line with Hippocrates' famous dictum : 'Physician heal thyself.'

Psychodynamic. An approach which emphasises the emotional content and meaning of all human experience and creates links between the dynamics of individual development and that of family and community life. In this book described as a broad approach which goes beyond a treatment modality and can be applied in a wide variety of settings such as education, the work force, health care, and early childhood development.

Psychopathology. A term that relates to problems and breakdown in mental functioning. Much of the knowledge about human development derives from an approach which focuses on illness rather than health. Current practice and research in infant development and studies of 'resilience' in children may begin to redress this balance. It may create a paradigm shift towards a better understanding of health rather than pathology, and help to focus on prevention rather than cure.

Psychosomatic. A recognition of the essential connection between mind and body which hopefully avoids a split between these two. In this book the essential psychosomatic relationship between the infant and mother is presented as a cornerstone of development.

Psychotherapy. Officially a form of psychological treatment based on psychoanalytical principles. Of a less intensive nature than psychoanalysis, which nevertheless focuses on the therapist/patient transference relationship. However, psychotherapy has come to be used as a generic term to cover almost any type of therapeutic help and orientation, and these therapies have little or nothing in common with psychoanalytic psychotherapy.

Psychotic. A state of mind in which the person is said to have 'taken leave of his senses'. This may take the form of extreme withdrawal or of delusions and hallucinations about family, friends and the broader community.

Regression. The natural process of taking one step backwards in developmental terms, from time to time, to an earlier stage of development. Most noticeable in children particularly at times of stress when they regress with regard to bodily functions such as bedwetting and soiling.

Reparation. The wish to restore and 'make good' difficult experiences, particularly in relation to one's parents. The capacity for reparation in children and young people is often underestimated but offers constructive opportunities for change. Derived from Melanie Klein's theory of child development.

Reverie: maternal and paternal. The period of preparation before the birth of the baby. It encourages parents' dreaminess, playfulness and appropriate self-absorption that are part of their mental preparation for the arrival of the new baby. Derived from the work of Donald Winnicott.

Splitting. A term that refers to the need to keep good and bad separate. This process can be seen in family life : 'Mum is good because she lets me do what I want. Dad is horrid because he won't.' In organisations there may be, for example, splitting between the 'good workers' and the 'bad management'. See also *integration,* the opposite process of splitting.

The good enough mother. A phrase used to enable parents to set themselves realistic goals, rather than to be perfect parents. Derived from the work of Donald Winnicott.

The Object or *Object of study*. Technical terms that denote an aspect of the internal structure of the personality which has developed a characteristic style or quality as a result of the early infant/parent interaction.

Transference. A term that refers to the relationship between the analyst and patient. It enables the patient to relive earlier conflicts in the 'here and now' experience of the analysis.

Transitional experience and *transitional space*. Terms used that suggest the need for an 'in between' stage to enable a move from one phase of development to another. Acknowledging the need for transition in child and adolescent experience is an important aspect not only of parenting but also educational and social life.

Transitional object. Term used to describe the blanket or soft toy used by the young child as a substitute for the mother, which enables him to create a space between himself and his mother and to make the transition from his relationship with her to the outside world. Derived from the work of Donald Winnicott.

Trauma. An overwhelming experience often associated with loss. Because of its extreme nature it is experienced as a major attack on the self. It may be difficult to make sense of or to process such an experience. So often traumatic events become clouded in amnesia (out of memory) although they may appear in a disguised form in turbulent and difficult current relationships.

Working through. The mental emotional work which takes place in children, adolescents and adults to make sense of a problem or difficult experience. Working through requires an appropriate time frame and the support of significant others such as relatives, friends or counsellors.